How To Size Up People

By
John E. Gibson

Popular approaches to
basic psychological
principles

CARILLON BOOKS

HOW TO SIZE UP PEOPLE

A CARILLON BOOK
Carillon Books edition published August, 1977

ISBN: 0-89310-015-3 (hard cover)
ISBN: 0-89310-016-1 (paperback)

Library of Congress Catalog Card Number: 77-78111

Copyright ©1977 by Carillon Books

CARILLON BOOKS is a division of
Catholic Digest
2115 Summit Avenue
St. Paul, Minnesota 55105
U.S.A.

INTRODUCTION

John Gibson's work in the field of popular psychology is internationally known through his magazine articles appearing in the U.S., England, Canada and Australia. He works generally from research reports of sound scientific value and reduces their content most often to an easily understood list of questions and answers.

His list of topics pretty well blankets the field in investigating the ordinary workings of the average human mind, the things you need to know in sizing up people. There is no effort in this volume to abnormal psychology nor such things as as diseases of the nervous system. His point is that you should know how to react to the day-to-day actions and sayings of your friends and the people about you in your everyday life. Your life and often theirs can improve with this knowledge.

He progresses from the specific activity named in the title, sizing up people, through self-analysis, the influence of mind over body, the emotions of love and hate, to the "battle of the sexes." That chapter, however, is chauvinistic from neither male nor female viewpoint, in fact instead of relating anything unpleasant, it deals with the interplay, usually delightful, of those human traits which are either distinctively feminine or exclusively masculine.

—Kenneth Ryan

CONTENTS

iv

Are You Ever Too Old To Fall In Love? Can The
"Other Woman" Steal Your Husband?

I.

OTHER PEOPLE AND THEIR HUMAN NATURE

OTHER PEOPLE AND THEIR HUMAN NATURE

*To size up people you have to understand them.
To understand any one of the countless varieties of
human beings you have to know not only the basic
facts of psychology but also a good many of the
minor quirks and what would be footnotes in the
textbook.*

WHY PEOPLE BEHAVE LIKE PEOPLE
A Few Tips on Understanding Human Nature

Surveys have shown that most of us are more interested in people than in anything else on earth. Behavior scientists are trying to find out more about why people behave like people. Here are some of their findings.

Is it true that one of the quickest ways to get to know a person better is to ask him about his first name?

Yes. Studies have shown that asking a person about his first name ("Do you like your name?" "Do you have relatives who have the same name?" and so on) will often produce very intimate and sometimes surprising responses. The authors of the study conclude that this simple approach is an effective means of gaining insight into another's personality. They also recommend it as an excellent way to draw shy people out.

Does familiarity breed contempt?

No. According to recent studies at the University of Michigan, "Familiarity does not breed contempt at all; it's quite the opposite. The more often a person comes in contact with something or someone, the more favorable he tends to feel toward them." Novelty is likely to be associated with uncertainty, which produces tension. But familiarity is comfortable. These findings seem to explain the hesitancy many

3

persons have about meeting new people. Everyone feels more at ease with someone he knows.

Does being in a crowded room make people more likely to argue, and show resentment or hostility?

Yes. Studies at Georgia State University have demonstrated that people tend to behave differently toward each other in a crowded room than elsewhere. In close proximity to one another, "The subjects tended to feel under pressure. They were disagreeable and unfriendly, had feelings more conducive to arguing than enjoyable conversation."

Does it take a special kind of empathy (insight) to understand another person?

Yes. One psychological study shows that there are two kinds of empathy: 1. "Sensitive empathy," the ability to be aware of the apparent expressions, speech, facial changes, and general behavior of a person and make accurate judgments in ordinary situations. 2. "Reflective empathy," the ability to detect concealed meanings which may lie beneath a person's words, gestures, and mannerisms; an acute sensitivity to another's inner feelings despite what he shows.

Women, investigations have shown, tend to be better at the second kind of empathy than men are, possibly because they are more emotionally motivated.

Is the length of a letter of recommendation an indication of how much your boss really likes or dislikes you?

Yes. Studies by a team of University of Oregon psychologists show that the shorter the letter of recommendation, the more reservations the boss has about you. He is likely to be writing it only because he feels obliged to give you some kind of reference. The longer the communication, the more highly the boss esteems you.

Other studies had similar findings. They also show that this principle applies to both verbal and written communications, and is by no means restricted to the boss-employee relationship. If you ask a friend what he thinks of someone, whether he replies shortly or at length is more significant than what he says.

Is it true that your friends' friends tell a lot about what you are like?

Yes. Sociologists at the University of Michigan studied the friendship patterns of more than 1,000 persons. They found that people whose friends didn't know each other had completely different personalities than those whose friends all knew one another. Persons in the first group were likely to be openminded and politically independent. They were able to enjoy themselves without the company of others; they seldom discussed their personal problems with friends, and had few rather than many. They also tended to be individualistic.

But, the study found, "If you are a member of an interlocking network of friends, each having a close relationship with the other, you are likely to differ from all of the preceding characteristics. You are gregarious, have many friends, and see a great deal of them."

'IF YOU COULD ONLY UNDERSTAND!'
Helping People to Get to Know Other People

In universities and research foundations, scientists have been trying to help people understand each other better. They have discovered many things that make us like or dislike each other.

Psychologists have found that some persons communicate their emotions with ease, and that others cannot. Some get their signals mixed. They feel anger, but convey surprise; or they may feel disgust, but the feeling they communicate to another person can be something different, perhaps boredom.

Psychologists agree that one of the biggest sources of discord between husbands and wives, sweethearts and friends is that one person may communicate a completely different emotion from the one he feels, producing confusion in the relationship. Here is a test that psychologists gave to students at the University of Florida to determine how well their facial expressions communicated their feelings and emotions.

Each student was seated so that only his face could be seen by the judges. He then attempted to portray ten emotions: happiness, love, fear, determination, bewilderment, surprise, anger, suffering, disgust, and contempt. (Try this at a party, with guests serving as judges.)

Happiness was the easiest emotion to communicate; it was correctly identified 70% of the time. Contempt was identified only 33% of the time. Women had the more expressive faces, and they were much more effective than men in communicating happiness, love, fear, and anger. The men did not score much better than women for any emotion, though they were slightly more effective in expressing determination.

Here are the emotions, listed in the order the students found easiest to communicate, beginning with the simplest and going on to the most difficult.

1. Happiness
2. Surprise
3. Fear
4. Love
5. Suffering
6. Disgust
7. Bewilderment
8. Anger
9. Determination
10. Contempt

There are two telltale speech mannerisms which easily reveal whether a person is self-confident or ridden with anxiety. But first match your own insight against the findings of the experts. You start by eavesdropping on three persons talking. Two of them are lacking in self-confidence. One is not. See if you can tell which is which by listening to them.

First person: "That was . . . it will be two weeks since I told him about that. I wanted to . . . I felt he should have another chance."

Second person: "I think . . . ah . . . that considering the . . . circumstances you were wise in . . . ah . . . handling it that way."

Third person: "I agree. Because we . . . we got along pretty well together. He was . . . he was sharing the office, you know."

Yale University researchers found the two most significant speech mannerisms to be these: 1. *Sentence change:* Stopping midway in a sentence to change its meaning or content, as, "That was . . . it will be two weeks . . ." 2. *Repetition:* The superfluous repetition of one or more words, as "Because we . . . got along pretty well together. He was . . . he was sharing the office." The more frequently they occur in your speech, the more anxiety and the less self-confidence is indicated.

Tests showed, however, that the frequency with which a person's speech was disturbed by the familiar *ah* had no bearing on anxiety or self-confidence. It was found that when a person pauses in his speech and says "ah" he is likely to be deliberating over what he is about to say, searching for just the right word to express his thought. The use of the expression *ah* was the only type of speech disturbance which the investigators found bore no relation to anxiety.

Psychological researches at the State University of New York have shown that people who get the most pleasure out of eating also get the most enjoyment out of life. The results of the study showed that people who eat merely to "keep themselves going" don't have nearly as much gusto for living as do people who look forward to mealtime with anticipation and have a well-developed appreciation for good food.

Psychologists at another university approached the matter

in a different way. After giving students a battery of personality tests, the investigators noted each person's attitude toward food, his likes or dislikes for specific dishes. They found that those who like most foods and had relatively few food aversions tended to have decidedly different personalities than the finicking eaters who had higher good-aversion scores.

People who liked the most foods, had few aversions, and enjoyed eating tended to be positive-minded, enterprising, vigorous, and resolute, with a genuine fondness for people in general. They were capable of expressing themselves articulately, and were seldom inclined to repress their emotions. When faced with problems, they were inclined to seek the company of others and to confide in them.

People in the second category were characterized by restraint, tenseness, and need for privacy. They preferred to be alone when faced with trouble or grief. They were slow to form close relationships with others, having only a few intimates. Their behavior tended to be introverted. They had a high degree of self-awareness, and were also acutely sensitive to their surroundings. Unlike those who looked forward to lunch or dinner as one of the highlights of the day, these people ate quickly, anxious to have it over with, caring little for service, ceremony, or fancy dishes.

In a University of Texas study investigators made a series of psychological tests on students to find out the things which determine whether person A is going to be like person B. The study showed that even when there is a difference of opinion on other things, people are predisposed to like or dislike each other because of the following considerations.

1. We like someone who likes someone we like.
2. We like someone who dislikes someone we dislike.

The psychological tests showed the principle also works this way:

3. We dislike someone who likes someone we dislike.
4. We dislike someone who dislikes someone we like.

Sometimes this principle may be outweighed by other considerations which bring people together, but the effect of the principle is nevertheless evident.

UNDERSTANDING THE OTHER FELLOW
Don't Jump to Hasty Conclusions

Your happiness is determined, to a very large extent, by your ability to understand people. The more sensitive your insight into the personalities of the people around you, the better you are going to get along.

If you have difficulty in understanding your spouse, you are going to have difficulty in getting along with him regardless of how great your love. And your chances of success in any endeavor will depend to a great extent on your ability to understand the people with whom you work.

Since understanding people, getting an accurate "feel" of their personality characteristics and how their minds work, is so important, psychologists try to determine precisely what "secrets" and principles are involved in the process.

Psychologist Verne Kallejian and his colleagues completed an intensive two-year study of the factors involved in "understanding the other fellow." To take the subject completely out of the realm of theory and insure practical and scientifically tested findings, Dr. Kallejian used 98 leaders in business, education and community groups as guinea pigs.

These persons were assigned at random to five groups of approximately 20 persons each, and met in these groups for three hours daily over a period of weeks.

Psychological tests were designed to determine how well each of the 98 subjects understood one another and how closely one subject could appraise the character and personality tendencies of the others.

Persons who made high "understanding" scores were analyzed to determine specifically how they were able to achieve them. Those who scored medium, fair, and poor in their insight into others, were subjected to similar analysis.

Example: Jones, after being in the company of Smith for a period, gained an impression of the latter's character and personality which proved to be highly accurate. He did the same with various other subjects. Black on the other hand, tended to gain impressions of his colleagues which were subsequently proven to be highly erroneous.

What did Jones do or what was there about his attitude or manner which enabled him to obtain a better insight and understanding of the others than Black did? And why did the Blacks of the group "miss the boat?" What were the barriers which kept them from really understanding various others in the group?

Findings of the study not only reveal the answers to these questions, but they provide a simple, foolproof test by which you can determine how good you are at really getting to know people.

The subjects who made the highest "understanding" scores were those who did not form snap judgments nor jump to conclusions regarding the other fellow's characteristics.

They were invariably good listeners; they drew the other fellow out and postponed making final decisions about him until they felt sure that all the evidence was in. The high scorers took their time, and frequently reversed or modified their conclusions several times, in the process of getting to know another person.

The low scorers tended to do just the opposite, being influenced largely by their first impressions and being prejudiced by them to such an extent that they were blind to significant aspects of the other person's character. They also tended to be self-centered and more intent on expressing themselves than listening to the other person and assessing his actions and reactions.

The individuals, who scored poorly on sizing up others, had another significant trait in common. Psychological tests showed that they tended to be rigid-minded, and given to stereotyped thinking (all businessmen are conservative reactionaries; all professors are impractical and absent-minded; most short men dream of being Napoleon; and so on).

It was also found that they tended to judge people on the basis of superficial characteristics, such as their body build, profession, social and economic status, or nationality.

When it was demonstrated to these subjects that their rigid-mindedness impaired their ability to form accurate judgments of others, many of them followed the suggestion that they make a conscientious attempt to overcome this tendency. To the extent that they were successful in this, their "understanding" scores went up sharply on later tests.

Another finding of the study: People tend to believe that the better they like a person, the better they understand him. The tests showed this assumption to be generally untrue; and that the best insight into another's personality is obtained when you neither strongly like nor dislike him.

Says psychologist Kallejian, summing up the findings on this point: "We tend to believe that we understand best those people we like the most and feel that they are like us. In reality, great difficulty in understanding occurs with those whom we strongly like. We tend to see them as we want to expect them to be, rather than the way they actually are. The same difficulty occurs with those we dislike, since we tend to see in them characteristics which we dislike in ourselves."

For example, there is a tendency to describe disliked persons as hypocrites, while the identical behavior in a liked person is considered merely tactful. The aggressive businessman is seen as greedy if you dislike him, and quite astute if you like him.

If you want to increase your ability to understand the other fellow and sharpen your insight into his character and personality, the findings and conclusions of the two-year study provide a simple set of rules:

Six Rules to Help Increase Understanding

1. Don't jump to conclusions about people. Hold your appraisal of them in abeyance until you've had the opportunity to assess the various aspects of their personality.

2. Cultivate the art of listening sympathetically and intently.

3. You can toss a leading question into the conversation now and then but do it casually. Never give the impression of probing.

4. Don't try to put people into categories. (He's the such-and-such type.) They won't fit.

5. Don't be hypercritical. Instead of looking for faults, cultivate an attitude of tolerance and acceptance toward

people who think and feel differently from the way you do.

6. Remember that people want to be understood and that the art of understanding them lies principally in just easing the stumbling blocks out of the way.

Here is a test by which you can rate your own ability to judge others. It will reveal just how capable you are of understanding another person, and how well you can judge how he reacts or responds. It is recommended that you try this test with a number of different persons. The more persons you try it with, the better it will index your ability to understand people in general. The test is a shortened version of the one devised for the collegian study.

Here is how you take it:

First, pick out any person you wish.

Second, in the blank space following each of the test statements, indicate how you believe the selected person will respond, noting after each item T (true), PT (only partly true) or F (false).

Third, ask the person you selected to indicate on the same form the extent to which he feels each statement applies to him. He is to use the same designations: T, PT and F. (*Remember, answer each item exactly as your insight into the other person leads you to believe he will answer.*)

How to score: In each case where you have correctly surmised the other person's response, give yourself one point. A score of 10 to 12 is phenomenal, and indicates you are a person of rare insight. A score of seven to nine is excellent; four to six good; and a score of less than four indicates that your insight, at least into this particular person leaves something to be desired.

1. I usually make up my mind and stick to it.

                    T____PT____F____

2. I become uncomfortable when others criticize me.

                    T____PT____F____

3. I become uncomfortable when praised.

                    T____PT____F____

4. I need somebody to push me in order to get things done.

                    T____PT____F____

5. I usually lack self-confidence when competing with others.

T_____ PT_____ F_____

6. I would rather listen than become the center of attention.

T_____ PT_____ F_____

7. I make allowances for my own prejudices in forming opinions of others.

T_____ PT_____ F_____

8. I like to have others depend on me for help or supervision.

T_____ PT_____ F_____

9. I like to stay with a job until it is finished.

T_____ PT_____ F_____

10. I am reluctant to express opinions before hearing what others have to say.

T_____ PT_____ F_____

11. I keep control over my emotions.

T_____ PT_____ F_____

12. I like to have things carefully planned and carried out according to plan.

T_____ PT_____ F_____

IS HIS PERSONALITY SHOWING?
Telltale Mannerisms Make it Easy to see the Real Person

How much can you tell about a person just by looking?
Well, science has found that if you know the signs to look for
you can frequently tell far more than you'd ever suspect.

The Cleveland Clinic's Dr. Leonard L. Lovshin has spent
many years carefully checking, testing, and cataloguing the
various telltale signs which give away personality secrets and
make a person as easy to read as an open book.

Take the wearing of dark glasses, for example. Now there's
nothing wrong about wearing dark glasses outside and when
the sun is shining. But Dr. Lovshin has found — and leading
clinicians agree — that the wearing of dark glasses indoors, or
outside on days when the sun doesn't shine, is a strong
indication of neurosis. The dark glasses act as a shield for the
emotionally insecure person to hide behind. Also, as
Dr. Lovshin points out, it is typical of many high-strung and
overly nervous individuals that they cannot tolerate light even
though it is not bright by normal standards.

There are, of course, cases where a person who is perfectly
normal will wear dark glasses when the sun isn't out;
prominent persons traveling incognito or people who have
eye trouble, for example. But these are exceptions, not the
rule.

Tinted lenses, incidentally, have the same connotation as
the wearing of dark glasses. "It is exceedingly difficult to fit
glasses for a tense, high-strung, worrisome type of person,"
Dr. Lovshin points out, "and every eye specialist has had the
experience of having such a person protest plaintively that
the glasses did not fit right, even after they had been changed
three or four times. In desperation, the ophthalmologist
often prescribes a tint for the lenses and the patient is somewhat happier with them."

Dr. Lovshin's investigations also show that women (entertainers excepted) who pluck their eyebrows and pencil in a
line may be neurotic.

And though the fact that a woman dyes her hair was found

to have no particular personality significance, brunettes who bleached their hair platinum blonde very definitely tended to be maladjusted. (So take a look at their hair roots.)

What about people who wear toupees? The wearing of a toupee, Dr. Lovshin finds, is not in itself clinically significant. But a badly matched or poorly fitted toupee is something else again. And the person whose hairpiece doesn't look as if it quite belonged there isn't likely to have a well-balanced personality. But if you can't detect that the fringe is phony, there's no penalty on this one.

Other signs found to be associated with a neurotic or emotionally unstable personality were a whining or weepy voice, widely dilated pupils, and repeated sighing.

But the sign of greatest significance, Dr. Lovshin finds, is the presence of fluttering eyelids. Eyelid-fluttering simply does not go with a well-balanced personality. To be really proficient at this, a woman must be hysterical — or at least have a full-blown neurosis. This type is frequently observed in doctors' offices.

"The typical picture," says Dr. Lovshin, "is that of a delicate 'sissy' type of young woman who tells the doctor all her 'horrible' symptoms while managing a sweet, brave smile and a chaste fluttering of the eyelids. The mechanism of this fluttering is not known, but it cannot be reproduced voluntarily to the same delicate degree."

He also finds that the middle-aged woman who paints her lips in a tiny cupid's bow is almost always emotionally immature; and if a baby-like voice is included in the picture, you've got an almost sure bet that she's neurotic. If she also wears clothes that are too young for her, your bet is a sure thing.

The technique of exaggeration in speech, says Dr. Lovshin in summing his findings, is easily recognized and is a *positive* sign of neurosis. For example, the neurotic woman always has *terrible* pains and *horrible* aches; nothing is just ordinary — all the complaints are terrific. It's significant to note in this connection that women are much more addicted to this practice than men, and that studies have shown those who are addicted to be far more neurotic and emotionally unstable.

Dr. Lovshin also finds that this technique of overstatement can give away more about a person than perhaps any other characteristic. For example, he has found that the woman who keeps repeating that she has the most wonderful husband in the world has a marital relationship that is definitely suspect; and the woman who insists that her husband is the most wonderful man in the world, even before she is asked, is actively trying to hide her disappointment in him.

With a little practice, the average person can learn to make a great many shrewd deductions about others, simply by noting the things about which they make exaggerated statements. It's the same psychological principle Shakespeare used when he wrote: "The lady doth protest too much, methinks . . .," the Queen's remark to Hamlet about one of the actresses in the play within the play.

It should perhaps be emphasized that Dr. Lovshin's provocative tip-offs on how to size up others are by no means arbitrary judgments and opinions, but are based on careful clinical observations. But when you use them to X-ray the other person's ego, there's just a word of caution: take a look and see that your own personality secrets aren't showing.

IS HE A DAYDREAMER?
Get Him to Talk About It

Tom Jones is sitting at his desk. The expression on his face is blissful. But as you look closer you can see that his eyes are just staring out into space, not focused on anything at all. He's oblivious to the sounds around him. Typewriters click. Buzzers sound. But Jones doesn't hear them. The boss has approached, stands quietly by his desk. "Jones," he says . . .. But Jones doesn't hear. He's thousands of miles away — on a south sea isle fringed with coconut palms, attended by beautiful grass-skirted maidens. Or maybe he's dreaming of winning the Irish sweepstakes, or marrying the boss's daughter, or fishing in a quiet, secluded lake. The boss frowns slightly, his hand touches Jones' shoulder. Jones starts suddenly. His eyes blink and come back into focus. "Excuse me, sir," he says with a nervous laugh. "I — — I guess my mind was on something else."

Several desks away, two colleagues exchange glances. "He'll never get anywhere — that Jones," murmurs one. "Spends too much time daydreaming." Is he right? It's an interesting question. And science can supply us with an equally interesting answer. For studies show that whether a man daydreams little, much, or not at all provides an important clue to his character, abilities and chances for achievement.

At the Institute of Psychological Research of Teachers College, Columbia University, psychologist Jerome L. Singer and his associates completed a study of daydreaming in hundreds of men and women of various ages and walks of life. They discovered that nearly nine persons out of ten do some daydreaming. They divided the remaining subjects into two classifications: Those who daydreamed frequently and those who indulged comparatively seldom. Persons in both categories were then subjected to a battery of personality tests.

It was found that the frequent daydreamers differ startlingly from the others in personality, abilities and general outlook on life. These findings make it possible for you to gain instant insight into another person's character simply by jockeying the conversation around to daydreams, then asking if he indulges in them frequently or seldom.

First, however, we'll give you a quick run-down on what the investigators discovered about daydreaming in general. People daydream about everything from romance to murder. They daydream in bathtubs, in elevators (these are quickies), and while driving to work (this is a fine way to become an accident statistic), but the study showed that most daydreams occur shortly before sleep when the person is in bed. City people daydream more than country people. And people who daydream frequently have far more colorful and vivid daydreams than those who do it only occasionally.

A high percentage of daydreaming relates to love and romance ("I imagine myself clasped in the embrace of a warm, loving person who will satisfy all my needs"). Incidentally, it is intriguing and perhaps significant to note that bachelors and spinsters don't indulge in romantic daydreams any more frequently than married people do.

When it comes to judging feminine characteristics, looks and manner can sometimes be quite deceiving. So here's a tip: A quick way to find out if a girl is warmly responsive and completely feminine is to ask her how much she daydreams. The investigators found that girls who daydreamed frequently tended to be extremely feminine in every sense of the word. This was not true for girls who seldom did.

Most people's daydreams tended to serve a useful purpose and were attempts to explore the future through "trial actions." They were efforts to determine in advance the consequences of certain acts and situations — somewhat like trying on different pairs of shoes for size before committing oneself to an actual purchase; or, in other cases, like sending up a trial balloon to see if destiny shoots it full of holes.

For example, a young man pictures himself married to one of the girls he has been dating. This begins as a blissful reverie. Then, as he contemplates the girl's various traits and tendencies and pictures how she would act under various situations, his daydreams gradually becomes less rosy. He realizes suddenly how many characteristics she shares with

18

her mother — who is mercenary, calculating, shrewish and domineering. He recalls then that the girl's father gave the impression of being hen-pecked and brow-beaten. The young man's flight of imagination descends abruptly from the clouds. He decides this is definitely not for him.

Another man wonders if he should accept a job offered by an oil company in Arabia. He takes the information he has about the job, working conditions and locale, tosses it into a kind of mental daydream mixer, and adds a dash of imagination. He then projects himself into the picture and tries to "live" it and feel it as vividly as possible. If he likes what he experiences in his mind's eye, he's apt to take up the offer. If not, he passes and waits for fate to deal him a new set of cards.

The study showed that people who daydream frequently tend to differ markedly from those who do not, in the following personality traits:

The frequent daydreamer was found to have a higher degree of self-awareness, to be more acutely conscious of himself as a person. Being better acquainted with his innermost urges and desires, he is better able to provide them with adequate means of expression. If he translates his greater self-awareness into action, he has a definite edge over others in achieving goals that will bring him the greatest self-satisfaction. But if he fails to translate his insight into action, he will remain a frustrated dreamer, never able to achieve his real potential.

Frequently daydreamers were also found to have it over the others where creativity, resourcefulness and capacity for original thinking are concerned. If you fall in this category, you are most likely to distinguish yourself in a field requiring creative mental effort and flexibility in thinking.

On the other hand, the study showed that people who do *not* daydream frequently are more contented with their lot than the others, have a greater ability to take misfortunes and setbacks in their stride — and if they can't achieve their goals, they're more willing to compromise and make the best of the situation. In short, it takes less to make them happy. And they are far more willing to work hard for what they get.

People who daydreamed frequently, however, needed a

great deal to make them happy. They had a strong need for personal achievement. They set high goals — sometimes unrealistically high. And when goals were not achieved, they tended to become extremely frustrated and dissatisfied. They also had a strong need to "keep up with the Joneses," to acquire the material possessions and high social status associated with success and distinction. Moreover, they had a strong need to be liked and admired by others.

In short, the frequent daydreamer wants the best there is on the bill of fare, and if he channels his abilities astutely, he has a good chance of getting it. The study showed, however, that there is one characteristic in his personality that makes his opportunities fewer than they otherwise would be. It simply goes against his grain to climb the ladder of success the hard way, laboring persistently rung by rung. He lacks the patience to plod along when the grade is steep. He seeks an easier way, looks for shortcuts. And because he's ingenious and resource- ful, he often finds them. But just as often he doesn't.

People who daydream frequently tend to be nervous, sensitive, high-strung, keenly perceptive. Those who don't are much more calm, relaxed, methodical and matter-of-fact, down-to-earth rather than imaginative. The non-daydreamer doesn't aim as high as his colleagues in the other category, but he takes steadier aim and he's more apt to hit the marks he shoots at. Perhaps that is why, as the investigation showed, he enjoys greater freedom from worry and anxiety. As for the dyed-in-the-wool daydreamer, though many of his goals may be unobtainable, often he is able to turn the air castles he builds into realities. Then he can live in them — and he's really got it made!

HOW TO GET ALONG WITH ANYONE
The First Thing is to Understand Him or Her

The better you understand people — yourself included — the better you're going to get along in the world. How happy your marriage is, how effectively you can work with others, how adept you are in climbing the ladder of success, depends to a great extent on your ability to understand the people around you.

A team of behavior scientists, exploring the whys and wherefores of what makes people act the way they do, has come up with some fascinating findings which will make it a whole lot easier for you to understand your spouse, your boss, your fellow workers — and yourself.

They have found that everybody falls predominantly into one of four general personality types. Each type, in effect, lives in a completely different world — speaking, thinking, feeling, and reacting, in a different way from the others.

A candid camera profile of these four personality types is presented in an extensive study conducted by the research teams of Drs. Humphrey Osmond, Harriett Mann, and Miriam Siegler at the Bureau of Research in Neurology and Psychiatry at Princeton — who have found that each type not only lives in a different world of thought, emotion, and sensation, but even looks at time differently.

Here are the four types:

The Sensation Type. This type tends to live almost exclusively in the present. His headlights are focused on the now — the ever-present *present.* This absorbs him to such an extent that he has little time or inclination to contemplate either past or future. In the world he lives in, the present is the only reality. In his view, if you make the best of the present, everything else will take care of itself. The future isn't real to him until it becomes the present. And as for the past, except for a fleeting backward glance, he tends to regard it much as he would yesterday's newspaper.

Because, as the investigators note, all of his energy is concentrated on the present, and little or none is reserved for looking backwards or forwards, he is superbly effective when it comes to facing the immediate situation which confronts him and dealing with it.

They also observed that this type of person is so geared to the present (and so comfortable in dealing with it), that he sees much more in a situation than the other types can. He is a doer, not a planner. He doesn't like to plant seeds and then wait for them to come up. He is impatient and distrustful of delays. He believes in action *now*. It's not that he has no faith in tomorrow, it's just that his consciousness is so completely focused on the present that the future isn't quite real to him.

Once you understand this type's life style and the way he operates, no type is easier to get along with. But if you treat him like any of the other three types, it will just make for static.

The Intuitive Type. For this type the *future* is far more real than either the past or the present. He lives predominantly in the future, plans for the future, puts his faith in the future. He plants today what he reaps in his mind's eye tomorrow.

His intuition is highly developed. He is extremely sensitive to subconscious promptings and hunches, and constantly seeks to evaluate them. His acutely sensitive antenna — or sixth sense — is focused on future situations which are still in the process of shaping themselves. His capacity for intuitive thinking — involving lightening-like flashes of perception — is often amazingly accurate.

As the authors of the study observe: For the intuitive type, the present is a pale shadow, the past a mist; bright lights and excitement are to be found beyond the next bend in the road. Because of his faith in the future — his confidence in events and circumstances which have yet to actually materialize — this type often appears to others as flighty, impractical, and unrealistic.

The clock on the wall which emphasizes the presence of the *present,* is not music to the ears of the intuitive type — for his consciousness is geared to the future. As the investigators note, to be aware of time, to always be punctual, to have to keep to a schedule — these are demands which are both painful and bothersome to him. For it just isn't natural or comfortable for him to pay attention to time.

So, if for example, your husband happens to be in this category, pay attention to his hunches, but don't get angry if he keeps you waiting, or doesn't always get home for dinner on time!

The Feeling Type. He is most at home, and functions most effectively in the area of feeling and emotion. His heart rules his head — and he has a big heart, filled with compassion for others. He is, as the behavior scientists note, a warm, sensitive person who exudes joy, freshness, conviviality and companionship.

Basically this type tends to live more in the *past* than in the present or future. Things that happened to him last week, or last year, or ten years ago, are more real to him than the here and now. Before he can accept something new, he must be able to relate it to something he's already known. He's very likely to say: "Oh yes, this reminds me of such and such or so and so." As a result, it's difficult for him to be comfortable in a new situation. It's also hard for him to make a decision that might change his life drastically. Thus he may continue in a job or relationship he doesn't really feel happy in, rather than make a change.

It's easy for him to lose track of time. Thus — in common with the Intuitive Type — it's often hard for him to be punctual. If he becomes interested in something — conversation at lunch, for example — an extra hour or so may slip by without his realizing it. His penchant for being oblivious to the passing of time sometimes creates problems in various areas of his life. ("I had no idea it was so late. I just don't know where the time has gone!") And punctual people frequently show little patience with him. Another characteristic: once he has decided how he feels about someone, he is slow to change his feelings — even if the other person's actions may richly deserve it.

The Thinking Type. This type takes a logical, clear-headed view of the world — and sees time in the same way: as an endless ribbon linking past, present, and future. He is uncomfort-

23

able unless everything proceeds in an orderly, logical manner and sequence — and tends to reject anything that doesn't fit into this pattern.

The authors of the study point out that the Thinking Type is unbeatable in situations calling for logic, objectivity and clear-headedness. He is long on patience, and his foresight and ability to analyze and evaluate a situation give him a pronounced edge in many circumstances.

He is not, however, at his best under conditions demanding spontaneous, spur-of-the-moment action, because he needs time to make up his mind before he acts. One should take this into account when dealing with him, and not expect him to be at his best under impromptu conditions where planning and system are impossible and it's necessary to "play it by ear."

As the scientists observe: "It is only the thinking type who takes plans so seriously that they can be completely upset by having to change a prearranged schedule. There is, in fact, no easier way to confuse thinking types than to require them to deviate from the plan to which they were committed." These people want and expect life to proceed at the same, logical, clock-like sequences that *time* does.

They are, as the study shows, time oriented. "Thinking types do not trifle with time. Time for them is serious, real, and demanding." Let other types dream away the hours and kill time when they feel like it. Let them be late for appointments. Not the thinking type. He lives by it, sees it more objectively than any other type. He's always pretty certain to know what time it is. And even if he doesn't wear a watch, his mental clock — his sense of time — is usually pretty well synchronized with the one on the wall.

Few of us, of course, are *purely one type,* but — as the investigators observe in summing their findings — each person has a natural predisposition to one of the four attitudes. And science's findings make it clear that the secret in getting along with people — our spouses, our co-workers, and our friends — is to remember that people of the four key personality types live in what amounts to four different worlds, in the sense

24

that each experiences life quite differently. If our relationships with them are to be pleasant, productive and harmonious, we need to take into consideration their markedly different attitudes, abilities, and temperaments.

WHAT DO YOU KNOW ABOUT HUMAN NATURE?
You may be in for a Surprise
when you Match Wits with the Experts

Most of us find human nature a fascinating subject. Science does, too, and psychologists have come up with some very interesting discoveries in the what-makes-people-tick department. To match your wits with the findings of the experts, check which of the following questions you believe true or false — then read the answers.

1. You can increase your intelligence by associating with people who are smarter than you are. (True____, False____)

2. Where romance is concerned, absence makes the heart grow fonder. (True____, False____)

3. Happy people have the fewest automobile accidents. (True____, False____)

4. People who think nobody likes them are usually right. (True____, False____)

5. Time goes by faster when you are doing difficult work. (True____, False____)

6. The smarter you are, the easier it is for you to remember things. (True____, False____)

7. Take life easy and you'll live longer. (True____, False____)

8. In most cases, a person's voice gives him away when he tells a lie. (True____, False____)

9. Poor people worry more about money than those who have plenty of it. (True____, False____)

10. Women worry more than men do. (True____, False____)

Answers:

1. False. In wide-scale studies conducted by army psychologists, 400 trainees were separated into two groups: Those whose I.Q. was average or below and those who scored in the higher brackets. Men of lesser intelligence were then billeted with personnel of higher than average I.Q. for extended periods of time. Subsequent tests showed constant association with men of higher intelligence had no appreciable effect in increasing the I.Q. or general aptitude of the less-intelligent recruits. Conclusions of the investigators: Intelligence is something that won't rub off on others.

2. True for men, *False* for women. In studies conducted at the University of Redlands, psychological tests showed that where men are concerned, separation from their mate or sweetheart does tend to make the heart grow fonder; but with women it was found that such separation did not tend to increase romantic feelings toward the object of their affections. The study showed, in fact, that when the man she is interested in is absent for an appreciable period of time, a lady's affections are more likely to cool than grow warmer.

3. True. Psychological studies show that people who are happy and well-adjusted are the safest drivers, collect the fewest traffic scars such as dented fenders, smashed radiators, etc. For example, extensive studies conducted at the University of Western Ontario show conclusively that the motorist who has a happy outlook on life is far less subject to accidents than others.

4. True. University of London investigators made a study of this matter. Their findings showed that while unpopular people are particularly dense in sizing up the feelings of others about them, people who think nobody likes them are usually 100% correct.

5. True. Experiments at Duke University have shown that when you're doing work that is difficult and requires concentration, time appears to pass much more swiftly than when you are doing work that is easy for you.

6. False. University studies show that memory and intelligence are two distinct functions and that a man can be extremely intelligent and have a very poor memory — and vice versa. When memory tests were given children in New York city schools, it was found that the scores made by the mentally retarded were as high or higher than those of average or above-average intelligence.

7. *False.* New York University studies have shown that people who take life the easiest — who are the least active mentally and physically — age the quickest and are the least resistant to disease. Research at other universities bears out these findings and show conclusively that leading an active and busy life plays a vital part in longevity.

8. *True.* The odds are far better than even that you can tell when a person is lying just by listening to his voice. This has been demonstrated in psychological tests conducted at De Pauw University. In the experiment an audience of men and women students were asked to listen to the voices of hidden speakers and try to determine when they lied and when they told the truth. Investigators then asked the hidden speakers such questions as "How old are you?" "What do you weigh?" "What color is your necktie?" etc. They were instructed to answer some of the questions falsely and to lie in as plausible a manner as possible.

In the majority of cases, the listeners were able to correctly judge which of the statements were truthful and which were false.

9. *False.* Purdue University studies of persons in the various socio-economic brackets show that the class which has the least money does the least worrying about it. Sociologists found that people in the lower-income brackets not only worried less about money, but worried less about most other things. They showed a marked inclination to life for today and let tomorrow take care of itself.

10. *True.* Psychologists at the University of Southern California made a wide-scale study of men and women from various walks of life, found that women are more given to worry and feelings of depression than men are. Other investigations have shown that women are not only subject to a greater variety of fears and phobias, but that their anxiety reactions are more intense.

WALLS BETWEEN PEOPLE
"Getting to Know You" is Simple if You Understand the Rules

How many people do you really know? How many people really know you? When did you last have a conversation in which there was any real understanding? Does it seem that there is a wall between you and other people? Many persons are lonely, because they never get to really know others. Dr. Sidney M. Jourard of the University of Florida made a ten-year-study of loneliness.

Let's take a look at his findings.

Do most people wear a mask which prevents others from knowing them?

Yes, and this mark, or "public self," often has little in common with one's real self. It is adopted to impress others, or to help one play a role he feels is expected of him.

Dr. Jourard explains, "There are many reasons why we conceal our true selves from others; to protect ourselves against possible criticism, hurt, or rejection. But this protection is purchased at a steep price. When we are not truly known by the other people, we join the 'lonely crowd.'

His studies show that even within families, where you would expect people to discard their masks, each person may feel apart from the rest. "A husband," he says in his book, *The Transparent Self,* "can be married to his wife for 15 years and never know her. Often children do not know their parents; fathers do not know what their children think, or what they are doing."

Dr. Jourard's studies show that people often feel that they know another person, when in fact they do not know him at all. They have constructed a more or less imaginary picture of him in their minds.

What does it mean really to know a person?

It means to know what he thinks, feels, believes, wants, worries about, Dr. Jourard finds. And letting another person know what you think, feel, or want is the only really effective way you can make yourself known to another person.

How do you get another person to disclose himself to you?

By first taking him into your confidence. The study (based on the experience of hundreds of men and women from all walks of life) shows that self-disclosure begets self-disclosure. You must also, of course, have the other's confidence. He must feel that you are a person of good will, that you will respect his confidence, that you offer him understanding, and that you honestly care about him.

"Any man," Dr. Jourard observes, "will hide his real self from those who are not of good will, just as a poker player hides his hand from the other players."

Our lack of communication results in a frustrating social game in which, after observing the "I'm-so-glad-to-see-you's, we go on to say what the other person expects us to say. And each takes leave of the other feeling vaguely bored and dissatisfied without knowing why.

HOW TO LOVE THY NEIGHBOR
You Must First have Respect for Yourself

Millions of people seem unable to feel love. Psychologists have been conducting intensive studies to find out why. They have discovered that most people incapable of feeling affection for others lack esteem for themselves.

Psychologist Erick Fromm has observed that before a person can love and accept another person, he must first love and accept himself. Psychological tests show that anything that will raise a person's self-esteem or make him happier with himself will increase his ability to feel affection for others.

Low self-esteem accounts for more marital difficulties than any other single factor. The things which make so many marriages miserable, bickering, nagging, infidelity, in-law troubles, and excessive drinking are largely brought about by the fact that one partner has a low opinion of himself. Marriage counselors say that if a man is unhappy with himself he is likely to be unhappy with his mate.

Other studies bear out the fact that you tend to feel the same way about others as you do about yourself. Self-esteem (not conceit, but appreciation of one's own true worth) goes hand in hand with the ability to accept others, to tolerate human shortcomings, and to have positive feelings toward them.

University of Florida studies show that the more charitable a person is toward himself, the more he tries to give himself a break, the better his personality adjustment. The person who doesn't accept himself does not really see himself clearly. He is afraid to look for his virtues, for fear he might turn up faults which he does not want to acknowledge or accept.

Studies at the Massachusetts Institute of Technology prove that people who make low scores on self-acceptance tests have the strongest prejudices against others, including racial prejudice. Tests further showed that when psychologists were able to help a person to become more self accepting, his social prejudices decreased. Conclusion of the investigators: to change a man's attitude toward his fellow man, first change his attitude toward himself.

Why are some persons so lacking in self-esteem? A National Institute of Public Health study says the cause is simply an unrealistic attitude toward oneself, caused by the discrepancy between a person's ideal self-image and his actual self-image. His ideal image of himself sets such unreachable objectives that when he consistently fails to achieve them, he begins to dislike himself, feeling that he is not measuring up.

People with low self-esteem get that way because of self-defeating concepts which have little basis in fact. Dr. Richard F. Campbell, associate professor of family relations at San Fernando Valley State College, lists some typical false assumptions. Some people feel that one must be liked and approved of by everyone in order to be happy. Others feel that they must never need the approval or love of anyone. And some persons feel that they are complete failures if they have unresolved problems.

How can you raise your self-esteem? 1. Take a hard look at your ideal self-image: the way you wish you were. If it sets impossible goals, then cut it down to size. Remember that everyone has faults, so don't downgrade yourself because you fall short of perfection. Accept yourself as you are. 2. Listen to that inner voice of conscience. Try a little harder to do as you think you should.

Science's findings not only support the admonition, "Love thy neighbor as thyself," but make it evident that we cannot love our neighbor unless we live our lives in such a way that we are able to love ourselves.

If you can say, "I am what I am, and I find it good," you can love and be loved.

HOW TO WIN ARGUMENTS AND INFLUENCE PEOPLE
Some Things Non-Salesmen Don't Know

You will often hear someone say, "I have no influence with that person at all. Nothing I say makes any impression on him." Recently psychologists from leading universities and research organizations have been eavesdropping on arguments and discussions to learn who influences whom and why. Here are some of their findings arranged in true and false statments.

When you are arguing with someone and he raises his voice, you should raise your own voice just slightly above his, or you will be at a psychological disadvantage.

False. Raising your own voice is likely to have an antagonizing effect and get you nowhere. Your smartest move when the other fellow raises his voice is to lower yours until it is just audible, making it necessary for him to lean forward and listen carefully to catch what you are saying. This tactic forces him to pay closer attention to you; makes him automatically lower his own voice to the level of yours; and generally tends to throw him off his stride.

Women have built-in advantages for winning arguments.

True. Studies show that women are better when it comes to expressing themselves, and have a greater facility with words than the average man does. Investigations have also shown that a woman has a more acute insight into what goes on in another person's mind, can sense what lies behind his words, and can tailor her arguments accordingly. And when it comes to launching a verbal attack, Harvard University studies show that when a woman really tries, she can actually talk much faster than a man can. The findings suggest that most of men's verbal victories over women are hard-won triumphs. When a man wins one, he owes it to himself to celebrate.

The best time to persuade someone to your point of view is after you have treated him to a sumptuous meal.

False. This is a good time, but not the best time. Psychological experiments at Yale University show that the time he will be most susceptible to persuasion is while he is enjoying the meal. For, as the investigators note in summing the findings of the study: "The mood of compliance decreases in strength rapidly after the meal has been eaten."

Persons who are the easiest to influence find it the most difficult to influence anyone else.

True. Psychological studies at Canada's McMaster University show that nervous, high-strung persons who are highly intelligent are the easiest of all types to influence. They also, tests showed, are the most unsuccessful when it comes to influencing others.

Women are more easily influenced than men are.

True. Studies conducted by psychologists at Yale and elsewhere show that women tend to be more gullible than men, more susceptible to smooth-talking salesmen and glib con-artists. Men also are vulnerable to the fast pitch, but are more hard-headed and objective-minded than women.

It is easier to influence a friend than someone you do not know.

False. It is the other way around. People tend to be influenced by the opinions of strangers, and pay little heed to the counsel of a friend. ("I told her she ought to do that, and I'm her best friend. But it made no impression until someone she scarcely knew told her the same thing.") Perhaps because we recognize their fallibility, we tend to discount advice given us by persons close to us, friends, parents, relatives. Advice from an outsider seems somehow more authoritative.

A good-looking girl (or a handsome man) needs a special technique when trying to influence others.

True. Studies conducted at Syracuse University show that when a person is attractive he (or she) will be more successful in influencing another if, instead of using subtlety or finesse, he states frankly beforehand his intention to influence or persuade them to his way of thinking. ("Look, before we sit down, I should tell you I am going to try to talk you into something. Okay?") While the investigators found this technique increased the effectiveness of pretty girls and good-looking men, it did nothing to increase the persuasive ability of plain or average-looking subjects.

The worst time to sell a person on an idea, a project, or whatever is when he is bored.

False. Boredom decreases a person's resistance to persuasion. In scientific experiments, when men and women were subjected to conditions inducing boredom, they became more suggestible. This is why door-to-door salesmen may talk a bored housewife into purchases which make her wonder later what possessed her. It could likewise explain why people are sometimes persuaded to engage in outlandish behavior which is completely out of character for them. ("It seems crazy now, as I look back on it, but at the time Joe's suggestion seemed like a wonderful way to relieve the monotony.")

HOW WELL DO YOU UNDERSTAND PEOPLE?
Some Things it Helps to Know

You can tell whether a person is happy or not by his reply to a three-word question, and there is a best way to persuade anybody to do anything. You can match your own knowledge of human nature with that of the experts by seeing how many of their questions you can answer correctly without peeking at the text which follows.

Can you tell if a person is happy or not by the way he answers when you ask him "How are you?"

At Stanford University, Dr. Paul J. Moses made a lifetime study of voice patterns. His findings show that a person's voice is a mirror of his emotions; that while *words* may lie, *voices* seldom do.

He points out, for example, that the standard answer to the question "How are you?" is "Fine, thanks." Uttered in a high pitch, it indicates that the person is saying, "I really feel good." But said in a low or descending pitch, it means that he actually doesn't feel very good, and brings the answer close to complaint. And regardless of what a person may be saying, his tone of voice will often tell you far more about how he really feels than will his words.

Is it true that many people have a desire to be misunderstood and be made uncomfortable?

Yes. These are the people who seem to find a perverse kind of satisfaction in being at least mildly miserable. Almost everyone has a female relative in that category — a chronic kill-joy, with a thin-lipped upside-down smile that spreads good cheer like a wet blanket, and who appears to enjoy herself only when she is complaining of being put upon, neglected or unappreciated.

Menninger Clinic studies show that people like this have a deep-seated personality quirk which gives them a strong need and desire to be misunderstood and be made uncomfortable. And if circumstances don't provide this situation, they'll find some way to create it, or convince themselves that it exists.

Does eating make you more susceptible to persuasion?

Yes — particularly if it's something tasty. Recent Yale University studies show that you are much more likely to believe and be influenced by something you read if you are eating something appetizing *while* you are reading it. Tests showed that eating before or after did not have the same effect. (Note: Obviously the best time to impress your boss with that report you've prepared is while he's putting away some food or refreshment. And wives may want to show their husbands the ad for that new whatever-it-is-they-have-their-hearts-set-on-while — not after — he's relishing one of his favorite foods.)

What is the best way to persuade someone to do something?

To find out the answer to this question Yale University psychologists conducted a special study. They found that it depends on whether the person you wish to persuade has 1. a self-confident, optimistic outlook, and thinks well of himself; or 2. is lacking in confidence, feels insecure, and is given to self-doubt.

The study showed that the most effective way to persuade the person who is *lacking* in self-confidence is to stress how *bad* it will be — how much he may regret it — if he doesn't do what you feel he should.

The psychologists found that with people who are self-confident and self-assured, the best approach is to show him how *good* things will be — how well the situation will work out — if he follows your counsel. In other words, one responds best to the negative approach, the other to the positive. Mix 'em up and you'll get nowhere.

Which get angry more often, men or women?

Anger studies conducted at Columbia University and Oregon State College show that the average man gets angry and really loses his temper on an average of about six times a week, whereas the average woman gets angry enough to blow her top an average of only three times a week or only half as often as men. The study also showed that women "got mad" most frequently at other people (real or fancied slights, and assorted personal grievances). Men's tempers were more likely to flare up at inanimate objects (such as a flat tire, a missed train, or a faulty razor).

'LET'S SHAKE ON THAT!'
How You Do It Tells What You Are

The way a man shakes hands tells more about his character than anything he says. The hand is an extension of the personality. Many persons cannot express themselves without making gestures. A man's handshake is of great social significance.

Psychiatrist Sandor S. Feldman says that in a good handshake the hands of two people are clasped with equal pressure by both parties. If one person doesn't exert this pressure, the other feels let down, and his feeling is justified, for the other person's handshake shows how he really feels.

Dr. Joost A. M. Meerloo has made a study of what he calls the psychodynamics of the handshake: in nearly every greeting there is a mutual reaching out for approval and acceptance. Each person's feelings and their reactions to each other are transmitted. The man who greets you with a deadpan handshake is secretely looking down at you. Another may go through the business of shaking hands in a roughshod manner. He is trying to hide his own insecurity. Another may keep his handshake as sterile as aseptic as possible, giving nothing of himself, no feeling of either fellowship or respect.

Here are some other commonly encountered handshakes.

Limp. The fingers have the feeling of an overcooked noodle, and the grip is feeble. A Northwestern University study links this type of handgrip with a negative outlook on life. It is popular among pessimists, chronic doubters, and people who wear dark glasses.

Bone crusher. The person thrusts out his hand aggressively, enfolding yours in a vice-like grip until you flinch or show other signs of being impressed. It is used by people who have a need to impress others with their physical prowess. Such people tend to like body-building exercises and to keep in shape. They have pronounced feelings of inferiority and emotional insecurity. By developing their muscles, and cultivating an overpowering handshake and an aggressive demeanor, they seek to compensate for feelings of inadequacy.

Hesitant. He cannot seem to make up his mind whether he

wants to shake hands or not. By the time you decide he doesn't want to, and have your hand back in your pocket, he suddenly whips out his, and waits for you to shake it. He tends to be equally indecisive in everyday life. By the time he has decided to act on an impulse, he has lost the impulse.

Close-to-the-body. The arm is not outstretched; the elbow is bent at right angles; the hand is held close to the body with little more than the wrist extending. This marks the cautious, conservative person. He does not stick either his hand or his neck out very far.

Compulsive. He never misses an opportunity to thrust out his hand and shake yours vigorously. He will do this when he arrives, when he leaves, when he passes you on the street. He has even been known to do it to persons whom he is not quite sure he knows. His compulsion reflects insecurity and fear of non-acceptance. He gets a temporary reassurance by shaking hands, and anybody's hand will do.

Nongrip. This is not really a handshake at all, though it passes for one. The person keeps his hand stiff and extends only his fingers. He simply does not want to get involved with you, or with anyone. And after one of his handshakes, most people get the message.

Matter-of-fact. He grasps your hand without really seeming to be aware of it, or of you. He puts no feeling into it, gets none out. And the same applies to most of his personal relationships. He is so preoccupied with his own objectives that he tends to think of people more as objects than as fellow human beings.

Jackhammer. He grasps your hand in a mechanical way, as though coupling a freight car. Then he shakes your hand with a series of convulsive jerks like a short-stroke piston with a loose push rod. He tends to be determined, rigid-minded, strong-willed, and inflexible in attitudes.

Captive audience. Favored by high-pressure salesmen, back slappers, promoters, and similar types. He grasps your hand, shakes it, and then holds onto it while he begins his pitch. He keeps talking, but does not release your hand until he feels he is getting through to you. If you start edging away, he'll say, "Of course, I know you're a busy man," and shake hands again, holding on while he continues talking.

This man is an opportunist, who regards people as objects to be manipulated. If he thinks he can further his ambition by using you in any way, he will. The best defense is to keep your hands clasped behind you.

WHAT YOUR LAUGHTER TELLS ABOUT YOU
Robust Guffaws (when appropriate) are the Healthiest

Someone has observed that laughing is "feeling good all over, and showing it principally in one spot." And Thackeray said that a good laugh is sunshine in the house. All this is true, but there are many kinds of laughter and each has a different significance. Recent psychological investigations have turned up some new findings about laughter.

Is it true that your laughter often tells a great deal about you?

Yes. Laughter can be most revealing. Yet it is often used to *mask* one's feelings, a screen to hide behind. ("What did he say when you asked him that question?" "Oh, he just laughed and changed the subject.")

What does a man's laughter tell you about his sense of humor?

It can tell you whether he has any or not. You can use the same method researchers employed in a psychological study. Tell him a completely pointless joke. The harder he laughs, the less sense of humor he is likely to have. For the louder a person laughs at a pointless joke, the more he doubts his ability to distinguish between what is funny and what is not. To cover his lack of appreciation, he tries to play it safe by laughing at anything that sounds as if it may be funny.

But don't fault him for a faint smile or a polite chuckle. He is probably only trying to keep from hurting your feelings, and he has probably decided that *you* don't have much sense of humor.

Is it true that laughter provides an excellent nervous tension release?

Yes. Harvard Professor Robert Freed Bales, who has made a study of the subject, finds that laughter provides instant release for pent up feelings of all kinds. It serves as a means of "discharging conflicted emotional states that can no longer be contained," he says. The emotions, he notes, may be anxiety, aggression, affection, or any other. That is why, in a tense social situation, laughter can often do more to "clear the air" than anything else.

What about people who are hard to coax even a chuckle from, who habitually repress their laughter for fear of losing their dignity?

Just as laughter often allows the release of pent-up feelings, psychiatric studies indicate that *repression* of laughter, if done habitually, can lead to psychosomatic symptoms, such as a headache. The person who seldom permits himself to respond to a funny situation with robust laughter, who for fear of losing dignity allows himself little more than a tight smile, is a likely subject for one of the many stress ailments.

What about people who laugh frequently when nothing is funny?

Laughing when there is nothing to laugh at is characteristic of people who are unsure of themselves. Such persons usually score high on anxiety tests. Their mirthless laughter assumes various forms and guises. They will often make some quite ordinary comments and then give a depreciating little laugh (indicative of lack of confidence or self-esteem) as though to say, "What I said probably didn't amount to much and may sound rather silly, but I couldn't think of anything else to say."

One psychiatric study observed that "the bizarre laughter of schizophrenics closely parallels that laughter of normal persons who laugh when there is nothing funny to laugh at."

Do some people use laughter as a weapon?

Yes, unfortunately that is true. A hostile person may use

it to vent his feelings on another. For, as one of the pioneer investigators of laughter says, "Two factors make laughter a most powerful weapon: 1. The humiliation normally felt by the person who is its object, a degradation similar to that of a beaten person. 2. The fact that, for some inexplicable reason, derisive laughter is contagious: even neutral bystanders are tempted to join on the side of derision."

How many kinds of laughter are there?

Psychological investigators agree that the varieties of laughter run a wide range, from the robust belly laugh to the nervous high-pitched giggle. The authors of one study observe that although laughter is a common expression of joy or delight, it does not always have that meaning. There is "hollow laughter," the laughter of fear and embarrassment. "Laughter," they conclude, "appears to be a fundamental reaction to limiting situations for which one has no ready reply."

And then there is bitter laughter. Psychiatrist Edmund Bergler, who made an exhaustive study of various forms of laughter, defined it as "one of the by-products of injustice-collecting." The injustice collector habitually magnifies trifles (examples of how he was put upon, or taken advantage of) because they fit into his constant inner need to prove to himself that he is the innocent victim of another's malice. So anxious is the injustice collector to justify feeling sorry for himself that even inanimate objects are used for this purpose. ("So, of course, when I had only ten minutes to get to my appointment, the car battery *would* pick that time to go dead." A statement like this is fittingly punctuated by bitter laughter.)

And then there is the fellow who laughs louder than anyone else at his own joke. He is an egotist.

There is also the person who habitually laughs without opening his mouth, the sound coming out of his nose in muffled rumblings and snorts. He represses his feelings the way he does his laughter; he keeps his emotions under tight reins. He rarely acts on impulse.

And then there is the flat, empty, humorless crackle. A humorless laughter of long standing is easily recognized. His mouth is likely to turn down at the corners.

What about laughter in dreams?

Dr. Martin Grotjahn, Clinical Professor of Psychiatry at the University of Southern California, has made a special study of laughter in dreams. He finds that dreams in which the subject is amused to the point that he bursts out with hilarious laughter are by no means uncommon. His findings show that it takes a lot less to make a person laugh in a dream state than when he is awake. A situation or joke which strikes a person as uproariously funny when occurring in a dream would be likely to strike a person as silly or pointless if it took place when he was awake. For we respond to primitive, childish forms of humor in dream states, humor which would hardly rate more than a wry smile if we were awake when we heard it.

SIX QUIRKS OF HUMAN NATURE
Psychological Studies have Discovered some
Surprising Facts about People

Since we're all human it's no wonder that surveys repeatedly show that the subject most people consider most interesting is human nature, why people behave as they do. Science is continually making new discoveries in this realm. Let's take a look at some of them.

Can you tell by a person's eyes whether or not you're making a good impression on him?

Yes. You can tell by noting the amount of time he maintains eye contact with you during conversation. Psychological studies at the University of California show that if each time he glances at you he looks quickly away, you're not making much of an impression. But if, with each glance, his eyes stay on yours for an appreciable interval, you're making a good impression on him.

Is a husband or a wife the better judge of whether or not the spouse is telling the truth?

The wife. In tests at DePauw University, psychologists found that even when she looks at her husband through rose-colored glasses, a woman is much more proficient than a man in judging whether he is lying or telling the truth just from the sound of his voice.

What do your dreams tell about your personality?

In dream research conducted at Washington State University, investigators separated students into several categories, according to the type of dreams they had, then subjected them to a series of personality tests. These were their findings:

Tension dreamers: those whose dreams tended to reflect anxiety, frustration, or hostility as the major theme. These people were found prone to worry about their physical health — with a tendency toward hypochondria.

They also tended to be distracted easily, found it difficult to sustain work activity, and were inclined to set aside an unfinished task to take up something else. They were particularly intrigued by novelty, change-of-pace, or diversion.

Social dreamers: those who dreamed of relaxed, pleasant relationships with other human beings. (Meeting or having dinner with an interesting person, attending an enjoyable party, or other social event.) Social dreamers actually tended to be introverted in real life, and were frequently inclined to shrink from contact with others. They were able to realize in their dreams situations which they had difficulty achieving in waking life.

Reward dreamers: those whose dreams featured such themes as achievement, status, and recognition (getting a raise, a promotion, receiving a gift). These dreamers were found to be dominating individuals, desiring leadership responsibility and the attention of admiration of others. They were more self-confident than the people in the other groups and tended to have greater intellectual facility.

People who report *no* reward themes of any kind in their dreams tended to be subject to depression and moodiness. They also were inclined to be pessimistic and to harbor more than their share of fears, anxieties, and compulsions.

Is a short, heavy-set person easier to fool and more suggestible than a tall, slender type?

Studies conducted on hundreds of subjects at Sweden's University of Lund have shown a definite relationship between a person's body build and his susceptibility to persuasion. The well-proportioned, athletic type tended to be the easiest to influence. The tall, slender type was more resistant to persuasion and harder to fool. And men and women of the short, stocky type tended to be the most independent minded, the least gullible, and the least susceptible to persuasion and outside influence.

Do most people enjoy meeting strangers?

Most people don't, according to a study recently conducted at a leading university. The psychologists arranged a group of six chairs an equal distance from each other in a waiting room. Sixty-six men and women were taken, one at a time, to the room under various pretexts and asked to sit down. Note was taken that two of the chairs were the most popular, probably because they were the most comfortable and afforded the

44

best view.

The experiment was then repeated — with a difference. This time when the person entered, there was someone sitting in the chair next to the most popular ones. Results: *Not one* of the 66 subjects would sit next to the other person, even though it meant sitting in a less comfortable place.

What is the best way to persuade someone to do something?

Yale University psychologists found that it depends on whether the person you wish to persuade has 1. an optimistic outlook, and thinks well of himself; or 2. feels insecure, and is given to self-doubts. The study showed that the most effective way to persuade the person who *lacks* self-confidence is to stress how *bad* it will be, how much he may regret it, if he doesn't do what you feel he should.

With people who are self-assured, the best approach is to show him how *good* things will be, how well the situation will work out, if he follows your counsel. In other words, one responds best to the negative approach, the other to the positive.

PEOPLE ARE FUNNY THAT WAY
More Seemingly Odd Quirks that are Common to Most of Us

Nearly everyone finds human nature fascinating. Science does, too, and psychiatrists and psychologists have recently made some interesting discoveries about people. Here are some of the findings:

Is it true that people who are the most worth knowing are the hardest to get to know?

Studies at Purdue University found the opposite to be true. The investigation showed that people who are the most difficult to get to know, or who don't like to reveal their true selves to another person, tend to be conflict-ridden, unhappy with themselves, and incapable of a really rewarding relationship with any other human being. They wear a mask, or public self, and they are quick to resent it when anyone shows enough interest to probe more deeply to find out what they are really like.

The same studies showed that happy people, who had few conflicts, showed no tendency to hide their real selves behind surface appearances of affectations. They were the same all the way through, liked being known and understood by others, and enjoyed cultivating close relationships with people they were attracted to.

Is it true that a person will return to the scene of his crime in hope of being caught?

This is seldom so, according to studies by Dr. Sandor S. Feldman, professor of psychiatry at the University of Rochester. "It is popularly believed," he says, "that conscience forces a person to return to the scene hoping to be caught and so be relieved of his guilt. This is not so. In most instances, it is quite the opposite; he goes back in order to prove to himself that he will not be caught. Sometimes he fails, and is apprehended, but he is willing to take that chance to convince himself that he is free of suspicion."

Is it true that people want to be liked even by their enemies?

A psychological study of both men and women sponsored by the National Science Foundation has demonstrated that a person finds it embarrassing to discover that someone likes him more than he likes them. And the investigation showed that most people find it upsetting indeed to find that they are highly esteemed by someone they think of as an enemy. They prefer to be disliked by people they dislike.

Are men better than women at reading emotion in another person's face?

No. Psychological studies show that women are superior to men when it comes to judging what a person is feeling from his facial expression. Tests also show that women are better at judging what a person's character is like just by looking at him.

Does hot weather make you more accident prone?

Yes. Studies conducted by the Economic and Social Research Institute, which made psychological in-depth surveys in several countries, found that when temperatures rise, both anxiety and accident proneness tend to increase. The thermometer may provide a good index to your chances of crossing a busy intersection without an accident.

Is it true that a well-adjusted person seldom blames himself for the fact that he isn't happier or more successful, feeling that such things as luck or chance, which are outside his control, are far more likely to be responsible?

No. Duke University researchers gave selected students standard personality tests, then compared the attitudes of the well-adjusted with the less well-adjusted. Conclusion of the investigators: the well-adjusted person who has high self-esteem, perceived himself as largely responsible for what happens to him. He doesn't blame society, or the fact that someone else got a better break, or his own lack of opportunity.

Would you be happier if you could have everything you wanted?

No. If you had everything you wanted, there would be nothing left to work for, nothing to look forward to, no challenges to pit your abilities against. The fruits of hard-won victory are far more sweet than unearned good fortune. Psychologists agree that it's a lucky thing most people don't get everything they want, for few of us really know what's best for us, or even what we really want.

Is it true that if you do a person a favor, it makes him like you better?

Recent psychological tests at Stanford University show that when you do a person a favor, it usually has no effect on how he feels about you or how much he likes you. What it does do, in the investigators' words, is "to create a feeling of obligation in the other person which can be eliminated only by reciprocating the favor." So doing a good turn for someone will make him want to do the same for you.

But it will not affect his liking for you one way or the other. If he is unable to return the favor, it may damage your relationship, since most people dislike the feeling of being obligated.

DON'T SCOFF AT OLD WIVES' TALES
They may be Trite, but Time has Proved
a Lot of Them to be True

How many things that you have taken for granted all your life aren't true? And how many "myths" that you've laughed at are actually fact?

In universities and research foundations popular beliefs have come in for some serious scrutiny. Truth has been separated from half-truth, fact from fallacy. Some alleged old wives' tales have proved to be well-founded, and things which have long been accepted as true have become exploded fallacies.

To check your own beliefs against what science has found out, try this quiz. Examine each statement carefully, and then indicate whether you believe it to be true or false.

1. Fright can make your hair turn white overnight.

T. [　] F. [　]

2. If you don't worry, you'll never get an ulcer.

T. [　] F. [　]

3. The better a husband and wife understand each other, the happier their marriage is likely to be. T. [　] F. [　]

4. Many people can predict weather changes by the way their feet feel. T. [　] F. [　]

5. Churchgoers are kindlier and more honest than the rest of the population. T. [　] F. [　]

6. People who are psychologically well-adjusted can work better under noisy conditions than those who are neurotic or emotionally unstable. T. [　] F. [　]

7. Eating certain foods can cause you to dream.

T. [　] F. [　]

8. People of the working class are more neighborly than those in the upper classes. T. [　] F. [　]

9. Though their minds may be warped, most murderers have a high I.Q. T. [　] F. [　]

Answers

1. *True.* Until recently medical authorities regarded hair turning white as an old wives' tale, believed it physiologically impossible for hair to suddenly whiten. But some cases have

now been scientifically accredited. Leading dermatologists, including Dr. Agnes Savill, author of *The Hair and the Scalp* and Dr. Lee McCarthy, author of *Diagnosis and Treatment of the Hair,* agree that sudden whitening of the hair does occasionally occur. It may be caused by emotions such as extreme fright or grief, or by severe nervous shock. Medical authorities also cite cases where a man's mustache or beard has turned white overnight.

2. *False.* It has long been established that worry can be — and frequently is — a *factor* in producing ulcers. But medical authorities agree that there are many other things besides worry which can cause an ulcer. As a matter of fact, babies are sometimes *born* with an ulcer. One leading pediatrician estimates that more than 1% of all infants suffer from ulcers just as their worried elders do, and he believes that the incidence may be even higher because of failure to recognize the symptoms in children until very recently. If you're a worried businessman with an ulcer, the odds are that your mental state is at least partly responsible. But on the other hand, who knows? Maybe you were born with them!

3. *False.* Psychological studies recently conducted at the University of Chicago show that your happiness in marriage does not depend upon how well you understand your wife (or husband).

On the contrary, the investigation showed that there is no evidence at all that understanding your mate is a factor in marital happiness. In fact, the wife who has such insight into her husband's personality that she can "read him like a book" isn't likely to be one bit happier than the one who shrugs resignedly and says: "Men! I simply can't understand them."

And there is, as a matter of fact, evidence to suggest that the husband who regards his wife as an unpredictable enigma, impossible really to fathom, may be much happier than the husband who knows his wife too well — and can correctly analyze her motives and attitudes.

4. *True.* Science has found that Grandpa's corns and bunions weren't kidding when they told him a storm was brewing and that sensitive feet can forecast weather changes

within a 24-hour period with surprising accuracy. Studies by Dr. William J. Stickel, former executive secretary of the National Association of Chiropodists, show that: "Feet, particularly in tight shoes, are sensitive to changes in atmospheric pressure — and a painful corn can quickly indicate changes in barometric pressure."

5. *True*. A recent survey shows that, on the whole, people who go to church are more apt to possess these qualities than non-churchgoers.

Other investigations have shown, incidentally, that people who go to church tend to be better educated, and more successful in their relationships with others, and enjoy higher income on the average, than non-churchgoers. And some interesting studies conducted at the University of Colorado show that persons who are the most religious-minded are the most courteous and considerate drivers, and average the fewest accidents on the road.

6. *False*. Here's a real surprise: People who are poorly adjusted work significantly better under conditions of loud noise than do persons with well-adjusted personalities, according to recent studies at the University of Oklahoma.

7. *True*. Foods can cause you to dream. And studies conducted at Ohio State University have shown that foods most likely to cause dreams are watermelon, fresh pineapple, cucumbers, bananas. The study showed, incidentally, what a lot of people already suspected — that you are far less likely to dream if you don't eat just before going to bed.

8. *False*. Recent wide-scale sociological studies show that people of the upper classes are, on the whole, far more neighborly than are working people belonging to the lower and lower-middle classes.

Sociologist Judith T. Shuval believes that this phenomenon may be largely due to the fact that people in the lower socio-economic classes "have less time, are subject to greater fatigue from harder physical exertion at work, have fewer available means for entertaining, and may lack facilities for receiving guests in the home."

9. *False*. The popular impression fostered by mystery

stories and movies that most murderers are scheming, crafty Fu Manchu types has no basis in fact.

Studies made by professional criminologists show that I.Q. of most murderers ranks far below the average; and that they are on the whole, less intelligent than any other type of criminal. One researcher, for example, discovered that only one murderer out of four possessed as much brain power as the average citizen does.

After a careful study of 200 typical murderers, Pomona College psychologists concluded that most homicides are committed because the individual lacks the intelligence to deal with an intimidating problem or situation — except by direct and primitively violent means.

YOUR CHILD IS MORE CREATIVE THAN YOU THINK
Recognize the Signs of Special Ability and
You can give Special Support

Every child is creative. But parents often fail to recognize the signs of creativity. They may misunderstand or even unintentionally discourage the expression of budding abilities. Children may hesitate to express themselves for fear of rebuffs.

Recent studies make it easier for parents to recognize and encourage creativity. For, as the studies make clear, your child is likely to be far more creative than you think.

True creativity is not merely an aptitude for art, writing, music, designing, and so on. Creativity is a way of life. It distinguishes outstanding work from the ordinary in every field of endeavor: science, mathematics, medicine, law, economics.

What are the ways in which children's creativity shows itself?

Dr. E. Paul Torrance, of the University of Georgia, has specialized in the creative potential in children, and carefully evaluated the findings of other leading studies. Here are the characteristics he finds closely associated with creativity in children. 1. A good sense of humor. 2. Sensitivity. 3. A liking and appreciation for color. 4. Enjoyment of reading. 5. Daydreaming: often gets lost in thought. 6. Ability to amuse self with simple things in imaginative ways; finding unusual uses for toys other than just the intended ones. 7. Original ways of doing things that are different from the standard directions. 8. Questioning beyond the single "why" or "how"; sometimes curious to the point where parents may find it annoying. 9. A flexible mind, with the ability to shift from one approach to another in his thinking. 10. Fluency and originality; producing a wide variety of ideas, including unusual solutions to problems.

Can a child of only average I.Q. have important creative ability?

Yes. The creative process differs from the ability to think and reason. The U.S. Office of Education sponsored an

53

extensive psychological study of young children, directed by psychologists Michael A. Wallach and Nathan Kogan. It found that children fell into four specific categories: 1. High creativity and high intelligence. 2. High intelligence but not high creativity. 3. High creativity but not high intelligence. 4. Not high in either creativity or intelligence.

Children in the first category were found to be bright in the classroom, with a long attention span and a high capacity for concentration on academic work. They also were found to be "the most socially well-adjusted of any of the groups. They had the strongest inclination to be friends with others. Others also had the strongest inclinations to be friends with them. They also were the least likely to harbor doubts about themselves, their actions, or their work."

Children in the second category also possessed "strong capacities for concentration on academic work and a long attention span." But there were marked differences between them and the first group. They were more conservative in their behavior, less excitable, more hesitant about expressing their opinions, and least likely of all four groups to indulge in eccentric or unpredictable behavior in the classroom. They were more conventional in their life style. The investigators describe their attitude as characterized by coolness or reserve in their relations with their peers; a tendency to conform to expectations; and an extraordinary ability to adjust to conditions and fit in harmoniously in their environment.

Children in the third category found it more difficult to maintain attention in class. They were more likely to let their minds wander than concentrate on what may seem to them a dull or difficult textbook. Nevertheless they did have the innate capacity to distinguish themselves in whatever area their ability tended. The authors of the study observed, "Children in this category give evidence of the same kind of creative thinking found in the high-creativity, high-intelligence group." But they did show a marked tendency to be lacking in self-confidence, to become discouraged. To compensate for this tendency, parents and teachers need to give these children much encouragement and reassurance.

Children in the fourth category, whose scores were not high on either I.Q. or creativity tests, were not likely to astonish the world, but they were found to possess in generous measure qualities essential to happiness and contentment. Observations showed them to be exceptionally gifted in the art of getting along well with others, both in teamwork and at play. They were much less hesitant about expressing themselves, were much more serene and self-assured and more confident of their ability to get along in the world than many of the more brilliant children. The psychologists noted that these children seem to have worked out an approach to life which makes them comfortable with the people around them.

What does it mean if your child has imaginary companions?

Studies show that if your child has one or more imaginary playmates he is highly creative. Researchers at Fordham University interviewed hundreds of people who had distinguished themselves by creative achievements, and hundreds of others with no such distinction. Those in the more creative group reported the existence of imaginary companions significantly more often than did those in the other group.

What other characteristics are associated with creativity in a child?

The most creative children, studies show, tend to be open rather than close-minded, welcoming and sorting out all new concepts and ideas, even those which at first may seem out-landish. They also are likely to be impulsive, spontaneous, heart-rules-the-head people, often given to acting on the spur of the moment; and frequently arriving at decisions by intuitive leaps, rather than taking time to think a thing through.

Does the time of day have anything to do with a child's creative ability?

Yes. Most children who are introverts tend to function better in the morning. But tests show that extrovert children do better in the afternoon. This introvert-extrovert difference has been demonstrated by psychological studies conducted at Cambridge. So if your child shows creative ability in music, painting, or writing, for example, the most productive time of the day to pursue this activity would depend on whether he is predominantly introverted or extroverted.

What distinguishes the life styles of the most creative children as they grow into adolescents and approach maturity?

Michigan State University investigators made a study of adolescents with marked creative ability. In many respects, their characteristic life styles had much in common with highly creative younger children. They were found, for example, to have ideas on a very wide range of subjects, from art to zoology. And they wanted the opportunity to share ideas with others.

Other findings: "They were highly sensitive to intellectual dishonesty, especially in their teachers. They were critical of drill or repetitious and recitation-type classroom procedures. They wanted more independent study opportunities. Though they expressed strong criticisms of society, they appeared to be optimistic about man and his future. Almost all of the girls and over half of the boys were interested in understanding themselves and others. Almost all had at least one adult in their families with whom they closely identified."

Do highly creative children have special problems?

The more creative a child is, the greater the differences between him and most of his playmates. As these differences widen with the development of his creativity, he may sometimes find it difficult to be accepted by his fellows. Unless he is well-adjusted socially, he may come to be considered "different" and somehow alien by the children around him at school and at play. He may even become what one authority has termed "a minority of one."

Parents can do much to help the exceptionally gifted child cope with such problems. But this requires sensitivity and understanding on their part. If your child's outstanding abilities make it difficult for him to get along with other children in the neighborhood, you can try to find children with similar talents for him to play with. You also can devote more time and consideration to him yourself, thus cultivating a closer and more rewarding parent-child relationship. Children who may be jealous of your child's endowments may try to belittle him whenever they can. You can offset this by helping him to feel a sense of his own worth.

Dr. Torrance observes, "Since creativity involves independence of mind, nonconformity to group pressures, or breaking out of the mold, it is inevitable that highly creative children experience some unusual problems of adjustment. It is important that parents and educators understand and appreciate this fact."

How can you increase your child's creativity?

One of the most effective ways is to encourage him to use it. Get him to solve various tasks and problems, encourage him to express his ideas both by writing them down and by communicating them verbally. Encourage him also to increase his vocabulary, so that he will completely understand more of what he reads and be able to communicate more of what he feels. Creativity without adequate means of expression tends to wither. A child should be continually encouraged to "talk out" his feelings about anything and everything under the sun, and to express himself as fully as possible. All psychological tests show that facility with words is closely related to creative thinking, with each stimulating the development of the other.

What else can you do to help your child develop his C.Q. (Creativity Quotient)?

Even if his never ending curiosity about things gets you down sometimes, do not discourage it. If you do not know the answers to questions he wonders about, try to find someone who does, or look up the answers in a reference book or encyclopedia. And as soon as he is old enough, show him how to look up things for himself.

Study those subjects he shows special interest in, so you can discuss them with him intelligently. Bring up intriguing aspects of the subject that may not have occurred to him. When he makes controversial assertions about this or that, challenge him to support them. A spirited discussion of a subject which interests him sharpens any child's creative thinking prowess.

HOW MUCH DO YOU KNOW ABOUT PEOPLE?
For Understanding, the More the Better

Human nature has often been called the most fascinating subject in the world, and a nationwide opinion poll has shown that most people regard it as such. Science is similarly intrigued by the reasons human beings behave the way they do.

Can you think faster when you're on your feet?

Yes. Where quick, active, vigorous thought-action is required, recent psychological studies at Long Island University show that you'll do better standing up than in any other position. However, tests showed that for passive, contemplative, or imaginative thinking a reclining position is best. And while sitting upright was found to be more conducive to fast thinking than lying down, most people's mental reactions are swifter when they are on their feet.

Are poor people friendlier than rich people?

Generally speaking, no. Sociological studies at two leading universities have shown that people in the middle and higher-income brackets average appreciably more close friends and casual acquaintances than do those in the lower-income brackets. The investigations also showed that people who are comfortably endowed financially are much more likely to be on good terms with their next-door neighbors.

Is it true that most people who fail to succeed in life do so because they don't know enough?

No. A wide-scale industrial survey of employment records has shown that for every man who fails because of lack of knowledge of education, two fail because of personality factors. These personality qualities, which were found to be the chief stumbling block to success, including inability to get along with others, lack of dependability, laziness, and similar characteristics. In another survey, hundreds of top executives were polled as to the chief reason men in their organizations had failed. In their responses, "personality factors" occurred 11 times more frequently than "lack of knowledge."

Do brain workers live longer than manual workers?

Yes. Extensive studies conducted by a leading life insurance company show that people who earn their living with their brains live appreciably longer than those who earn their bread with their muscles. The reason people in professional and managerial positions average the longest life-spans is attributed to the fact that their generally higher standard of living affords better protection against disease, exposure, and occupational accident hazards. (For example, a lumberjack can be killed by a falling tree, but an executive isn't likely to suffer fatal injuries from a pencil sharpener.)

Is it true that your state of mind frequently controls how well you can hear?

Yes. Research at the Illinois Institute of Technology demonstrates that our emotional attitudes have a direct effect on how acutely our hearing sense functions; that we tend to hear best the things we want to hear — and vice versa. The investigators offer typical examples of this selective hearing perception: A child hears "ice cream" much easier than the similar sounding "wipe clean", a mother may fail to waken when her alarm clock goes off, but is roused immediately by a slight shimper from her baby's crib, and so on. (The husband who protests that he didn't hear his wife tell him to do something is probably telling the truth. He didn't hear because he didn't *want* to.)

Is it true that hunger makes people lonely?

Yes. University of Minnesota studies show that hunger — like anxiety — tends to make people want to be with others. Indeed, tests showed that the hungrier a person gets, the more his desire to be with other people increases.

Is it true that the higher your social class, the earlier you mature — mentally, physically, and emotionally?

No. The reverse is true. University of Chicago sociologists studied hundreds of people from all classes and all walks of life. They found that people from the lower social levels spent less time in high school, left home sooner, got their first jobs sooner, married, and had children earlier. Said the investigators in summing their findings: "The higher the social class, the later in life each group reached each of these events." The study also showed a similar relationship between social status and the beginning of various physical changes associated with maturity.

Do brunettes show their age earlier than blondes?

No — it's the other way around. Studies at the University of Miami School of Medicine show that blondes tend to show their age quicker, the texture of their skin being more delicate and more susceptible to the effects of sun, wind, and weather.

Is it true that you can sleep best in a room that's completely dark and free from noise?

No. Psychological studies at Indiana University show that people relax and sleep better in a little noise and light than they do in a dark, sound-proofed room. A room that is completely dark and completely quiet, the investigators found, tended to promote restlessness — increasing muscular tensions and stepping up circulatory activity.

II.

WHAT'S TRUE OF THEM IS TRUE OF YOU

WHAT'S TRUE OF THEM IS TRUE OF YOU

A famous French preacher of the last century was once asked where he had learned so thoroughly the workings of the human heart. By "heart," of course, the questioner meant what we would call the mind and emotions. Modern scientific studies have undoubtedly added to the store of knowledge the preacher had, but they only prove that his answer was right. He said, "I learn about the hearts of others by looking into my own."

A first-hand experience of any mental reaction is the best way to learn about it. To size up other people, you have first to size up yourself. Analysis of your own moods, prejudices, preferences and sensibilities will tell you as much about other people as it will of yourself.

WHAT KIND OF PERSON ARE YOU?
A Single Phrase can have Depths of Meaning

People frequently complain that nobody understands them. It's not surprising, since nobody really understands himself as well as he'd like to. It's fun getting to know yourself better. The following test is based on the findings of a series of studies conducted by psychologist Robert H. Knapp and his colleagues at Wesleyan University. Each of the phrases used in the test has been pretested on hundreds of men and women, and found to provide an amazingly accurate index to their characters. Here is a list of key phrases which the psychologists find most effective in revealing personality. To take the test, select from the eighteen phrases the *one* which most closely symbolizes the image you have of yourself. Then to find out what this tells about you, check the analyses.

	A
An electric generator	[ ]
A surging tide	[ ]
A humming teakettle	[ ]

	B
A shaft of light	[ ]
A lilting melody	[ ]
A bird rising in flight	[ ]

	C
A leafless tree	[ ]
A waterworn pebble	[ ]
A weathered anchor	[ ]

	D
A racing horse	[ ]
A cracking whip	[ ]
A plunging waterfall	[ ]

	E
A tangled string	[ ]
A boat lost in mist	[ ]
A trapped moth	[ ]

	F
A gently swaying tree	[ ]
A wandering cloud	[ ]
A balloon floating in the sky	[ ]

ANALYSES

A. The psychological study showed that men and women who select a phrase from group A tend to be forceful, dynamic and brimming with self-confidence and initiative. The tests show these people to be go-getters in every sense of the word. They are self-starters who itch to get going and are irked by idleness.

B. If the phrase you check is from group B, the tests show this indicates a cheerful and optimistic outlook, a capacity to dominate in social situations and a marked ability to influence the feelings and attitudes of others. People in this bracket are not easily discouraged, have a strong liking for others, and place a high value on friendship.

C. The psychologists find people who check group C to be calm, patient and forebearing. They are inclined to let their heads rule their hearts and to form judgments in an impersonal, matter-of-fact manner. These people expect to have to work for whatever they get. They don't believe in something for nothing; rather, they are inclined to feel you're lucky if you get something for something.

D. People who identify with a phrase in group D were found to be fast-reacting, energetic and impetuous individuals who are apt to act on impulse, and are motivated more by feelings and emotions than by analytical thinking. Personality tests show that people in this category are inclined to react with quick sympathy to the plight of others. They are also quick to anger, but are not likely to hold a grudge long. They make up their minds quickly, but are subject to change, and how they feel today about something may be very different from how they feel tomorrow.

E. Men and women who pick a phrase from group E tend to find life confusing and frequently frustrating, but they share a dogged determination to overcome obstacles that seem to them to stand in the way of their goals. They are willing to struggle and persevere to achieve their ends, even when they feel, as they frequently do, that the cards are stacked against them.

F. If you find yourself best symbolized in a group F phrase, you are in select company. People in this bracket are distinguished by some very enviable characteristics. Despite the pressures and hustle and bustle of everyday life, they tend to be serene and tranquil, to view the world and the people around them with a calm and unruffled perspective. Instead of worrying over problems, they are inclined to regard them reflectively or meditatively. They manage somehow to separate themselves sufficiently from earthy turmoil and emotional turbulence to achieve peace of mind or at least a reasonable facsimile thereof.

HOW NORMAL ARE YOU?
Here's a Scientific Yardstick to show how Closely Your Attitudes Agree with those of Other People

Are you different from most people? Do you have attitudes, inclinations and idiosyncrasies which set you apart from others? Do you hate work? Do you want to get away from it all? Think you're underpaid? Have trouble with your in-laws? To find out how things are with most people, psychologists and sociologists have been conducting countless surveys and studies. Collectively, they've felt the pulse and probed the attitudes of hundreds of thousands of representative men and women from all walks of life. Here is a round-up of their findings. How do they compare with your own ideas and beliefs?

Is it normal to hate work?

It's normal to be unenthusiastic about irksome chores and tedious jobs, but if you're allergic to work *per se* that's something else again. Psychiatrist Bernard S. Robbins has made a study of the type of person who hates work and finds such an attitude a symptom of neurosis. Normally a person should *want* to work and should derive from it a feeling of usefulness, self-confidence and satisfaction.

Despite gripes about unpleasant aspects of their jobs, most people *do* gain a real sense of personal satisfaction from work and would feel lost if they didn't have it to do. A large life-insurance company polled a representative cross-section of over 3,000 men and women on their attitudes toward work. Each was asked, "Would you like to lead a carefree existence, free from responsibilities, with the leisure to do exactly as you pleased and not have to think about working for a living?" The great majority, over 75%, turned thumbs down on the leisured, carefree existence, said they'd prefer to go on working, doing something useful and productive.

But isn't it normal to want to "get away from it all"?

Yes — but not permanently. In a study conducted by University of California psychologists, the wishes of 16,000 men and women were carefully evaluated and classified.

One of the most frequently expressed desires was to get away from it all for a while, to take a trip to the South Seas or a junket to Europe. But studies also show that after such a sojourn, most people are just as happy to return as they were to leave. But it's the most natural thing in the world to want to leave the work-a-day world completely behind once in a while and take a really king-sized coffee break.

Is it normal to feel that you are underpaid?

Yes. National surveys conducted by the Office of Public Opinion Research at Princeton show that over two-thirds of the people feel they aren't being paid as much as they should be. Most professional people were extremely dissatisfied with their earnings. Best satisfied — irrespective of income bracket — were businessmen and farmers.

Is it normal for a woman to be more emotional than a man?

No. As a matter of fact, studies conducted at the University of California Institute of Personality Assessment and Research show that most women are not more emotional than men. It was found that men feel things just as keenly and are just as subject to emotional reactions as women are. How the sexes differ here is that men are more inclined to keep their emotional feelings under wraps and don't display them as openly as women do. And other studies have shown that under some circumstances men are even more apt to be carried away by their emotions than are women.

Is it normal to suspect you're abnormal?

Yes. It's the rare person who hasn't suspected himself at times of being irrational and "off the beam." It's interesting to note in this connection that in many cases people who really *have* slipped a cog mentally or emotionally are likely to have no self-doubts whatsoever.

Is it normal to crave certain foods when you're feeling sorry for yourself?

Yes. Wide-scale studies conducted by Dr. William Kaufman show that when people are feeling sorry for themselves there is a tendency to crave sweets — most particularly chocolate.

Is it normal for most women to have difficulty in retelling a funny story?

Yes. Dr. Martin Grotjahn, professor of psychiatry at the University of Southern California, has made a study of sex differences where humor is concerned. He finds that the notion that few women are capable of telling a joke properly is completely valid. Some women can retell a humorous anecdote just as skillfully and effectively as any man — but such women are exceptions. The average woman, his studies show, is apt to try to tell a funny story and fail.

In his book *Beyond Laughter* he cites a typical illustration of female misunderstanding of a joke, as follows: A charming and attractive woman with a fine sense of humor and intelligence was frequently teased because of her inability to retell jokes. Because of the teasing of her friends, she developed an ambition to tell jokes well. One day she listened to the old story about a Chinese executioner who was so skillful that sometimes his victims did not know what had happened to them. One time, however, the head did not come off after the blade slipped through the neck of a prisoner, who addressed the executioner with the words, "Sir, you forgot me." Said the executioner with a superior smile: "Nod!" implying, of course, that then the head fell off.

Later the lady tried to tell this joke as follows: "A Chinese executioner lined up the prisoners he was going to decapitate. As they were all standing there, he told them to nod their heads. End of story. I must have forgotten something."

Is it normal to have in-law trouble?

A Cornell University survey of married couples shows that one couple out of three has difficulties with in-laws, ranging from a kind of armed truce, marked by mutual wariness and suspicion, to open and undisguised warfare. It was found, incidentally, that women have more trouble than men in getting along with in-laws.

Is it normal to worry?

Yes. Worry is a natural, normal emotion. To feel no anxiety or concern in the face of hazards, dangers, threats to one's security is abnormal. As the distinguished psychiatrist, Dr. Judd Marmor, points out: "To be unworried when faced with distressing reality situations is likely to indicate a serious

mental disorder." There is nothing abnormal about worrying —
if you've *really* got something to worry about. But chronic
anxiety over improbable or imagined hazards is an entirely
different story.

How do you define a normal, well-adjusted personality?

One of the best and most succinct definitions of a well-
adjusted personality is offered by the well-known psychologist,
Dr. Gardner Murphy: "It is one which utilizes effectively and
without conflict all that it possesses." In other words, the
man with a well-adjusted personality doesn't waste energies
on self-doubts and inner conflicts but applies his full power
to the expression of his abilities. He's like a finely tuned
automobile that delivers its maximum horsepower to the
wheels and achieves its greatest potential.

'I REMEMBER, I REMEMBER . . .'
What Your First Memory Tells About You

A person's first memory tells a lot about his personality secrets and gives penetrating insight into his character. Dr. Domeena C. Renshaw, clinic director at Loyola University Medical Center, Chicago, found the evidence.

Why should the first thing that a man remembers about his life be fraught with such psychological significance? Dr. Renshaw's studies confirm what the late Alfred Adler observed: when a person looks backward into his early past we can be sure that what his memory turns up will be of great emotional significance. Dr. Adler would never try to analyze a personality without asking for the first memory.

Dr. Renshaw points out that a person's first memory is expressed in terms of his present attitudes and feelings, and is therefore a good indication of how he is likely to act in his current situation. The focal point of the study is the simple, short test of asking the person specifically for his first memory, and then analyzing its content: "Tell me the very first thing you can remember as a child. Try to give the story in detail, how old you were, other people in it, and what happened."

You can take your own simplified version of the test. It will not have the clinical accuracy of the test itself, which is designed for use of professionals, but it will give you an idea of the way it works. Just jot down your first memory: the first thing that made a sufficiently strong impression on you to be permanently retained in your consciousness. Then a little later you can find out what your recollection indicates.

A simple, short method of analyzing a first memory was developed in the study, which was also participated in by nine psychiatrists. The method was carefully tested on scores of subjects of varying personality types, and it proved most effective in providing a valuable insight in an extremely short time. Here is how the analysis works.

1. The manner in which the first memory is related, and the way in which the episode is depicted.

a. The memory is related in an orderly way with great

attention to detail. ("I remember there were three steps leading up to a walk, where a dog with spots was playing with my black-and-white cat. My mother came out of the house. She had on a blue dress and was carrying a package.")

This form of presentation was found to indicate a marked tendency to be overconscientious. The person is likely to have a great capacity for work, but a limited capacity for "letting go."

b. The memory is related in a dramatic way, with color, animation, and excitement. This was found to reveal a tendency to do things impulsively, without reflection; to act on the spur of the moment, with the heart ruling the head.

As an example, "There was this great dog that looked like a wolf who was chasing me, and he seemed about ten feet tall, with wild eyes, and teeth that snapped, and a look on his face as if he was going to eat me. I escaped by climbing as fast as I could up a ladder that was leaning against our apple tree in the back yard, and I threw green apples at the dog until I finally hit him and he went away."

c. The memory is depicted in an indecisive, apologetic, or guarded manner. ("It was such a silly thing, really. There were these people asking me who I was and I was lost or something, and I forgot what I said exactly, but then a woman came up. I'm not sure, but I think it was my aunt, and she said . . ..")

This was found to indicate a person who is extremely sensitive to real or fancied slights, who is watchful under circumstances which are even slightly suspicious. The study also showed that people who detailed their first memory in this fashion tended to be worriers, often feeling anxiety without justification.

2. It was found that *the role a person described himself as playing* in his earliest memory tended to give an accurate picture of the way he currently viewed himself. Subjects who depicted themselves as shy or misunderstood by others in their first memory tended to see themselves the same way now. ("I must have been around two or three years old, and I hid under the bed when some people I didn't know came to dinner. I didn't want to face them.")

3. The way a person remembers conducting himself in the

first episode that he recalls about himself was found to be related to his present life style, the way he deals with the world. A memory such as this would indicate a person who is self-confident, quick-tempered, aggressive, and action-minded: "I was sitting there in my high chair, and there was this uncle I didn't like who was itchy-cooing me, and I picked up my dish of oatmeal with both hands and let him have it right in the face." A person of this type would be quite unlikely to retain throughout the years an early memory of his behaving in a frightened or sheepish manner.

A person who feels that he is not getting a square deal from the world, that it is the other fellow who gets all the breaks, is likely to retain as his most vivid early memory one which shows him being deprived of something. ("There was this big bag of candy that I found on the shelf by reaching on tiptoe, and grandmother found me eating it and took it away. I found where she hid it, but she caught me and took it away again before I got to eat any more of it.")

When the test, which is designed for clinical use as a diagnostic tool, is administered by specialists, it shows an even wider variety of personality traits and tendencies, including "environmental response," and other behavioral factors more the concern of the professional.

But a further finding of general interest is what is revealed by a first memory which is "devoid of detail as well as human objects." Dr. Renshaw cites as an example this first memory, from the case history of a subject in the study: "I remember the farm. The animals, they were chickens. I was three." Persons who responded in this manner tended to have these characteristics in common: they were reserved in disposition; kept their feelings very much to themselves; were self-contained, and generally preferred to keep their own counsel.

Dr. Renshaw says that the study raises a very interesting question: does the first memory ever change? There is reason to suspect that changes in the personality, becoming more out-going or more withdrawn, for example, may alter the first memory, so that "a new, perhaps earlier, memory will be remembered, and that the new character of the person allows this new memory to come to consciousness."

72

ARE YOU AN INTROVERT OR AN EXTROVERT?
Either Way, Science Has News For You

If you have ever wondered about whether you're an introvert or an extrovert, you're probably an introvert. For the extrovert seldom speculates about what kind of person he is. Few of us fall completely in either category, but most of us have marked tendencies toward one. One of the simplest ways to determine which side you identify with, is to ask yourself how you behave when you are upset.

Prof. Raymond B. Cattell of the University of Illinois supplies us another easy-to-use yardstick: the extrovert is concerned about what others think; the introvert is more an individualist.

Whether you tend to be the reflective and idea-minded introvert, whose world tends to center within himself, or the highly social, hail-fellow-well-met, action-minded extrovert, who would rather *make* the world go round than understand *why* it goes round, you'll be interested in the findings of science. You can match your own opinions with the experts' conclusions. Just check each statement as true or false before reading the answer.

Extroverts are easier to influence than introverts.
(True_____. False_____.)

True. This doesn't mean that the extrovert isn't strong-minded, but it is important to him to be liked by others, and he scores high on such traits as amiability and willingness to "go along." This makes him more readily influenced by others.

Extroverts can stand pain better than introverts.
(True_____. False_____.)

True. The extrovert can take in stride aches and pains which would cause an introvert to grit his teeth in anguish. It's not that the extrovert is necessarily any braver; it's just that extroverts have a greater tolerance for pain.

The extrovert tends to be negligent of his ailments, and often does not take proper care of himself. The introvert is likely to be over-attentive to aches and pains, and to read more into them.

If you're an introvert, you are likely to fall in love with an extrovert. (True_____. False_____.)

False. Studies show that in the great majority of cases, like personalities very definitely tend to attract like. More often than not the introvert has difficulty in understanding the extrovert.

There are, of course, cases where the two types do fall in love, marry, and succeed in adjusting happily to each other's differences. Dr. Paul Popenoe, director of the American Institute of Family Relations, says, "The problems of introversion and extroversion in marriage are great. An extrovert wife, for example, may spend years nagging her introvert husband to go out with her more. Similarly, the extrovert husband may hurt the feelings of his sensitive introvert wife."

Extroverts have a better sense of humor than introverts. (True_____. False_____.)

False. This question is guaranteed to provoke controversy. Most extroverts consider the average introvert's sense of humor to be sadly in need of a shot in the arm, and vice versa. Neither has any appreciable edge. The difference lies in the *type* of wit and humor that each prefers. A joke or situation which an extrovert considers uproariously funny may not tickle an introvert at all. And the extrovert may completely miss the point of wit which the introvert finds highly amusing. In *The Structure of Personality,* psychologist H. J. Eysenck cites studies which show that the introvert prefers subtle wit; the extrovert prefers broader humor.

Introverts are better at reading another person's mind. (True_____. False_____.)

False. In studies at Duke University, extroverts made significantly better scores on mental-telepathy experiments.

Introverts and extroverts are born that way. (True_____. False_____.)

True. Studies at the University of London indicate that introversion or extroversion is as hereditary as intelligence.

Introverts have the greater capacity for happiness. (True_____. False_____.)

True. And they have a greater capacity for unhappiness as well. That is because by his very nature the introvert is more sensitive to his own feelings and emotions.

LIKE TO TAKE A CHANCE?
Everyone Must Take Risks, but the Kind You Prefer Indicates the Type of Work You Should be Doing

Being born is a risk, life itself is a gamble with different odds for every person, and there is no way at any age to avoid risks.

The big difference between people is not whether they take risks or not, but the kind of risks they are willing to take. If you prefer situations where there is a higher element of risk, but a greater reward if you are successful, you will answer Yes to most of the following questions.

1. Would you prefer a job with a high salary but only slight security over a job which offered you high security and a small salary?

2. Do you think of yourself as a driver who likes to get the most out of an automobile in performance rather than as a conservative driver who always stays within the speed limit?

3. Would you prefer investing for a fairly high return involving some risk to a more conservative investment with a lower rate of return?

4. Are you more attracted to sports like auto racing or skin and scuba diving than to billiards, bowling, tennis, hiking?

5. When you travel, do you often arrive at the airport with barely time to catch your plane?

If you answered No to most of these questions, you are the type of person who prefers situations where success brings a smaller reward, with less risk of failure. The category you fit into is a guide to the type of work in which you would be happier.

At the University of Massachusetts, psychologists Bernard Cameron and Jerome L. Myers gave students special tests on the type of risks they preferred. Students were then given a standard personality test.

The study showed that the students who preferred situations involving higher risks with higher rewards tended to be aggressive in their attitudes. When they felt that other persons were infringing on their rights they showed resentment. They said witty or clever things; enjoyed telling others of their personal experiences and achievements, and liked attention. And they like to use words that others didn't know and to ask questions others couldn't answer.

They tended to have dominant personalities, to argue strongly for their own point of view, to govern group decisions, settle arguments and disputes between others; to exert influence over others and to persuade them toward their own lines of thinking. Their ability to attract followers, coupled with their ability to supervise the actions of others, made them very happy when they held positions of authority.

People who favored lower risks and lesser but more certain reward had totally different personality traits. What they valued most was independence from others; being self-directed and able to express themselves freely. They tended to be highly individualistic; disliked being fenced in by custom or convention. They liked to stick to a job until it was finished, and were able to concentrate for long periods at a time without being distracted from their work. Key words describing people in this group are *patient, persevering, freedom loving, individualistic.*

Not everyone, of course, fits completely into one of these two classifications, just as few people are completely introverted or extroverted. However, everyone will have a tendency in one direction or another.

Studies further show that the person who prefers to take extremely high risks or extremely low risks tends to be lacking in self-confidence. His desire to avoid failure is stronger than his drive to achieve success. However, a person who prefers medium risks tends to be self-reliant and assured.

HOW DO YOU LOOK AT THE WORLD?
Are You Realistic and Materialistic or Imaginative and Impractical?

How you look at the world tells a lot about you. Read
each of the following statements, and check whether you agree
or disagree with it. Then go on to find out what you are like.

1. My world consists largely of my own neighborhood and
the people whose lives touch mine. (Agree____ Disagree____)

2. I am as strongly concerned with the welfare of people all
over the world as I am with those in my own community.
(Agree____ Disagree____)

3. The other side of the world seems a long way away from
me and seems apart from the realities of my life. (Agree____
Disagree____)

4. I am concerned with the whole world and its peoples
rather than just the part that I know and work in. (Agree____
Disagree____)

5. I find self-expression principally in my home, job, family,
close friends; and in my own immediate community.
(Agree____ Disagree____)

6. I take a world view of humanity. I think of the world as
a whole. It seems to me that my responsibility to the people
in other parts of the world is as great as my responsibility to
people in my own neighborhood. (Agree____ Disagree____)

If you agree with statements 1, 3, and 5 your world tends
to be bounded by the things, people, and places near you,
friends, family, business associates. Your world is a personalized
one.

If you found yourself agreeing with statements 2, 4, and 6,
you are world-minded in your outlook, and tend to think of
humanity in terms of mankind rather than just in terms of
persons whose lives touch yours.

A series of studies conducted by psychologist Erich P. Prien
gave several personality tests to a large group of college students.
The results showed that a person's attitude toward the world
goes hand in hand with specific personality characteristics, and
that the two kinds of persons not only had different world out-

looks, but different personalities, different emotional responses, and a different way of looking at almost everything.

The first were found to have these characteristics in common: they were conscientious, persevering, painstaking, and self-controlled. They were inclined to be more prudent than adventurous, and preferred to plan things ahead rather than act hastily. They were less flexible in dealing with others than were the second group, and they were more respectful of tradition and precedents.

They believed in the virtues of hard work, and were guided by a desire for achievement and recognition.

They were concerned with the welfare of others, and often identified with philanthropic projects, but they were also inclined to place emphasis on what they as individuals could achieve.

People of the second group were outgoing, friendly, idealistic, and enthusiastic. They enjoyed having lots of people around and liked to meet new people. But their personal relationships were not always harmonious.

They were adaptable to changing situations, and welcomed ideas. But they found it easier to think up ideas than to put them into practical application, and often found it difficult to stick to a task after their first interest had worn off. They liked excitement and adventure, and sometimes acted impulsively, not thinking about consequences.

They had a sympathetic attitude toward most people, and a concern for the welfare of those less fortunate than themselves. They placed a comparatively low value on the material things in life, and were not much concerned with personal prestige.

They tended to think of themselves as promoting the welfare of mankind as a whole. The first group were inclined to think of the second as impractical visionaries. The first group think of themselves as practical, levelheaded, and realistic; the second group tended to regard them as self-centered and materialistic.

Which type is it best to be? Which is happier? Neither one nor the other, necessarily. As for which makes the greatest contribution to mankind's welfare this is a question which has two sides. But since each has qualities that complement the other, it looks as though the world needs both of them. For in our world, idealistic dreamers are as important as doers.

Before a dream can be made a reality, someone must dream it. And before the dream can become a reality, someone must do it.

If your answers did not fall entirely into one category or the other, you share the attributes of both types. This may show a more rounded personality, but it could suggest some conflicts of interests.

LITTLE THINGS THAT TELL A LOT ABOUT YOU
A Few Drops of Lemon Juice — or the
Way You Chew Candy — May Tell as Much About You as
Hours of Conversation on a Couch

Would you believe that by squeezing four drops of lemon juice on a person's tongue you can tell whether he's an introvert or an extrovert? That you can judge his character better by listening to him than by seeing him? That you can tell what kind of personality he has by the way he eats a meal, or even just a piece of candy?

In what might be termed a "mouth-watering" experiment conducted at Cambridge University in England, scientists demonstrated that introverts can be distinguished instantly from extroverts — with no personality testing whatsoever — just by putting four drops of lemon juice on a person's tongue, causing an immediate increase in saliva output.

Their discovery that people who were known to be introverts unloosed more saliva than those previously determined to be extroverts caused quite a stir in scientific circles. To put the findings to the acid test — or perhaps the *citric* acid test — an even more extensive study was conducted by the noted British personality-testers, Sybil and Dr. H. J. Eysenck. They tested a scientifically selected sample of 100 men and women — four drops of lemon juice on the tongue for 20 seconds. The results bore out the Cambridge University findings in every respect!

In the meantime, in another psychological study sponsored by the National Institute of Mental Health and conducted by Dr. Norman R. F. Maier and research associate James A. Thurber at the University of Michigan, 200 men and women students were tested on their ability to judge honestly under three conditions: (1) watching and hearing an interview; (2) listening to a tape recording of the interview; and (3) reading a transcript of the interview.

The students were asked to tell, by a person's responses to questions during the interview: (1) when he was telling the truth (2) when he was being evasive and seeking to deceive or conceal something; and (3) when his response consisted of an outright lie

Surprise! The listeners and readers were found to be better judges, by a wide margin, over those who had both seen and heard the interviews. Concluded the investigators: "The watchers were distracted by facial expressions, gestures, etc."

The results of the Michigan study could have a far-reaching effect in influencing techniques in hiring and firing, says Dr. Maier. An employer could make more accurate judgments if he did not conduct the interview himself but based his decisions later on a tape or transcript, say, of what the applicant *said* to a third party.

As for your enjoyment of food, recent psychological research at the State University of New York, reported at the annual meeting of the Eastern Psychological Association, shows conclusively that people who don't enjoy eating don't get nearly as much fun out of life as those who do.

At the University of Texas, too, psychologists were able to link food with life attitudes. Results of a test on 400 students showed that those who liked most foods tended to be assertive, energetic, sociable and affectionate, and had a love of comfort and relaxation. They tended to have dominant personalities and were able to communicate their feelings freely.

Researchers found that those students who did *not* eat with gusto, on the other hand, had almost exactly the opposite type of personalities.

Along this line, science has found that another way to get a quick line on a person's character and personality is to watch how he eats candy. In a survey directed by a team of industrial psychologists in London, a national sample of more than 1,200 people were interviewed about their candy-eating habits (were they "crunchers," "chewers" or "suckers"?) and then given personality tests.

About a third of them preferred to suck their candy — and these turned out to be the best adjusted and the most emotionally stable but sometimes smug and lacking in initiative. Half of the candy-eaters were chewers and these, the study showed, tended to be cheerful and optimistic — but were apt to lack discipline and had a tendency to start things without finishing them. The remaining 17% — the crunchers — tended to be highly excitable and impulsive, but unpredictable in their reactions.

So, the next time a hostess passes around a tray of food or assorted candy, or a dish of lemon drops, be wary. The way you eat it — or the way you look her in the eye, and say, "No thanks, I'm on a diet" — may tell her more about the real you than you're ready to reveal!

QUESTIONS WITH X-RAY EYES
Your Offhand Attitudes Reveal Your Personality

Seven seemingly casual questions can reveal your personality to depths beyond your imagining.

To make it more fun, simply answer these following key questions as honestly as you can, then see what your answers reveal about yourself. (Also try them out on your friends: fun game, conversation starter, breaks the ice at a party.)

Do you like your first name?

Your attitude toward your first name is a measure of your self-esteem. Columbia University studies show that persons who answer Yes to the question, "Do you feel your name is you?" tend to think much more highly of themselves than those who do not like their names. Of the 400 subjects of the study, those who disliked their first names were also markedly dissatisfied with themselves.

Do you frequently recall your dreams when you awaken in the morning?

At the University of North Carolina, psychologists conducted a study which showed that persons who recalled their dreams frequently were the most creative-minded, valued ideas and feelings more than material considerations, and were inclined toward contemplative thought. They could express themselves more easily than those who seldom recalled their dreams. The latter tended to be matter-of-fact and material-minded, were less given to self-doubts and anxieties, vastly preferred action to contemplation, and took a dim view of introspection.

Do you prefer warm colors (such as red, orange, yellow) or cool colors (such as blue, green, violet)?

A study of hundreds of university students of various backgrounds and nationalities brought out personality differences revealed by color preferences. The warm-color people were more emotionally responsive, more impulsive, than those preferring cool colors. They also had quicker reactions, and tended to be more sensitively aware of their environment and more stimulated by it. Persons who preferred cool colors had a greater ability to concentrate on mental tasks, tending to be

82

more single-minded and less easily distracted or influenced by the people or activity around them.

Are you overweight, underweight, or about normal?

Temple University research shows that being overweight, underweight, or normal tends to go hand in hand with specific personality traits. Subjects were selected from a group of more than 400 college women, who were divided into three weight groups and then tested.

Normal and overweight people tended to be more aggressive, to dominate others, while underweight persons were inclined to be more submissive.

Psychologist Joseph Friedman, who directed the study at Temple, suggests that this may be because "underweight persons, due to their more fragile physiques, have learned to avoid the pressures and possible dangers of boldness in interpersonal relations."

The normal-weight people averaged better scores on mental ability. They were able to reason more clearly and objectively, avoiding emotional bias or prejudice. The more a person's weight deviates from normal in either direction, the more likely he is to be hypersensitive, on the defensive emotionally.

If you were asked to locate the center of your "self," to select some one point or area of your body that you feel is "you," where would that be?

Both men and women students were asked this question at New Mexico State University. About 50% of each said they felt that their head was the center of "self." But almost three times as many women (35%) as men (13%) located the central part of their being in the chest or heart area. Women *do* tend to be more emotional than men, and less given to thought than to feeling. This suggests that the site a person regards as the center of his "self" tells whether he is ruled by his heart or his head.

Do you daydream frequently?

Two university studies show that frequent daydreamers tend to be nervous and high-strung. They scored high on anxiety tests. Many inveterate daydreamers were so anxiety prone that having nothing to feel anxious about did not stop them. They simply generated a kind of vague, free-floating anxiety that did not need any outside stimulus. They were also found to be very sensitive and perceptive. Infrequent daydreamers tended to be matter-of-fact, easygoing, less imaginative, and not inclined to fret or worry.

If you had equal opportunity of winning a desirable prize by 1. competing for it in a contest of skill, or 2. letting the outcome be decided by a game of chance, which would you choose?

Persons who prefer to rely on skill rather than chance tend to excel in judgment, foresight, and planning ahead.

This is shown by researches of Veteran Administration psychologist Dr. Rayman W. Bortner. Such persons have a greater self-confidence and a more realistic outlook on life. But those who preferred to rely on chance tended to see the world around them as threatening. They were fearful of criticism. They avoid responsibility and decisions; and, since they play no active roles, they avoid criticism.

HOW'S YOUR MENTAL BATTING AVERAGE?
It Isn't the Size of Your I.Q. that Counts —
It's the Way You Use It

How well you get along in this world and how successfully you are able to solve your problems depends not so much on how much intelligence you have, as on how effectively you use it. Authorities have found, as a matter of fact, that most people possess far more intelligence than they are able to use effectively.

In view of this fact, scientists in leading universities have been conducting exhaustive surveys and experiments to find out as much as possible about how people's minds work — and how to get top performance out of people. Their discoveries not only explode popular misconceptions, but reveal many valuable secrets which will enable you to perform any type of mental work more easily and more efficiently.

Regardless of where you rank on the I.Q. scale, science can now tell you how to evaluate your thinking ability. Let's take a look at their findings.

Does your intelligence vary with the seasons?

Yes. If you're like most people, your brain will function better in the spring than during any other time in the year; and second best in the fall. And you'll have a lot more on the ball mentally in winter than you will in summer. During hot weather your brain is likely to be slower at coming up with the answers than at any other time.

The noted scientist, Ellsworth Huntington, compared the findings of leading studies and surveys assessing the intelligence of all types of individuals during the various months and seasons. And he found them to be in general agreement on the above points.

Though science cannot wholly explain this interesting phenomenon, it has established that temperature and climate do have a very direct bearing on how well our mental faculties function, and that cool weather is far more conducive to creative thinking than in summer heat. The same factors that stimulate all nature in the spring may be responsible for man's mental acceleration during that time of year.

These findings suggest that people might do well to tackle their most critical problems during those seasons of the year when their brains develop their greatest power. And as for the summer — well, that seems a good time to take as long a vacation as possible.

Does your manual dexterity provide an index of intelligence

Yes. Contrary to popular opinion, Dr. Maurice H. Fouracre of Columbia University finds that intelligence and manual dexterity tend to go together; and that the person who is adept at working with his hands is likely to rank appreciably higher in the I.Q. department than the man who is not. His findings completely upset the commonly held belief that the individual who is lacking in intellectual prowess is likely to excel in manual skill.

What are two simple steps you can take to step up your mental power?

Studies show that your brain can't function at top efficiency without an ample supply of oxygen and blood. Don't permit yourself to slump at your desk — and do cultivate a posture which permits proper breathing and adequate oxygen. Also get enough exercise to insure a good circulation of blood.

Studies conducted at the University of Oregon Medical School show that shallow breathing — or any other condition which limits oxygen intake — causes the brain cells to function less efficiently. And poor circulation was found to have a similarly adverse effect.

And at the University of Illinois it was found in laboratory tests that when students' oxygen intake was restricted, scores made on I.Q. tests took a sharp drop. The study also made it clear that the mental performance of thin people is most affected by breathing habits which restrict the intake of oxygen. Least affected because of his greater lung capacity is the short, stock, barrel-chested individual.

Is your ability to think affected by what you eat?

Yes. If you want to get the best performance out of your gray matter, scientific evidence indicates that you'd better eat an adequate, well-balanced diet. And the further you depart from it, the more your mental abilities are likely to suffer. In a University of Minnesota study, for example, subjects were fed on a low-nutrition diet, then given mental tests to check the effect. In almost 90% of the cases, mental abilities were found to have been adversely affected.

Studies also have shown that the average person's capacity for sustained mental effort is appreciably lower when he starts the day with a skimpy breakfast.

Can you think better when you concentrate intensely?

Contrary to what many people believe, you can't. Studies conducted by the noted psychiatrist, Dr. David Harold Fink, show that intense concentration actually tends to slow your mental processes. Here's why: The harder you try to concentrate, the more tense you become. And tension inhibits all types of mental effort — including memory (next time you're trying to remember something, instead of cudgeling your brain, try relaxing, you'll find the desired information will come to you much quicker).

To illustrate how tension interferes with our ability to think, Doctor Fink points out that when tension becomes extreme as in a severe fright or anxiety — our mental powers may become completely paralyzed, and refuse to function at all.

There's another factor, too. Psychologists have long recognized that man owes much of his brilliant thinking to his subconscious faculties. And your subconscious or intuitive faculties can't operate effectively when your conscious mind is tied up in knots. That's why some of a man's best ideas are likely to come to him while he's shaving, or in the bathtub — when his mind is at ease.

How can you improve your daily performance of mental work?

Productive ideas are likely to occur to you anywhere — frequently in the most unexpected places. But exhaustive studies conducted by psychologist Harold E. Burtt of Ohio State University show that you can increase everyday efficiency if you have one particular place which is used only for brain work – and nothing else. The brain soon becomes conditioned to this, and when this work-place association has become thoroughly established, just sitting down there is enough to start the mental wheels rolling.

But, Professor Burtt's studies show, if a man's desk is used for purposes other than work (social conversations, reading the papers, serving refreshments), this conditioned reflex no longer works – and instead of going into high gear, the mind is apt to be distracted from top-level performance by thoughts of bull sessions, news stories or snacks.

Professor Burtt's studies would seem to indicate that it's better to take a trip to the water cooler to carry on a social conversation or hear the latest funny story; and that the practice of sending out for sandwiches to eat at his desk is likely to subtract from an executive's overall mental performance.

Will you get smarter as you grow older?

It depends on your I.Q. Studies show that the adult of average or below-average intelligence tends to exhibit decreasing mental capabilities with age. However, research recently completed at the University of California and at Stanford, shows that people of above-average intelligence tend to become smarter as they grow older. In these studies, present I.Q. ratings of more than 1,000 persons of above-average intelligence were compared with the scores made by the same persons 12 years previously. They were found to be measurably smarter.

Is it true that the size of your vocabulary is a reliable index to your intelligence?

Yes. There is general agreement among most leading authorities on this. Tests have repeatedly shown that a man's ability to assimilate new knowledge, his ability to reason, and his capacity to solve mental problems are closely related to the number of words he knows.

Furthermore, the University of California's speech expert, Martha Gowdy Mason, finds a very definite correlation between success in life and an individual's vocabulary. Says she, "It has been said that language is the dress of thought and every time we talk, our minds are on parade. Certainly it is impossible to express ideas and thoughts, to communicate with others, unless one has a good vocabulary and words come easily.

"In industry, the boss almost invariably has a larger vocabulary than those he directs. He did not acquire that vocabulary as the result of being a top executive, but through long practice in the efficient expression of his thoughts to others. The words which are his tools are precision sharp, and his vocabulary is a steadily growing factor in his success."

Authorities also make another point. A limited vocabulary tends to slow down a man's mental processes by making it difficult for him to verbalize his thoughts to himself.

Can you increase your intelligence merely by adding to your vocabulary?

This is an interesting question. Most psychologists agree that you cannot increase your innate mental capacities merely by mechanically enlarging your vocabulary. And, as UCLA psychologist James T. Bugental points out, memorizing new words and their definitions will do little — alone — to add to your mental stature. If the knowledge is retained, however, artificial or forced vocabulary expansion can enable you to understand and assimilate more of what you read and help you express your thoughts more effectively.

Remember, however, that a man is not intelligent because he has a good vocabulary. It's the other way around. A person of high I.Q. naturally acquires a good vocabulary to satisfy the demands of his intelligence.

The more intelligent a man is, the more important it is for him to have words which will permit him to express his thoughts with exactitude.

That's basically why men of higher intelligence tend to have larger vocabularies than do persons of lesser mental endowment. They have them for the same reason that a skilled cabinetmaker has a better assortment of tools than a rough carpenter has. The rough carpenter might do somewhat better work if he possessed all the cabinetmaker's tools, but the mere possession of these tools would certainly not transform him into a skilled wood-worker. And the same principle applies to vocabulary and intelligence.

HOW IS YOUR SENSE OF HUMOR?
A Test to Measure the Accuracy of Your Funnybone

A good sense of humor may not be necessary for success and happiness, but psychologists agree that it helps. The better your sense of humor, the more enjoyment you get out of life and the less likely you are to become depressed. One who can laugh at himself is not likely to waste time feeling sorry for himself.

If you have a good sense of humor it does not necessarily mean that you are smarter than most people or likely to be more successful. But psychological studies show that on the whole people who do well on sense-of-humor tests also tend to make higher than average scores on intelligence tests. Researchers at two leading universities have found that people with wit and humor tend to be more emotionally stable than those who seldom find anything very amusing.

On the other hand, University of Michigan studies have established that a person who is addicted to some forms of humor (the punster, for example) may have strong inner conflicts and unresolved personality problems. His conflicting feelings find expression in making a play on words.

Some people pride themselves on their sense of humor whether they have one or not. Others don't give themselves the credit they deserve. The following quiz gives you a chance to test yourself.

1. Do you secretly feel that a great many of the jokes people tell you are somewhat pointless? Yes_____. No_____.

2. Does it make you angry when something happens to make you lose your dignity? Yes_____. No_____.

3. Do you think the world would not be in the shape it is today if people took things a little more seriously? Yes_____. No_____.

4. A well-known psychiatrist says, "In overcoming our fears, a sense of humor is even more important than will power." Do you think his statement should be taken with a grain of salt? Yes_____. No_____.

5. In looking at the cartoons in a magazine, do you look for errors the cartoonist may have made? (A lot of people do!)

Yes_____. No_____.

6. Do you hate to tell a joke on yourself? Yes_____. No_____.

7. Do you think the importance of a sense of humor is frequently overrated? Yes_____. No_____.

8. Do you think that people who do things just for the fun of it are likely to be irresponsible? Yes_____. No_____.

9. When somebody else is telling a story, are you often so busy trying to think of one yourself that you only half listen? Yes_____. No_____.

10. A poet once admonished, "Wrinkle not the face with too much laughter, lest thou become ridiculous." Does this strike you as sound advice? Yes_____. No_____.

For each question answered with a Yes, you score nothing. For every question answered with a No, give yourself 10 points. A score of less than 50 indicates that you are an extremely serious person, inclined to view things too literally; and though you have some sense of humor, you haven't given it a chance to develop.

A score of 50 or 60 indicates that your sense of humor is fair. If you scored 70 points, that is average; but psychologists point out that the average person's sense of humor is not all that it might be. They agree that he would be happier if he would take things less seriously. A score of 80 is good; 90 or 100 excellent. Things don't bother you much if you score this high, for you have learned to laugh at yourself.

WHAT ARE YOU AFRAID OF?
Researchers Have Found the Best Way to Conquer Anxieties

Are you afraid of losing your job? Worried about the state of your marriage, your bank account or your blood pressure? Exhaustive studies have been made to ascertain the chief sources of fear and worry for Americans. In addition, leading research foundations have been developing methods to enable you to keep your fears from getting you down.

Let's take a look at some important findings:

Question: What are most people afraid of?

Answer: Rather surprisingly, not war and the H-bomb. At the Illinois Institute of Technology psychologists made a careful study of the fears and anxieties of a representative cross-section of American businessmen. They found that they are subject to 10 chief fears:

1. *Financial* — 80% were afraid they were going to lose money or not make enough.

2. *Job security* — 74% worried about losing their jobs, as a result of shakeups, business falling off, inter-office policies, or competition from younger men.

3. *Health* — 69% were worried about real or imaginary ailments.

4. *Personal appearance* — 59% were fearful that their dress and manner were handicapping their chances of success.

5. *Politics* — Apprehensions and anxieties in this area affected 56% of the businessmen polled, and centered around government trends, such as taxation. Broader political worries were typified by such comments as, "Too many people in the country nowadays want to ride on the shirttails of someone else who will foot the bill for them."

6. *Marital difficulties* — 44% were worried by incompatibility.

7. *Lack of self-confidence* — 40% feared they didn't have enough "on the ball."

8. *Religious and philosophical convictions* — 37% were worried over what to believe.

9. *Sexual morality* — 34% were subject to worries and conflicts arising from temptations and/or transgressions.

10. *Trouble with relatives* — Anxieties in this department affected 33%, and ranged from the fear that "my mother-in-law is going to drive me out of my mind," to how to get rid of the wife's brother before he wrecks the business.

Q. Is it true that we are most subject to specific fears and anxieties at certain ages?

A. Yes. The same study showed that, so far as the average businessman is concerned, during his late 20's he worries most about personal appearance and the impression he makes on other people. At 30 he worries most about sexual morality. At 33 qualms regarding his religious and philosophical convictions reach a peak. At 35 his No. 1 fear is money. At 39 it's job security, health and marital difficulties. (This is a rough year!) But in his middle 40's, the emphasis shifts to politics. From here on, fears tend to level off, with no more peak years.

Q. What is the best way to deal with the ordinary "garden-variety" fears and anxieties that all of us are subject to?

A. Much advice — good, bad and indifferent — has been given out on this subject. Scientists at the University of California decided to separate the wheat from the chaff and to determine by actual psychological tests what method *really* works best.

First they carefully evaluated the findings of all other leading authorities. Next, Drs. Jurgen Ruesch and A. Rodgney Prestwood, who directed the study, subjected every means of alleviating worry and anxiety to careful test. They observed the effects on men and women from various walks of life. And they found only one method that effectively does the job. That method boils down to this:

Share your fears and anxieties with another person. Don't let them accumulate. Don't bottle them up. Don't try to conceal them. The worries you don't get off your chest do the mental and physical damage.

Q. How can the investigators be certain of this?

A. In summarizing the findings of their exhaustive studies, the university scientists state flatly and unequivocally that: "The successful management of worry and anxiety seems possible only through the process of sharing and communicating . . .."

How can the scientists be so sure? Largely because of one incontrovertible fact brought out by their investigation: fears and anxieties have the most damaging effect on those persons who habitually *conceal* their worries beneath a calm surface; and the least effect on individuals who "discharge them in interpersonal relations."

Q. Does it matter particularly whom you share your worries with?

A. Yes. It's important to exercise care and discrimination in choosing the person you unburden yourself to. It should be someone in whom you repose complete confidence, someone you can rely on for sympathetic understanding. The university study showed that this system works best of all when the confidant is a *loved one,* and is far less effective with strangers or casual acquaintances. (Note to husbands and wives: unburden your worries to each other — and don't delay.)

It is significant to note, in this connection, that the incidence of nervous breakdowns and other stress ailments caused by anxiety is a great deal higher among bachelors and spinsters than among married persons.

Q. What else can you do to keep your fears and anxieties from getting you down?

A. Many of our fears stem directly from an overactive imagination — and have no basis in reality whatsoever. Most fears of this type can be eliminated by the simple process of not crossing your bridges until you come to them. Don't *generate* anxiety by speculating as to the possibility of the bridge being out.

Many of your fears you can completely eliminate just by going into *action* — instead of merely "stewing" about them.

Sort your fears and anxieties into two piles: those which result from conditions beyond your control and those you can *do* something about — and take immediate action on the latter.

The late psychologist, Dr. Henry C. Link, found that a great many fears result from an overactive mind and underactive body, pointing out that "we generate fears while we sit; we overcome them by action."

YOUR FRUSTRATION INDEX
It is One Key to Your Character

Frustrations are part of life. They range from the waiter who brings you the wrong order to the gas-station attendant who keeps you waiting while he chats with another customer.

The way you react to frustration is a key to your character according to studies conducted at Whitworth College by Psychologists Robert L. Schalock and Patricia MacDonald. They have devised a frustration test to be used by psychologists and personnel consultants. Their principles have been adapted to a short, easy quiz. To test yourself, check your reaction to each of the following situations.

1. You are standing in line at a sale and someone, who has crowded into line just ahead of you, buys the last of the articles on sale, leaving you to go home empty-handed. Which comes closest to expressing your feelings?

   a) "Grrr! That pushy so and so!"

   b) "I guess I should have gotten here earlier."

   c) "Oh well, it doesn't really matter. Besides, she probably needs it more than I do."

2. The telephone jars you awake when you are sleeping late in the morning, and it turns out to be someone trying to sell you something you don't want. Which of the following expressions would come closest to your thoughts?

   a) "He should break a leg with my compliments!"

   b) "I really shouldn't lie in bed all morning anyway."

   c) "It's nothing to get upset about. It's his job, after all."

3. A store clerk curtly refuses to let you return a purchase because you have lost the sales slip. How would you react?

   a) Tell the clerk that he ought to recognize his own merchandise; and what kind of store is he running anyway?

   b) Tell yourself that it is your own fault for not keeping the sales slip.

   c) Shrug off the incident, reminding yourself that the clerk was only following the rules.

4. If someone borrowed a coat from you and returned it badly soiled, which feeling would you be most likely to have?

a) "I'll never lend him anything again!"

b) "I suppose I shouldn't have lent him a thing that soils so easily."

c) "I'm sure he didn't notice it was soiled, or he would have had it cleaned."

5. If an acquaintance passes you without speaking, which are you likely to say to yourself?

a) "Well! What has she got her nose in the air for?"

b) "I suppose I should have spoken to her first."

c) "She probably had her mind on something else and just didn't see me."

HOW TO SCORE

In all cases, the investigators found, people reacted to frustration in one of three ways.

1. By blaming others (or the situation or environment) and becoming angry. You are in this category if you scored mostly *a* responses in the quiz.

2. By blaming themselves. This is your category if you scored mostly *b* responses.

3. Blaming no one. The frustrated person may be embarrassed, but is not angry. This is your category if you scored mostly *c* responses.

ANALYSIS

Psychologists Schalock and MacDonald found that people who blame others or the environment for their frustrations (psychologists call it being *extrapunitive)* had these personality traits in common.

The *men* found it difficult to control impulsiveness and impatience in all social situations. They tended to be restless, with energy to spare. They were tense, excitable, and their quickly changing moods ranged from elation through anxiety and depression. They were also cautious in their dealing with others.

The *women* in this category were inconsistent, whimsical, and capricious; they tended to avoid tasks that required them to be thorough.

Both sexes in category 2, those who blamed themselves (psychologists call this being *intrapunitive),* were steady and

and dependable. They were cheerful and optimistic. They were also adaptable, adjusting to a situation rather than trying to make the situation adjust to them. They were tolerant of others, and inclined to take them at face value. They seldom worried.

The subjects in category 3, rather than blaming themselves, others, or their environment, tried to ignore their frustrations in the hope that refusing to recognize them would make them go away. (This was termed being *impunitive.*) There were marked differences between men and women in this category.

Tests showed that the women tended to share these personality traits: they were prudent, discreet, cautious, and disliked taking unnecessary risks. They preferred to save for a rainy day rather than gamble on finding an umbrella. They tended to be shy, particularly in situations involving persons they did not know very well.

The men, on the other hand, were self-confident and assured. They were also inclined to keep their own counsel; were "strong, silent men." Not the easiest people in the world to make friends with, but when you did, you had gained a genuine friend.

WHAT MAKES YOU ANGRY?
Pent-Up Resentment Needs a Safety Outlet

Studies of nearly 200 college students in American universities show that the average man gets angry about six times a week, while the average young woman loses her temper only three times. Women lose their tempers most at people, men at inanimate objects. Only in about one case in three was a man's anger aroused and directed at an individual. What burnt up the young women mostly was feeling slighted, or otherwise ill-used by people with whom they came into contact.

The investigators also found that there are certain times of the day when people are more apt to get angry than others. Almost 50% of the cases of violent anger, it was recorded, occurred either just before lunch or during the hour before dinner.

Facial expressions don't definitely give an indication of anger. Psychological tests show that anger is one of the most difficult emotions to detect by looking at a person. Professor Dallas Buzby, in his studies, confronted 716 students with photographs of extremely angry persons and asked them to identify the emotion from the facial expressions. Only 2% made correct judgments; anger was most frequently judged as "pleased."

It might be thought that emotionally unstable people would become angrier than normal well-balanced persons but a study of 200 normal individuals and 210 abnormals by psychology professors proved that this assumption is wrong.

They tested the reactions of the two groups to maddening situations of every type and variety such as being laughed at and ridiculed, being repeatedly disconnected on the telephone, accidentally hitting their thumb with a hammer and so on. In almost every instance the anger reaction of the normal group was much more intense than that of the abnormal one.

The lesson to be learned from this is: don't worry if you show a tendency to blow your top when you kick your shin in the dark or when your sweetheart goes out with someone else. You are merely a normal individual and not mentally unbalanced.

Some people are quicker to anger than others because, as the tests show, they are too tense. In many cases it was found circumstances that arouse anger in a physically tense person won't have any effect at all when the person is relaxed.

Other studies have shown that it is virtually impossible to sustain any unpleasant emotion while you're relaxed. A leading psychiatrist gives temper-ridden patients this advice: "Don't worry about flying off the handle. Just release that physical tension and 'let go' completely. Remember you can't get really mad when you're physically relaxed."

One of the reasons why tense people fly into a rage quicker than others is that when the millions of pain nerves in the body are even slightly disturbed they flash a pain impulse to the brain, which weighs this message, and evaluates it in terms of so much pain or discomfort.

When a state of tension exists it causes the brain to over-value pain impulses — thus causing you to feel far more uncomfortable than you otherwise would. But, when you are relaxed, pain messages tend to be evaluated on much lower scale. Tests show that up to 75% of the pain (or disagreeable sensation) which exists when a person is tense vanishes entirely when he relaxes.

An interesting point that showed up is that persons who have had serious illnesses at any time tend, in later life, to become more quick-tempered than others and to react more violently to anger-provoking situations. Psychologists found this to be particularly true when the critical illness occurred during childhood.

The same study also showed that an eldest child is apt to be more grouchy and bad-tempered than others. The evidence indicates, according to psychologist Dr. George M. Stratton, that the first-born is apt to be more irascible. He believes this tendency to bad temper in the first child is due to the attitude of parents toward it which is apt to be different from their attitude toward subsequent children. Psychologists have observed that the first offspring is more likely to be spoiled or overdisciplined than children who follow.

There are distinct trends noticeable about the after-effects of anger, more than 70% showing that their anger experiences left them feeling irritable and fatigued. Only 15% reported feeling better.

The key to the after-effects of anger is whether it is expressed or bottled up. If anger is continually repressed and not provided with means of expression, tests show it will do actual physical harm. In fact, medical researchers have established that repression can cause permanent damage to health. Anger which is "bottled up" builds severe tensions and these affect the functioning of muscles, heart and entire circulatory system.

Many medical men go further and declare that continuous repression of anger can result in malignant high blood pressure and other diseases such as colitis and hypertension. Its role in producing the "sick" headache is already well established.

The best way to avoid the after-effects of anger, of course, is to avoid situations that are likely to lead to upsets. But when you do get mad, authorities agree that you should find some means of expressing that anger.

Frequently this may call for a high degree of discretion. For example, you can't very well tell your boss to go jump in the lake without losing your job; if you punch that discourteous bus driver in the nose you are apt to wind up in the police station. But there are safe and sane outlets for pent-up resentment.

For example go down to the gymnasium and pretend that the punching bag is your boss. Women often find relief from anger in a shopping spree. But before you try that, you'd better make sure it won't just lead to more temper — on the part of your husband.

Virtually any form of sport or exercise will serve to release the dangerous and vitality-sapping tension that suppressed anger builds up.

SPEECH MANNERISMS THAT GIVE YOU AWAY
Of Course, To Be Frank, I Don't Care —
But Would You Do Me a Favor?

How much can you tell about a person just by his mannerisms of speech? Plenty, according to scientific findings.

The University of Rochester's Dr. Sandor S. Feldman has
made a ten-year study of telltale mannerisms. Dr. Feldman,
clinical professor of psychiatry at the university's medical
center, suspected that mannerisms were hiding places for
personality quirks.

Let's look at some of the interesting findings of the study.

"To be frank . . ." or "to be honest . . .." When a person
begins a sentence in this manner, it's a giveaway that he is
not always frank and honest. If he were, he would not feel
the need to proclaim his honesty. Dr. Feldman's investigation
showed that when a man prefaces a statement in this manner,
he is likely to be telling only a partial truth and is trying to
emphasize the truth part by saying *honest.*

"Am I right?" We've all met people who interlard their
speech with "Am I right?" The person who does this,
Dr. Feldman finds, is so unsure of himself that he needs a
yes man. He expects to be told that he is right; and if he is
not told, he is hurt and annoyed. He asks because he lacks
the courage of his convictions. He needs approval in order to
give him enough assurance to continue talking.

"I wouldn't do it for a million dollars." When a person says
this, it means he *would.* In all of us there is a struggle between
temptation and conscience. And the psychiatrist's studies
indicate that a person's statement that he would not violate
an ethical code is highly significant. The very fact that he
expresses the thought, even though negatively, is a giveaway
that he is toying with the idea of committing the deed if the
monetary stakes are high enough.

"I can't find the words to describe . . .." Chances are that
this speaker is completely insincere. The expression, Professor
Feldman affirms, is used to avoid betraying the fact that the
speaker has *no* feelings regarding the matter. Also people who

"cannot find the words" often don't even try because they are envious or because they are lazy. The professor points out that everyone should be able to find a way to express his emotions effectively, in a few simple words, if the feelings are sincere.

"Would you do me a favor?" When somebody buttonholes you with this approach, beware! The cards are stacked against you. Says Dr. Feldman, "The use of this sentence is unfair; it is blackmailing. The speaker traps the listener, who has to listen to the request or be rude. And in giving consent to listen the listener is placed in a dilemma by the word *favor*. He has to grant a something against his own best interests, or to appear in an uncharitable light. Watch out for him!"

"Bye-bye." The phrase "bye-bye" seems innocent enough, off hand. But Professor Feldman points out that "bye-bye" indicates greater closeness to a person than does "good-by." Women, particularly young ones, use "bye-bye" when parting from people with whom they do not have, but wish to have, a close relationship. They think by using the phrase that the other person may accept the familiarity graciously. Sometimes, however, the person to whom the phrase is addressed finds it irritating, because he is uncertain whether he should allow himself to be involved by the "bye-bye." He has to answer "good-by," to indicate to the woman that she is in no position to say "bye-bye."

"Of course." This is another phrase that reveals a great deal. Says Dr. Feldman in summing his findings: A wife asks her husband, "Do you still love me?" If the husband replies, "Of course I love you, dear," the wife will not be satisfied. She wants to know whether her husband loves her in the same way he did when he was courting her. A simple Yes would mean to her that he "really" loves her; that she alone attracts him; that she is always on his mind, in a word, that he is crazy about her. The "of course" tells, in a thinly veiled way, the truth: "I love you, but no longer as in our romantic days."

"I don't care." In most cases when a person uses this phrase he actually cares very much. For example: "The boss didn't ask my opinion, but I don't care"; "She didn't invite me, but

I couldn't care less." It was found that if a person says *without being asked* that he does not care, then it's very likely that he *does* care and is attempting to hide his real feelings.

WHAT YOUR CLOTHES REVEAL
ABOUT YOUR PERSONALITY
Don't Let Them Make You a Liar

Researchers find that a person's character is revealed to a remarkable extent by the clothes he wears and the way he chooses them. Let us take a look at their most interesting discoveries.

Does the way you choose your clothing reveal a great deal about your character and personality?

Definitely. This is especially true of women. In a University of North Carolina study, hundreds of women undergraduates were interviewed and given a clothing-attitude questionnaire. Then they were subjected to a battery of personality tests.

The women who chose their clothing principally for *comfort and practicality* tended to be self-controlled, dependable, socially well-adjusted, with a genuine liking for people. They were also painstaking and thorough in performing their jobs or household duties; and were inclined to defer to authority rather than question or resent it.

Women who were very clothes conscious, placing strong emphasis on the *latest styles and fashions* in selecting their apparel, were found to be conscientious, conventional, stereotyped in their thinking, and inclined to be nonintellectual. Tests also showed them to be generally sympathetic and gregarious.

Women who stressed *conformity* in selecting their clothes ("I don't feel comfortable in dresses which make me stand out from the crowd") tended to be conservative in their general attitude and outlook, with a strong feeling for tradition and propriety. They were inclined to emphasize economic and social values, and to be less concerned with arts and literature.

Those who stressed *economy and thrift* ("I don't spend much time reading about fashion — and I usually buy my dresses at the end of the season") tended to be conscientious, alert, efficient, precise, and controlled. Personality tests also showed that high scorers in this category were inclined to be "markedly intelligent individuals interested in the discovery of truth."

Can you tell anything about a person's character and personality just by asking him his choice of costume to go to a fancy dress ball?

You can, indeed. Lawrence Langner, who has conducted extensive studies on clothing and personality, says, "The selection of the fancy dress costume is *never an accident* when there is full freedom of choice, but is an expression of a conscious or unconscious desire of the wearer."

He also notes the extent to which our clothing can affect our state of mind. As a matter of fact, one's whole attitude and outlook can be altered by switching to different attire ("I feel like a different person in that outfit").

Children are much more likely to get into mischief, commit nuisances, and otherwise engage in obstreperous behavior when they are sloppily dressed (shirts hanging out, dirty jeans). When a youngster is dressed up, he tends to change his behavior to conform with the attire.

Are the best-looking men and women usually the best dressed?

No. As often as not the man or woman who spends the most time in selecting clothes is trying to compensate for a real or fancied lack in looks or personality. Extreme preoccupation with clothes indicates the person is unsure of himself and lacks self-confidence. A really attractive person is likely to "look good in almost anything." He (or she) knows this, and thus can afford to take a more casual attitude toward wearing apparel.

To what extent do people judge us by our clothes?

To a much greater extent than many of us may realize.

Cornell University psychologist Mary Shaw Ryan reports that the clothes of a person you never met before influence your estimation of him. The way a friend is dressed can tell us the mood he is in, whether he is tired, or what he is planning to do next. A careless or bedraggled appearance is likely to convey a low mood, where the individual cares little about the impression he makes or what others may think of him. On the other hand, as the psychologist observed, the person who is "dressed up," who presents a well-groomed appearance, is perceived as being in good spirits and looking forward to having a good time. And this is quite likely to be so; for people tend both consciously and unconsciously to put on clothing which fits their mood.

A person's attitude toward his personal appearance provides an important clue to his general morale and emotional well-being. When a patient tries to improve his grooming, the psychiatrist considers the patient recuperating. But a patient completely disinterested in his appearance is having a bad day.

What about persons who have difficulty finding clothes that suit them?

Studies show that persons who have this type of clothing problem tend to have similar problems in adjusting to family, friends, and job. People in this category include individuals who "haven't a thing to wear" despite a closet full of clothes; or those who have difficulty buying apparel in which they feel comfortable. ("I just can't seem to find anything that's right for me. If it's the right style, it's the wrong color, or it doesn't fit, or the price is exorbitant.")

What kind of clothing should you wear?

Whether you are a man or a woman, you should wear the kind of clothing in which you feel most comfortable and at ease, and which best reflects your personality. Clothing can facilitate human relationships, and serve as a short cut to getting acquainted with others. If you wear the type of apparel which reflects the kind of person you are, it helps to clue the other person in on what you are like, and he will not have to spend time trying to figure it out, and perhaps come to a faulty conclusion. On the other hand, clothing which does not fit your personality, or belies your character and outlook on life, can mislead the other person completely. Do not let your clothing say things about you that are not true.

WHAT YOU WEAR TELLS WHAT YOU ARE
Clothes Don't Just Make the Man —
They Reveal Him, Psychologists Find

This may surprise you, but psychologists have found that your clothing preferences provide a key not only to how well-balanced you are emotionally, but to how intelligent you are. To top matters off, the experts have found that man's clothing habits even reveal his philosophy and general outlook on life.

Well-groomed. In studies conducted at Columbia University Teachers College, a number of teen-age girls were divided into two groups: 1. those who presented a good appearance in terms of neatness, taste and appropriateness of attire, and 2. those who did not — i.e., tended to dress sloppily or in poor taste, and whose general grooming left something to be desired.

Marked personality differences were found between the two groups. Those who presented a good appearance tended to have the following traits in common: they were well-adjusted emotionally, possessed self-confidence, enjoyed social activities, had a strong liking for others and placed high value on friend-ships with members of the opposite sex.

On the other hand, those who scored low on dress and general grooming tended to be poorly adjusted socially and to have a generally negative outlook on life.

Other general tendencies in this group included the desire to be self-effacing or inconspicuous. These findings indicate general tendencies — there are, of course, many individuals who are exceptions.

Slipshod. The Columbia University study showed that the well-dressed persons tended to be appreciably smarter on the whole than those who were careless, slipshod or showed lack of taste in their attire. The median I.Q. for the "good appearance" group was 104, while that for the "poor appearance" group was only 95. Other studies have also shown a relationship between clothing selection and mental ability.

There are exceptions, of course — the high-I.Q. genius who doesn't give a hang about his personal appearance, and the empty-headed dandy who is impeccable in his dress — but evidence seems to indicate that such cases are far from typical.

Extremist. Studies conducted at New York University indicate that excessive concern over clothing and appearance suggest personal and social maladjustment.

It's a natural and normal thing to want to look one's best and to choose clothes and accessories which will contribute to a pleasing appearance. However, when a person goes to the *extreme* in this direction it is frequently an indication of personality maladjustment, psychologists find. The man, for example, who spends 10 minutes before the mirror painstakingly adjusting the knot in his tie, the angle of his hat or the set of his jacket is more than likely to have neurotic tendencies. Likewise,the woman who, after having spent hours at the dressing table, still isn't sure that she looks right, and worries over whether she should have worn this instead of that, etc.

Color-Crazy. A study conducted at the Drexel Institute of Technology in Philadelphia showed marked personality differences between those who like a wide variety of colors, and those who did not. The individuals who were color-minded tended to be extroverted, to enjoy the company of others, to be reasonably self-sufficient and confident, and to have dominant personalities.

On the other hand, personality tests have showed that those who were partial to *few* colors tended to have the following traits in common: to be lacking in self-confidence, and to have difficulty in making decisions.

Fashion's Slave. Psychologists and sociologists have explored women's craving to keep up with the latest fashion. A consensus of their findings indicates that a chief reason why women pursue styles and fashions is to relieve feelings of insecurity or inadequacy.

Another major reason for a woman's intense interest in clothes, is, of course, competition for male attention. But psychologists point out that strong preoccupation with fashion frequently represents a clear-cut case of compensation for a woman's sense of inferiority in a world of men.

Six Clothes Types: This interesting question has been perhaps most thoroughly and scientifically explored by the noted psychologist, Professor George W. Hartmann. His findings indicate that one of the things that reveals facts about a man's personality and general character is his preference in clothes, and his attitude toward them.

Dr. Hartmann suggested, as a result of his studies, that a man's "clothing behavior" linked him with one of six established personality types:

1. *The intellectual type.* He has a passion for knowledge, and a coolly objective mental attitude toward life. When this man buys a suit of clothes, he is principally concerned with the *properties of the material* — how well it will wear, if it will hold its crease properly, show spots easily, etc. — and with having it *fit* perfectly. If it measures up on these two counts he's likely to be satisfied.

2. *The economic type.* He falls into the efficient, hard-headed, materialistic-minded category. When he buys clothes, his concern is getting the most value for his money, and he keeps a shrewd eye open for bargains.

3. *The esthetic type.* He is acutely sensitive to the beauty in nature and the various arts; and his ability, or at least the urge, to create. When this type chooses a suit or a tie, he does so on the basis of "if it's good-looking, nothing else matters."

4. *The humanitarian type.* This person is dominated by love of his fellow men, and feels a strong sense of responsibility for the well-being of others. It disturbs a man of this type to wear the kind of clothes that his neighbor cannot afford. He buys a suit more because he needs one to keep warm than to indulge his personal tastes or preferences. He is less concerned by the cut of his topcoat than by the fact that there are those less fortunate than he who do not even possess one.

5. *The political type.* He seeks power and prestige — political, social or financial; wants others to look up to him; enjoys having people jump when he snaps his fingers. This type chooses a tie or suit not necessarily because he personally *likes* the pattern, cut or fabric, but because he believes others will regard it as impressive.

He is not particularly concerned with the cost and quality of his wardrobe — except as they contribute to the over-all effect of making him appear important.

6. *The religious-philosophical type.* The least materialistic of any of the key types, this man's world is dominated by spiritual values. He favors simplicity in clothes, dresses conservatively and tends scrupulously to avoid ostentation.

There are, of course, notable exceptions to these classifications — and there are many persons who are a combination of two or more types. These groupings are tentative and obviously incomplete. They are based, however, on conclusions dictated by carefully evaluated psychological findings.

SO YOU HATE TO GET UP IN THE MORNING
Often it is Much More Exciting to Sleep

If you hate to get up in the morning it may be that you lead a more interesting life while asleep. Studies show that many people's dream lives are more exciting than their everyday existence, sometimes the opposite of their lives during the day. A person who is feeling depressed may pass each night in happy dreams.

Still, many persons lead a much pleasanter life in their waking hours than they do in their dreams. (Perhaps these are the ones who like to get up in the morning.)

In dreams you can do a great deal of living in a very short time. Studies made at the Institute of Psychology of the University of Oslo found that people frequently had dreams in which months of action, adventure, and excitement were crowded into a dream lasting only a few minutes.

Since we spend a third of our lives in a state of unconsciousness, science has taken pains to explore this world. Here are some of the findings.

People who lead active social lives dream the most. (True_____. False_____.)

False. Studies at the University of North Carolina showed that when subjects were socially isolated for some time, they spent more of their sleeping hours in dreaming. Dream activity seems to compensate for lack of social activity.

Some persons never dream. (True_____. False_____.)

False. Late studies indicate that dreaming is "an intrinsic part of normal sleep," an experience shared by everyone. But some persons seldom remember their dreams, no matter how colorful or how vivid. The easiest time to remember a dream is when you have been suddenly awakened. To remember a dream, write it down the instant you wake up. Otherwise, dreams may fade quickly. Psychological tests show that people who find it easiest to recall their dreams have the best insight into their own true feelings and desires.

People who dream in color also find life in their waking hours more colorful than those who dream only in black and white. (True_____. False_____.)

True. Psychological studies at Stanford University show that those who dream in color find life exciting when they are awake, and are vividly aware of everything that goes on around them. Color dreamers, particularly women, tend to be highly intuitive.

You can tell when someone is dreaming just by looking at him. (True_____. False_____.)

True. You can tell by watching his eyelids. Researchers have found that usually when a person dreams, his eyes may be seen moving rapidly under his eyelids, as he "watches" the sequences of his dreams. The more action there is in the dream, the more rapid the eye movements. If little or no action is experienced, the eye movements may be almost imperceptible.

Experiments at the University of Cincinnati showed that artifically inducing rapid eye movements in sleeping subjects, through mechanical manipulation or photo stimulation, could actually cause persons to dream, even influence the content of their dreams.

Sleepwalking occurs when the dream is so vivid that the sleeper feels impelled to take physical part in it. (True_____. False_____.)

False. Scientists report that sleepwalking seldom occurs during the dreaming phase of sleep; that it tends to run in families, is more likely to occur in children than adults, is aggravated by anxiety and worry. Unlike dreams, it is associated with temporary loss of memory: usually the sleepwalker has no memory of having walked in his sleep.

You will have a more interesting dream life if you go to bed thirsty. (True_____. False_____.)

True. Studies at New York University showed that subjects who went to bed thirsty dreamed more, and their dreams covered more subjects. They also had more dreams about food, and they woke up hungrier, with a bigger appetite for breakfast.

A person's dream life changes when he quits smoking. (True_____. False_____.)

True. University of California studies show that when heavy

111

smokers quit, both their sleep and dream patterns changed radically. They slept better and longer, and had less difficulty getting to sleep. They also dreamed more than before.

Sleeping pills keep you from dreaming. (True_____. False_____.

True. UCLA Medical Center's sleep-research scientists have discovered that sleeping-pill users "are fortunate if they dream very much at all." The investigators also report that when the drugs are discontinued, the dreams come back.

We do not think while we are asleep. (True_____. False_____.

False. Research reveals that our mental faculties and dream processes both function while we are asleep. Subconscious activity continues unceasingly at various levels, solving problems, interpreting our feelings, wishes, and desires. (How many times have you gone to sleep with a problem on your mind and awakened with the solution?) After an intensive study of the subject, University of Chicago investigators conclude that "dreams are only a part of a larger body of sleep mentation (brain activity)." In other studies, when subjects were awakened at various times by investigators and asked if they were dreaming, they frequently said, "No, I've been thinking." They regarded the sleep activity as thoughts rather than dreams. This occurred most often when the subject's eyes were not moving under the lids (indicative of dreaming). So active is our subconscious during sleep that the noted psychiatrist, Dr. Joost A. M. Meerloo, calls sleep just another form of wakefulness.

Studies at the Veterans Administration's Behavior-Research Laboratory show that people tend both to dream and to think in their sleep about problems, situations, or ideas which they find disturbing, upsetting, or baffling. Nearly all the subjects in the survey tended to dream about occurrences which they found confusing. It was as though things occurring in the course of the day which the conscious mind was unable to comprehend were referred to the subconscious mind during sleep.

USE YOUR (6TH) SENSE!
Science Finds Considerable Evidence for
Extrasensory Perception

How good are your hunches? Can you send a "think-o-gram?" Can you transmit or receive ideas and information through mental waves comparable to radio waves?

Science has been taking a close look at ESP (extrasensory perception) and made some interesting findings. Recent studies in universities and research foundations seek answers to many of the same questions you may have wondered about.

Do most people have ESP?

Yes. Studies conducted at the City College of the City University of New York have demonstrated that ESP is associated with other human capabilities, such as perception, learning, and thinking. As psychology Professor Gertrude Schmeidler observes, ESP operates in varying degrees in every-day occurrences: someone stares at you and you turn around. A neglectful friend phones you after a long delay and you suspect it is he before picking up the receiver.

The studies indicate that all forms of ESP — telepathy, sub-conscious promptings, hunches — are simply extensions and refinements of our ordinary sensory faculties. Why they function at one time but not at another has been found to be influenced by such factors as mood, personality characteristics, and general outlook.

Do some people lack ESP?

Yes, just as there are people whose intuitional faculties fail to function. Psychological studies at Oxford University show that in some people "there is a kind of censorship which tends to prevent ESP impressions from emerging into consciousness."

What personality type is best at ESP?

All studies show that people who consistently make the best scores on ESP tests are likely to be well-adjusted, emotionally stable, self-confident, socially outgoing, and have a good rapport with others. Other characteristics which they were found to share in common: a freedom from nervousness, negativism, hostility, or defensiveness. A relatively carefree, accepting, happy-go-lucky outlook on life in general was characteristic of a significant percentage of the high scorers on ESP tests.

A psychological study of elementary school boys and girls has shown similar findings, "with positive scores being made by children who were outgoing in temperament, and the poorest scores made by those who were psychologically withdrawn in their social relations."

Is it true that good memory and ESP go together?

Yes. Research at the Institute of Parapsychology in Durham, N.C., shows "a significantly positive relationship between the scores made by subjects on ESP tests and the scores made on memory tests." Conclusions of the investigators: "Our findings suggest that there are psychological factors common to both ESP and memory."

Are creative people better at ESP than others?

Yes. Investigations have shown that people with creative ability are more proficient in sensing others' thoughts, have better developed intuitive faculties, and a keener sense of perception. They can usually rely on the accuracy of their hunches (psychologists call this precognition). In studies conducted at the University of Wyoming, students who scored highest on creativity tests also made the highest scores on ESP tests.

Does your ESP work better when you are lying down?

That depends on whether you are sending or receiving. Studies at the University of California indicate that conditions highly conducive to thought telepathy exist when the state of mind of the sender (isolated from the other participant) is one of emotional intensity — and the receiver is lying down and relaxed.

Can you lose ESP?

Yes. Tests show that it may be present one day and gone the next. Loss of ESP may be either temporary or permanent. Psychological studies at the University of Virginia show that "many extra sensory subjects (who participated in the tests) apparently lose their ability after a more or less prolonged period of successful performance." Investigators have also noted that ESP, like other perceptive senses, is influenced to a great extent by mood, general attitude, and outlook, which may vary from day-to-day.

Are happily married couples better at ESP than others?

Yes. The closer you are to another person, the better you are able to sense his thoughts and feelings, and this holds true whether you are in the same room or isolated from each other.

In the studies made at Agnes Scott College, couples who share a close emotional relationship were pitted against couples who were not close, in a sender-receiver ESP test. (All couples were separated from each other in special rooms.) Couples in the closely related group did consistently better in every respect than the others.

Does it matter whether or not you believe in ESP?

Yes. In studies conducted by a team of University of California psychologists, more than 100 volunteer subjects, including both men and women, ranging in age from 14 to 65, were divided into two groups: those who believe in ESP and those who are convinced that ESP does not exist. Concluded the investigators: significant results on telepathy tests were obtained *only* with the group which believes in ESP.

Are some of our dreams really thoughts sent by someone else?

A series of studies conducted by scientists in the dream laboratory at Maimonides Medical Center, New York City, have demonstrated the ability of subjects to influence the content of another person's dreams from a distant room. In another controlled experiment, telepathic dream effects were achieved when "senders" and dreamers were separated by a distance of 14 miles.

"It is worthy of note," says psychiatrist Dr. Joost A. M. Meerloo, "that even in sleep, sensory stimuli from the outer world are registered on the brain. Many telepathic messages are received during sleep and dreams when the normal defensive 'warding off' of stimuli is at rest. We are now able to register some of these hypersensitive perceptions electronically, especially when assisted by computers."

This brings up the interesting question of how many of

our dreams originate in our own consciousness, and how many may come from someone else. Science has only just begun to investigate this phenomenon, but it is interesting to speculate on the possibility that the air may be as filled with vagrant thoughts as it is with equally invisible radio waves. If that is so we would do well to learn to be selective about the thoughts we "tune in."

VICTIMS OF THE ALPHABET
Treatment is Easier and Prognosis Better For
Women Than For Men

The receptionist looked around the roomful of job applicants. "To be fair to everyone, you will be interviewed in alphabetical order," she said. "The *A's* to *G's* will be seen this morning, the *H's* to *P's* we should get to this afternoon. The rest of you will have to come back tomorrow, except," she smiled apologetically, "for the *S's* to *Z's*. I'm afraid we may not be able to get to you until next week."

The lower-alphabet people exchanged sympathetic glances. "By the time they get to my name," one said, "the job will be filled five times."

If you are one of the millions of Smiths, Thompsons, or Williamses you are in the underprivileged part of the alphabet. Wherever you go or whatever you do, the world will not let you forget it.

Say you are a doctor. No matter what skills you attain you will always be at the end of the medical directory. So with the phone book, no matter who you are. Suppose you even appear in *Who's Who* some day? The same. You will never be up front.

No matter how far your surname separates you from the *A's*, you probably accept the situation unquestioningly because you never knew anything different. As you grew up, you began to realize the full extent to which alphabetical discrimination is practiced, usually in the name of fairness.

If you are beginning to suspect that the alphabetical order of a person's name may have a significant influence on him, on his physical health and his mental, emotional, and financial well-being, your suspicions are well-founded. For a British researcher, Dr. Trevor Weston, has made some startling findings.

As a first step he tried to determine if the alphabetical order of a person's name has a bearing on life expectancy. His findings: "For the population as a whole, life expectancy is about 71 years. Records of the ages of death over the last ten years of those with surnames beginning S to Z show how an average life expectancy of only 64 years."

So much for mortality. What about morbidity: ulcers, heart attacks, and so on? Dr. Weston's analysis of hospital records of peptic ulcers show there were roughly twice as many patients with S to Z surnames as could have been mathematically expected. So the S's to Z's were twice as likely as those ahead of them in the alphabet to get ulcers. For coronaries, the figures were even worse. Having taken every other possible factor into account, he found the odds three to one against people whose names began from S to Z.

Mental health? He reported his findings in Britain's *Medical News:* "The incidence of neuroses was found to be 50% greater among people in the S to Z category. It is clear that the strain of all the waiting, the indignity of always being last, renders a person much more likely to become morose and introspective, with a growing conviction that he may not, in fact, *be* as good as the *A's, B's,* and *C's.*"

What can be done for the victims? Nothing, says Dr. Weston, except change his name. For a woman, however, the answer is simple: marry someone in the *A's, B's,* or *C's.*

III.

SWEET SUCCESS AND HAPPINESS

SWEET SUCCESS AND HAPPINESS

*It's from an innocent kind of selfishness, but it is
true that your usual motive in sizing up other people
is the promotion of your own success and happiness.
There are no sure rules to follow in attaining them,
as is quite evident from the general state of humanity.
But a knowledge of what makes people happy will
certainly contribute to your own success, and the
secret of hanging on to success is to have it make
other people besides yourself happy about it.*

WHAT ARE YOUR CHANCES OF SUCCESS?
There Are Several Factors That Horatio Alger
Never Even Thought Of

What are the factors which determine how successful you
are going to be? Let's take this subject out of the realm of
conjecture and speculation. Let's concern ourselves with the
latest, practical, down-to-earth findings of the nation's top-
flight research scientists. These gentlemen, who burned the
midnight oil in universities and research foundations, have
explored the whys and wherefores of success. Let's examine
their findings.

Question: How can you increase your chances for success?

Answer: By engaging in the type of work that you most
enjoy doing; which means that you will choose the vocation
that brings you the greatest sense of personal satisfaction and
which provides for the fullest expression of both your abilities
and personality. It may take some experimenting to find this
vocation. But no matter how much trouble and effort it takes,
it's more than worth it — for sociological studies show that it
is likely to mean the difference between success and failure.
A nationwide survey has shown that of men who have distinguished themselves in their fields, over 94% were doing the
type of work they liked the best. On the other hand, studies

121

show than a man who doesn't particularly enjoy his work seldom excels in it, no matter how hard he tries. A mass of evidence indicates that most failures are simply misfits.

Q: What about the matter of changing jobs — is it true that a "rolling stone" gathers the least moss?

A: At Columbia University, a survey was made to determine whether it is best for a young man to remain with one concern for a long time and work up, or change about from one firm to another as better opportunities present themselves. They made a careful study of the vocational histories of hundreds of promising young men between the ages of 20 and 31. Conclusion of the investigators: "the popular idea that the young man who remains longer with a given firm will out-distance the one who changes more frequently finds no support from our investigation."

And a wide-scale study conducted at the University of Kansas showed that eminent men have shown a marked tendency to change jobs more frequently than their less-successful colleagues. Indeed it was found that men who had achieved top ranking in their respective fields tended to keep shifting until they found positions which offered the maximum opportunity for the expression of their talents and abilities.

Q: What one quality do all successful men have in common?

A: It is not a high I.Q. — many men of achievement have only average intelligence. It is not outstanding talent and ability. You can be successful and possess these qualities to a lesser extent than the average ne'er-do-well. The trait that men of accomplishment have in common is a very special quality which has been found so important to achievement that psychologists have been at some pains to define it and analyze its relationship to success. It is the greater willingness to spend time in accomplishing a task; it is the willingness to withstand discomfort, and the ability to persevere in the face of seemingly impossible odds; it is also the willingness to resign oneself to patient plodding when the load is heavy and the road is steep.

Scientists at Ohio University made a psychological study of the relationship of persistence to success. They found after

122

exhaustive tests on all types of persons that there is a very positive relationship between an individual's ability to accomplish any task and the time he is willing to spend on it. If you have this quality of persistence or can cultivate it, the odds are very great not only that you will find the vocation you're best suited for but that you will distinguish yourself in it.

Q: If you're not as successful as you feel you ought to be, what can you do about it?

A: Try to put your finger on the trouble spot; more often than not, the thing that holds a man back is pure laziness.

If there's any doubt in your mind about how you stack up in this department, here's a fast fool-proof, scientifically tested method of finding out. This test was developed as a result of exhaustive studies conducted by psychologists at Illinois Institute of Technology. They have found that a good vocabulary indicates that you're well endowed so far as I.Q. and ability are concerned. If you aren't making the grade with such fine equipment, it's simply because you're not applying yourself.

Q: Is it important to get started on your career as early in life as possible?

A: Yes. Aside from the fact that it may take appreciable time before you find the occupational groove that best fits your abilities, there is another even more important factor. Science has found that the man who gets an early start on his career is far more likely to distinguish himself in his vocation than otherwise.

Q: Are you more likely to be successful if your father was?

A: Yes. At Indiana University investigators studied a representative cross-section of successful Americans, who had distinguished themselves in their various fields. They found that the parents of these men tended to have specific traits in common. They were characterized by 1. mental alertness, 2. ambition, 3. energy, 4. a strong desire to improve their lot and to give their children better opportunities.

The survey showed that the great majority of the nation's most successful men come from better than average homes, and have fathers who attained some distinction in their profession or occupation.

Findings of the investigation showed that only a comparative minority of eminently successful men have Horatio Alger backgrounds. Thus, contrary to what many people think, it would appear that being born with a silver spoon in your mouth — culturally and economically — tends to spur rather than sap ambition and initiative.

At any rate, the study showed that those families who had to struggle hardest to make ends meet produced the fewest successful men.

Q: At what age are you likely to be the most successful?

A: Exhaustive studies conducted at Ohio University show that in terms of productivity and creative ability, you're likely to turn in the highest batting average between the ages of 30 and 40. This was found particularly true of men engaged in professional fields, such as science, medicine, research, psychology and kindred callings. The survey showed, however, that most business executives don't reach their top stride until appreciably later in life — between 50 and 60.

And so far as earning power alone is concerned, a survey of all age groups showed that most of the highest paid men are in their middle 50's.

Q: Do happiness and financial success tend to go hand in hand?

A: Only to a certain extent. People with extremely low or high incomes tend to be the least happy. The happiest are those who have achieved a halfway degree of financial success.

Indeed, evidence all up and down the line indicates that an income sufficient to provide for economic security is most conducive to happiness, enough to make ends meet comfortably, with some left over to add to the nest egg, but not enough to put you in the wealthy class.

Studies conducted by sociologist Judson T. Landis show, incidentally, that most people tend to be happier during that period in their lives when they are climbing up the ladder of success, rather than after they have reached the top.

Q: Is the man who gripes about his work less likely to

succeed at it?

A: If he's disposed toward griping he'll always find things to complain about — even though his job fits him like a glove. This attitude used to be regarded as a liability, but science's latest findings indicate that it may well be an asset.

The University of Michigan's Institute for Social Research did a four-year survey of the personnel of leading U.S. companies. They found that the man who gripes about his work, his boss or his company is more likely to succeed than the man who either has no gripes or keeps them to himself.

A man may gripe because he's a perfectionist, or because he envisions some better way of doing things and does not yet have the authority to put his ideas into practice.

But regardless of the motivation, the survey showed that the personality characteristics that dispose a man to griping also make him a better and more efficient worker.

"While this type," say the investigators, "will often spend a lunch hour denouncing his job and criticizing things in general, the driving urge to succeed will send this same subject back to work fired with more productive energy."

A spokesman for one of the country's largest insurance companies — whose employees were included in the survey — believes the investigation may produce startling results. "On the basis of the study," he observed, "it may be that instead of firing a guy who threatens to punch his boss in the nose, we should promote him."

HOW DOES YOUR JOB STACK UP?
You Can Tell From the Kind of Work You Do
How Smart You Are, How Long You'll Live and
How Your Neighbors Rate You

In leading universities and research foundations, scientific investigators have lately been putting the yardstick on virtually every profession and calling in the book. To find out how each one rates in various and sundry respects, they've conducted wide-scale polls, studies and surveys — covering everybody from doctors and teachers to ditchdiggers and night-club singers.

They can tell you exactly what standing your vocation has in the eyes of fellow Americans, which occupations have the highest I.Q.'s, and so on. To find out how your job rates, look at science's findings.

Question: How do the various professions and occupations rank as to prestige and social standing?

Answer: Consensus of public-opinion surveys conducted by leading research organizations and universities shows that doctors enjoy the greatest social prestige of any profession or calling. College professors rank almost as high, followed closely by scientists and bankers. In the next highest bracket, lawyers, architects and dentists enjoy about equal standing in the mind of the public.

Other gainful occupations, listed in the order of their social prestige, are as follows: novelists, schoolteachers, farmers, electricians, newspaper reporters, traveling salesmen, mail carriers and plumbers.

Public-opinion surveys likewise show that, among the occupations regarded as having a lesser social status, the barber ranks somewhat above the store clerk and the milkman; and the truck driver ranks slightly higher than the night-club singer.

Occupations regarded as having the least social prestige — listed in the order of descending status — are: taxi drivers, waiters, bartenders, janitors, garbage collectors, street sweepers and shoe shiners.

Q: Has there been any change in the social status of the various occupations in the last generation?

A: Comparatively little. Researchers at the University of Minnesota found only slight differences in results obtained by investigators three decades ago. Most notable changes: the physician has replaced the banker as the man with the most prestige; while the social status of farmers and traveling salesmen has dropped. Biggest gain in occupational prestige has been made by the insurance agent.

Q: It's a well-known fact that people in some occupations tend to be smarter than those in others. How do the various occupations rank in this respect?

A: During the last war, the Army had top psychologists analyze the findings of intelligence tests given to over 80,000 enlisted men in 227 occupations. The professions scoring in the highest I.Q. bracket were accountancy, engineering, medicine and chemistry. The second highest intelligence bracket included writers, teachers, lawyers and dentists. Ranking in the next bracket were pharmacists, draftsmen, reporters, and tool designers.

In the middle of the intelligence scale, machinists ranked ahead of policemen, who in turn averaged higher I.Q.'s than entertainers. Boilermakers and welders made somewhat lower scores, and were followed by plumbers, auto mechanics, bricklayers, carpenters and painters. In the next bracket, truck drivers made better showings than cooks and service-station attendants.

Generally speaking, the Army intelligence tests showed that those who used brawn rather than brains to bring home the bacon tended to be endowed accordingly. Occupations making the lowest scores of all being unskilled laborers, miners, farm hands and lumberjacks.

It's important to realize, however, that this survey does not pretend to evaluate the intelligence of each individual in the various occupations. It merely reports the averages for each calling. For example, some carpenters were found to have higher I.Q.'s than some accountants, and so on. But such cases tended to be the exception rather than the rule.

Q: On the average, members of which professions live the longest?

A: Sociologists at Westminster College made a study of the life spans of nearly 10,000 persons in virtually every profession. Educators and lawyers were found to average the longest lives. Engineers and scientists ranked next. Chemists, philosophers and theologians placed third in the longevity sweepstakes. Next came physicians, followed by musicians, painters, and mathematicians. Authors and actors averaged slightly shorter life spans. And shortest lived of all were poets and explorers.

The Westminster College study likewise showed that men who attain eminence in their profession tend to live appreciably longer than those who do not. Very possibly this is because they have more to live for. For studies have shown morale to be an important factor in longevity.

Q: What occupations have the highest rate of mental breakdowns?

A: To find out the answer to this question, the University of Chicago sponsored a wide-scale study. It checked the occupational background of virtually every man admitted to mental hospitals (suffering from a psychosis) in the Chicago area, over a 12-year period. This included over 12,000 persons. The vocations are listed in the order in which mental breakdown was found to occur, beginning with those which had the lowest rate.

1. Professional and executive group: doctors, lawyers, manufacturers, company officials, etc.
2. Major salesmen: stockbrokers, wholesale dealers, etc.
3. Small tradesmen: primarily minor retail dealers
4. Office workers: stenographers, bookkeepers, accountants, general clerical workers
5. Policemen and firemen
6. Clergymen and teachers
7. Engineers
8. Sub-executives: foremen, overseers, etc.
9. Semi-professional: druggists, designers, draftsmen, undertakers, etc.
10. Salesmen: store salesmen, traveling salesmen
11. Artists, musicians, actors, entertainers

12. Barbers, beauticians
13. Skilled workers: painters, carpenters, electricians, etc.
14. Minor government employees: postal clerks, mail carriers, city and county inspectors, etc.
15. Domestic workers: cooks, cleaners, porters, servants, etc.
16. Generally unskilled workers: laborers, elevator men, janitors, etc.
17. Peddlers
18. Waiters

Starting with the professional-executive group at the top of the list, the mental breakdown rate rose steadily with each occupation listed. For example, the percentage of barbers who went off the deep end mentally was over five times as high as for doctors and lawyers; and the rate for waiters was over nine times as great.

As sociologist Robert E. Clark points out, the study showed that occupational groups differ widely as to personality traits which have a bearing on the likelihood of a person becoming psychotic.

University of Michigan studies likewise show that a significant relationship exists between a man's adjustment and the occupation he chooses.

Q: What about the person who cannot make up his mind about the occupation he wishes to follow?

A: Studies conducted by psychologist Bertram R. Forer, of the Veterans Administration's Mental Hygiene Clinic, show that the man who cannot decide on a vocation — or has no preferences about one — is likely to be emotionally maladjusted.

"Emotionally disturbed persons," the psychologist finds "often do not know what is good for them occupationally. What they wish to do and what they should do may be quite different, and they will generally be highly resistant toward recognizing the fact."

This is borne out by other studies which show that the round peg in the square hole, or jack-of-all-trades-but-master-of-none type tends to be less well-adjusted and most subject to mental breakdown.

Q: How can you tell if you are in the occupation you are best fitted for?

A: Studies of industrial psychologists have repeatedly demonstrated that the best index to how well suited a man is to his job is how much he enjoys doing it. If you don't find your work interesting, and if performing it does not afford you a strong sense of personal satisfaction, then you have not yet found the occupation best suited to your abilities.

Furthermore, if you don't enjoy the work you're doing, the odds are that you lack the capacity to excel in it. Choose the type of work that best fits your temperament and ability — in other words, the job you enjoy. And the better the fit, the greater your chances for distinguishing yourself.

If there is any doubt in your mind as to the direction where your real abilities lie, take a vocational guidance test, and then pick your line of work accordingly. When you buy a pair of shoes, you measure the foot first. And you fit the shoe to the foot — not vice versa.

Consensus of studies and surveys in this area makes it clear that most vocational misfits did not choose their job — intelligently, that is. They followed the line of least resistance and let the job choose them.

TEST YOUR PERSONALITY
And Match Your Occupation to Your Life Style

One of the most important questions in your life is whether your occupation matches your life style.

Unnecessary frustration, failure, and disappointment can be avoided if you are filling the role in life for which you are best suited and equipped. A University of Connecticut psychologist, Dr. Kenneth Ring, and his associates have developed a test designed to show a person's life-performance style. Here is an adaptation of Dr. Ring's test with simplified scoring and analysis.

Consider each statement carefully, then check whether you find it true or false. Each item is designed to bring out the presence or absence of specific personality qualities.

1. I often feel like telling people what I really think of them. (True_____ False_____)

2. I would be uncomfortable in anything other than fairly conventional dress. (True_____ False_____)

3. I enjoy being with people who are suave and sophisticated. (True_____False_____)

4. When in a new and unfamiliar situation, I am usually governed by the behavior of others present. (True_____ False_____)

5. In social situations, I often feel tense and constrained. (True_____ False_____)

6. At times I suspect myself of being too easily swayed by the opinions of others, and perhaps too open-minded and receptive to other people's ideas. (True_____ False_____)

7. I usually have trouble making myself heard in an argument. (True_____ False_____)

8. I don't like formality. (True_____ False_____)

9. I feel I can handle myself pretty well in most social situations. (True_____ False_____)

10. I like to meet new people. (True_____ False_____)

11. I don't mind playing a role or pretending to like something I really don't if it serves some good purpose. (True_____ False_____)

131

12. I enjoy "putting people on" sometimes, and playing conversational games. (True_____ False_____)

13. I usually find it difficult to change someone else's opinion. (True_____False_____)

14. I like to do things that other people regard as unconventional. (True_____False_____)

15. I enjoy being the host (or hostess) of a party. (True_____ False_____)

16. I think a person should adapt his behavior to the group that he is with at the time. (True_____False_____)

17. I often find it difficult to get people to do me favors, even when I have the right to expect them. (True_____ false_____)

18. I should like to belong to several clubs or lodges. (True_____False_____)

19. I think it is important to learn obedience. (True_____ False_____)

20. I like to avoid situations which do not permit me to do things in an original way. (True_____False_____)

21. Just the thought of giving a talk in public scares me. (True_____ False_____)

22. I can fit in pretty easily with any group of people. (True_____ False_____)

23. In general, I find that I dislike nonconformists. (True_____ False_____)

24. It is usually easy for me to persuade others to my own point of view. (True_____ False_____)

25. I like to go to parties. (True_____ False_____)

26. I prefer to listen to other people's opinions before I take a stand. (True_____ False_____)

27. When in a group of people I have trouble thinking of the right things to talk about. (True_____False_____)

28. If I am with someone I do not like, I am usually diplomatic and do not express my real feelings. (True_____False_____)

29. I have the knack of recognizing people's talents and abilities and putting them to the best purpose. (True_____ False_____)

30. I like to follow instructions and do what is expected of

me. (True_____ False_____)

HOW TO SCORE

1. If your answer to this question was *False,* put the letter C here_____.

2. If your answer was *False,* put the letter B here_____.

3. If you said *False* on this one, write the letter A here_____.

4. If you said *True* on this one, write the letter C here_____.

5. If you said *True* on this one, put the letter A here_____.

6. If you said *True* on this one, put the letter C here_____.

7. If you said *False* on this one, write the letter B here_____.

8. If you said *False* on this one, write the letter C here_____.

9. If you said *False* on this one, put the letter A here_____.

10. If you said *True* on this one, write the letter B here_____.

11. If you said *False,* write the letter A here_____.

12. If you said *True* on this one, put the letter B here_____.

13. If you said *False* on this one, write the letter B here_____.

14. If you said *False,* write the letter C here_____.

15. If you said *True,* put down the letter B here_____.

16. If you said *True,* put down the letter C here_____.

17. If you said *False* on this one, put down the letter B here_____.

18. If you said *False,* write the letter A here_____.

19. If you answered *True,* put down the letter C here_____.

20. If you said *True* on this one, write the letter A here_____.

21. If you said *False,* put down the letter B here_____.

22. If you wrote *False* on this one, put down the letter A here_____.

23. If you said *True,* put down the letter C here_____.

24. If you said *True,* write the letter B here_____.

25. If you said *False,* put the letter A here_____.

26. If you answered *True,* write the letter C here_____.

27. If you said *True,* write the letter A here_____.

28. If you answered *False,* put down the letter A here_____.

29. If you said *True* on this one, write the letter B here_____.

30. If you answered *True* on this one, write the letter C here_____.

Now total the numbers of *A's B's* and *C's* which you scored. If you have more *A's* than anything else, you are predominantly an *A*-type personality. (See the analyses which follow.) Mostly *B's* indicate strong *B*-type tendencies; and a majority of *C's* indicates you are basically a *C*-type. It should, of course, be emphasized that few people fit wholly and completely into one category, but most people are predominantly one or the other. The more one letter outnumbers the others, the more completely your tendencies lie in the direction of that type. The total number of letters you have checked indicates the extent to which you share characteristics of all three types.

ANALYSES

The "A" Type Personality

A-types are highly individualistic, strongly opinionated, and have little patience with sham or pretense. The man or woman in this category is by nature frank and outspoken; he believes in saying exactly what he thinks. He is not socially adept or skilled in the subtleties of diplomacy. The roundabout approach is completely foreign to him. He is uncomfortable in situations where he cannot be forthright and direct. He wants to "be himself" at all times, and he expects others to do the same. His independent-mindedness may alienate people occasionally, but it would never occur to anyone to question his honesty or integrity. He believes along with Shakespeare that if you are true to yourself, you cannot be false to any man.

Type *A* people are happiest and most successful in occupations where they can be their own boss, or where they can be selective about their clientele, and do not have to meet the public at large. Such people may have many talents, and they possess strength of character, but they tend to lack skill in interpersonal relations and the ability to get along harmoniously with all types of people in various situations. It follows that a type *A* person would be least happy in such occupations as salesman, career diplomat, public-relations man, and personnel director. And one of the most unfortunate choices he could make would be to go into politics, or run for any public office. The type of people he gets along best with are other *A* people. He understands them, and they understand him. They do not always get along, but frequently an *A*-type person can be happy in a joint enterprise with them. But he is better off in an occupation where his rugged

134

individual life style will be an asset as in the arts (music, writing), or agriculture (farming, landscaping, forestry). In law and medicine the aggressive-minded and independent achieve outstanding success.

The "B" Type Personality

The B-type person is typically highly skilled in interpersonal relations. He is socially adroit, and verbally adept. He has an innate understanding of people. He is quick to grasp the underlying motivations of other people. This insight serves him in excellent stead when he wishes to gain control of a situation or enlist the cooperation of others who may have conflicting views. He not only understands people, he enjoys them. He rarely feels at a loss in any circumstance where *people* are involved. As the psychologists who conducted the study observe: A B person enjoys interpersonal relationships which would make an A personality feel excruciatingly uncomfortable, and knows precisely what to do and how to act in situations where an A does not.

The B person's ability as a strategist makes him highly effective in influencing others. However, these abilities make it necessary for him to guard against the temptation to manipulate people or use them to achieve selfish ends. For, more than any other talent, the ability to influence others can either be used positively or abused.

B people will be the happiest and function most effectively in occupations which involve salesmanship in any chosen field, organizing, group leadership, politics, jobs involving travel, breaking new ground, meeting new people. There is practically no occupation which involves dealing with the public that the B person cannot cope with.

The "C" Type Personality

One of the secrets of getting along in this world is the ability to adjust to conditions, roll with the punches, make allowances for other people's faults, and be appreciative of their virtues. The C-type people can get along with almost anybody, in any setting, and exhibit admirable patience even with difficult people under trying circumstances. They "pour oil on troubled waters" rather than "make waves." Their motto is "Live and let me live." They like to go out of their way to please others and do favors for people. Because of this they are sometimes taken advantage of and imposed upon.

Considerate, thoughtful, and sensitive to the feelings and attitudes of others, they have a strongly ingrained respect for convention and tradition. They are respectful of the rights of others, and will go out of their way to avoid antagonizing others. They are interested in what other people think, their concepts and ideas. And they are interested in what other people think *about them.* For it is important to them to have the respect and approval of others, and they strive to merit it. They are, however, indecisive sometimes, and need to guard against being too easily influenced by the opinions of others.

C people have the ability to work quietly, efficiently, and competently in practically any field which does not require them to be aggressive, impose their will on others, or mold others' opinions. They tend to be uncomfortable in jobs which require them to order people around, enforce discipline, become involved in conflicts of will. They feel more at home following rules and regulations than making them, are more comfortable carrying out orders than giving them. And they are happiest and most successful in occupations whose functions and boundaries are specific and well-defined. This opens up a wide variety of choices, which include accountant, engineer, dietitian, chemist, secretary, pathologist, statistician, computer operator, and technicians in every field from cosmetology to electronics.

WHAT DO YOU WANT MOST OUT OF LIFE?
Ninety-Nine Out Of A Hundred People Will Answer "Happiness," But When They Are Asked What Happiness Means To Them, They Have Vastly Differing Ideas

Do you feel that you would be happier if you had more money, if you had a better education, if you could live the life of Riley and do exactly what you pleased without cares or responsibilities, if you could live to be 100, or if you had a deeper and more satisfying religious faith? How do your dreams and aspirations compare with those of other people? Here's your chance to find out.

For psychologists and sociologists in leading universities and research foundations have conducted exhaustive polls, studies and wide-scale surveys to find out what most people want out of life. After probing the attitudes and ambitions of hundreds of thousands of representative individuals, they can give you a pretty accurate picture of what the average person feels would make him happy.

If you would like to find out how your wishes and desires stack up with those of other people, researchers have made it possible for you to do this. Psychologists at a leading university evaluated the wishes of 16,000 people from various walks of life. Each was asked: "If you could have anything you wanted, what would be the first thing you would wish for?" More than a third of the people wished for something which would enable them to "get away from it all," something which would provide a relief from the sameness of their everyday existence, such as a cruise to the South Seas, a trip around the world, or a sojourn in some far-off romantic spot. Roughly an equal number of this cross-section of men and women wished for something more practical, such as new furniture, adding a new room to the house, or getting a new car. Only 13% wished for luxuries such as a maid or a new fur coat.

If you are like most people, however, you would react differently if you were suddenly given a lump of cold cash — say a windfall of $1,000. Though your first wish might be to use it for pleasure, the chances are that you would be much more apt to invest the money conservatively, or keep it as a nest egg — and not spend it at all. In one poll, men and women from every class of society were asked the following question: "If you were given $1,000 tomorrow, what would you do with it?" The overwhelming majority said they would save it, invest it carefully, or use the money to help purchase a home. Fewer than seven people in 100 said they would shoot the works on "just having fun."

Most people, contrary to what you might think, would not like to forego their cares and responsibilities and lead the life of Riley without having to think about working for a living. A leading life insurance company surveyed more than 3,000 representative men and women on this question. And less than one out of four was intrigued by the prospect of a completely leisured and carefree life. The overwhelming majority — over 75% — said they preferred to keep on working even after they reached the age of retirement, or at any rate to continue "doing something useful."

As for wanting to live to be 100, just slightly over half of the people feel that they would like to be able to do this. The rest either take a very dim view of the idea, or else are undecided. A poll which interviewed men and women from all walks of life on this question showed that 57% wanted very much to be able to celebrate their 100th birthday — feeling that the longer you live the more you get out of life; 32% said definitely that they would not want to live that long, and 11% could not make up their minds. Ironically enough, far fewer women (the longer-lived sex) than men wanted to reach this age.

Another interesting finding of the survey: the older a person gets, the longer he wants to live. The biggest percentage of those who wanted to live to be 100 were middle-aged or over. The attitude of the younger people seemed to be: youth is the time that counts — and old age is strictly "for the birds."

Typical comments of people who didn't want to live to be 100 reflect their reasons: "There's just no point to it — I'm sure I'd have lost my usefulness long before I got that old" . . . "Old people are apt to be lonely and feel that the world has passed them by" . . . "I don't think living to be that old would be much fun. There are too many things you couldn't do" . . . "It isn't how *long* you live that's important, it's how *much* you live" . . . "I might be sick and helpless — just a burden on someone."

People who wanted their birthdays to stretch to the century mark looked at things from a different angle: "The older I get, the more life interests me. I want to stay alive as long as possible" . . . "Life is a fascinating pageant. I want to see as much of it as I possibly can" . . . "I want to live to see the marvels of the atomic age."

Studies show that if you are like the average person, one of the chief things you want out of life is a happy marriage. But when it comes to naming the ingredients most necessary for a happy marriage, only a small percentage place such qualities as love, faithfulness and devotion at the top of the list. On the contrary, wide-scale surveys show that the quality the average male regards as of greatest importance in a wife is that she be a good housekeeper and a good cook. And while many men placed love and devotion fairly high on the list of essentials, less than 4% considered them the most important qualities in a wife.

The majority of the women were inclined to sell love short too. Surveys show that the characteristics most women value highest in a husband are 1. that he be a good provider, 2. that he possess the qualities of faithfulness and steadiness, 3. that he be kind and considerate. Love ranked farther down on the list, just ahead of "intelligence and common sense." Only a small minority of the women gave love the No. 1 priority.

If you are a woman, the odds are better than even that you think men get more of out life than women do. For polls and surveys have repeatedly shown that most women feel that men lead more interesting lives than they do. And it has also been established that women envy men's lot much more than men envy women's. For example, the Canadian Institute of Public Opinion asked a representative cross-section of men and women this question: "If you had a choice which would you rather be — a man or a woman?" Twenty-nine per cent of the women said that they would much prefer being men. But a scant 6% of the men were intrigued by the thought of being a woman.

Ask the average person what he wants most out of life, and the odds are that a better education will be one of the things most prominently mentioned. In one survey, Gallup Poll interviewers asked people of all walks of life this question: "Everyone makes mistakes occasionally. Will you tell me what you consider to be the biggest mistake in your life so far?" By far the most frequent reply was: "Not getting sufficient education." This was mentioned far more frequently than mistakes having to do with choosing the wrong marriage partner, or the wrong career.

This thirst for a better education is by no means confined to those who haven't had much. On the contrary, investigations have shown that the better an education a person has had, the more apt he is to wish he had even more. Men with college degrees, researchers found out, had an even greater desire to further their education than those who have never progressed farther than high school.

Now we come to the question of what people want in life more than anything else. Ask 100 people this question, and 99 will probably say happiness. But what does happiness mean to them? To find out the answer, a leading public-opinion research organization polled a representative cross-section of the population. Having plenty of money was the answer given most often by men and women of all ages. Peace of mind and contentment ran a poor second; having a good family life ranked next; being in good health was fourth, and was followed by having good friends, and satisfaction from work.

These results bear out what psychologists and sociologists have long contended; that most people tend to overestimate the power of money to bring happiness, and to regard happiness and a fat bank account as practically synonymous. Studies show that people who regard having plenty of money as a requisite for happiness are really the least happy.

Actually, what are the things which are the most important to personal happiness? In one poll people were asked to rate themselves on a five-point scale, ranging from "very happy" to "very unhappy." The majority of those who rated themselves the happiest had four points in common: 1. they got along well with their families, 2. they didn't worry much, 3. they were engaged in work from which they derived real satisfaction, and 4. they enjoyed good health. Most of those who rated themselves as not happy answered negatively on every one of these points.

Sociological studies and public-opinion surveys show that most people wish for a deeper and more satisfying religious faith; and realize that they would get much more out of life if they would cultivate greater spiritual resources.

If you are like the majority, you are "too busy," too concerned with material considerations, to do a great deal about this. Nine out of 10 believe in God, in the efficacy of prayer — and its ability to provide you with a sense of inner peace and spiritual uplift. But for most it's difficult to "find time" from the distractions of everyday living to fully tap those sources whence come peace for the mind and sustenance for the spirit.

THE SIMPLE WAY TO HAPPINESS
The Great American Pursuit May Be Easier Than You Think

The U.S. Constitution guarantees our right to the pursuit of happiness, but doesn't tell us how to find it. Some people find it without looking; for others it is harder to find than uranium. To help us in our quest, scientists have been doing some fruitful exploring. Although happiness is strictly a do-it-yourself operation their findings give some good tips.

What is the chief cause of unhappiness?

Husband-and-wife fights contribute more toward unhappiness than any other single cause. Studies show that most marital disputes follow a specific pattern. They start over "little things," gain momentum, and suddenly flare into a full-blown quarrel.

Sociologists have found that such quarrels happen even in the best-adjusted families. What can you do about them? To answer this question, Columbia University investigators made a careful study. They found that there are certain periods in the day when family fights are most likely to flare up; the worst time is shortly before meals, so govern yourself accordingly.

Will a hobby increase your happiness?

Yes, indeed! Most people's jobs do not allow full expression of their talents or interests. They feel frustrated. A good hobby furnishes recreation and at the same time provides for self-expression. Psychiatric studies show that a hobby makes a person happier and healthier. Hobbies are far more common among well balanced persons than with those who have neurotic or psychotic tendencies.

There are times in everyone's life when unhappiness cannot be avoided. A hobby then is particularly important, according to psychiatrist Dr. William C. Menninger.

Are some persons allergic to happiness?

Yes. You probably know at least one person like that. They look at life through dark-colored glasses, and seem genuinely unhappy unless they have something to complain about. They enjoy feeling put upon, since it gives them the opportunity for self-pity. When something good happens to them they seem really uncomfortable until they can find some *flaw* in the picture.

Psychiatrist Dr. Edmund Bergler, who made a clinical study of the species, has described the kill-joy. He seems almost gifted with a biting irony which he directs at people who seem to be enjoying themselves. He gets pleasure from "freezing" other people by conspicuously not laughing at their jokes.

He has the general manner of a stern and disgusted governess confronted by a bunch of silly children. His motto seems to be the opposite of live and let live, yet he is never conscious of being a kill-joy. Avoid such people, for unhappiness, like happiness, is contagious.

How does a happy person differ basically from an unhappy person?

Studies at two leading universities show that happy persons place the greatest importance on such things as peace of mind, clear conscience, friendship and affection, love of one's work, enjoyment of nature. The less happy seek happiness in thrills, excitement, acquiring money, travel, new clothes, new cars, and all forms of entertainment.

Has it been possible to isolate the most important ingredient in happiness?

Yes. Scientists at the Harvard Research Center, working under sociologist Dr. Pitrim A. Sorokin, have scientifically demonstrated that love is the most essential ingredient in happiness: and that self-centeredness and unhappiness go hand in hand. Love was also found to be the best remedy for despondency.

In Dr. Sorokin's book *The Ways and Power of Love,* he says, "like other natural forces, love can be generated deliberately." Make the experiment. It will give you a warm glow inside, and it will be a good start toward lasting happiness.

What does it take to make a happy man?

It is hard to find a better answer than the one given by W. Beran Wolfe. "If you observe a really happy man you will find him building a boat, writing a symphony, educating his son, growing double dahlias in his garden, or looking for dinosaur eggs in the Gobi desert. He will not be searching for happiness as if it were a collar button that has rolled under the radiator. He will not be striving for it as a goal in itself. He will have become aware that he is happy in the course of living life 24 hours of the day."

IS EVERYBODY HAPPY?
Happiness Should Not Be Pursued,
Psychologists Say — It Must Ensue

Happiness is often hard to find, and even harder to sustain. In scientific studies, investigators have turned up findings which can help us make our own lives happier.

Are the happiest people those who have the fewest frustrations?

No. A University of California study tests men and women of various ages and walks of life in ways designed to measure degree of happiness, or, as investigators put it, "sense of psychological well-being." An inventory was taken of each person' life situation. Contrary to what might be expected, the people with the fewest trials, tribulations, disappointments, and frustrations were *not* the happiest. The happiest people, it was found, were those "with many resources (successes, accomplishments, windfalls) *and* many deficits (frustrations, blighted hopes, losses of various kinds)."

The investigators concluded that resources may compensate for so-called "deficits," and that the interaction of the two may actually enhance a sense of well-being. So occasional storms do help us to appreciate the fine weather that comes in-between.

What age do most people consider the happiest?

A recent university survey of hundreds of adults of all ages showed that middle age was generally considered the happiest time in life. It was felt that younger people had the most opportunities for enjoyment of life, and for happiness, but that those farther along in years were more successful in achieving it.

Can anyone find happiness if he will persist in his search for it?

No. As one psychiatrist points out in citing the findings of studies on the subject, "Happiness cannot be *pursued*. It must *ensue*. Happiness is available only as a by-product, a side effect of living. Once one has fulfilled his meaning or loves another human being, happiness occurs by itself. But the more one makes happiness an aim, the more the aim is missed."

Can overcoming some personal handicap or surmounting some obstacle be counted on to increase your happiness?

It is often assumed that overcoming some personal handicap which has resulted in hardship or frustration will automatically bring feelings of happiness and general well-being. Often just the opposite happens.

The reason, as one psychologist observes, is that "it removes a convenient cause on which to blame unhappiness. Once the crutch is removed, a person is forced to realize that his unhappiness originates in his own personality. No longer can he believe that the grass is greener on the other side."

Are religious people happier than others?

A survey which interviewed hundreds of people regarding how happy or unhappy they were showed that "unhappiness was approximately five times higher among nonreligious people than among those who describe themselves as 'very religious'." All evidence would seem to further confirm that man cannot live by bread alone without suffering spiritual malnutrition.

Does it take more to make us happy as we grow older?

Yes. Psychological studies have shown that an elementary school child's concept of happiness is very simple: wish fulfillment (a new bicycle, a trip to the circus, spending a summer at grandmother's). But with the approach of maturity, it was found, most people "equate happiness with feelings of love, success, and personal satisfaction." And middle-aged women were found to equate happiness most particularly with marital bliss.

Is there a formula for happiness?

Yes. The findings of all psychological studies indicate that happiness can be achieved by finding out what one is best fitted to do, and finding the opportunity to do it.

A PROFILE OF HAPPINESS
Scientists Find Real Differences Between
Happy and Unhappy People

New studies give us a searching analysis of happiness: the attitudes, personality characteristics, and world outlook which make people happy or unhappy.

How do happy people differ from unhappy people?

At the University of California, psychologists gave psychological tests to students and divided them into two classes.

1. Those who had open and outgoing personalities, who liked to reveal themselves to others, were easy to know and enjoyed having close personal relationships with others, sharing each other's thoughts, feelings, and ideas.

2. Those whose personalities tended to be closed, were difficult to know and preferred to remain that way; who kept their real selves hidden under a social facade, and resented attempts of others to get to know them. People in this category tended to be intensely jealous of the privacy of their inner world; to defend it against all comers; and to maintain a certain reserve in all relationships.

Questionnaires were given each subject to determine how happy or unhappy he rated himself, and how he was seen by friends and associates. Happiness scores for the two personality types were then compared. Results of the study showed that the open persons were far happier in nearly every respect than those who preferred not to be known by others.

Are there other basic personality differences between happy and unhappy people?

Yes. In reporting the findings of their ten-year study, psychologists Alden E. Wessman and David F. Ricks note these essential differences: "The composite self-picture presented by happy men in the study, both in moods of elation and depression, was that of a warm, friendly, candid person, comfortable in intimate relationships, conscientious, inventive, capable of taking things as they come, and not pessimistic." The people classified by the psychologists as happy were not immune to occasional feelings of depression, but they used the low periods

146

productively as "a time for taking stock, self searching, and looking for solutions to problems, with optimistic feelings that solutions would be found."

Unhappy men, on the other hand, described themselves, even in periods of elation, as unable to fully apply themselves, unproductive, cautious, hesitant, doubting, given to wasting time, and preoccupied with themselves and their own feelings. In depression they described themselves in much the same way, emphasizing that they never got what they really wanted.

Another difference between the happy and unhappy people was in their ideals and the things they deemed most important in life. The unhappy tended to place little value on anything but efficient work and the fulfillment of ambition. But people who were classified as generally happy valued warmth and friendliness just as highly as achieving personal goals. And they looked upon pretense, selfishness, and pessimism as much greater threats to contentment and well-being than failure to fulfill one's ambitions.

Another finding: the happy subjects in the study had a warm concern for others, a tenderness, honesty, and desire to comfort the less fortunate. The unhappy subjects tended to lack this quality, or have it in less measure.

Is the "pursuit of happiness" possible?

The surest way not to find happiness is to drop everything and look for it. People of unlimited wealth have spent fortunes and looked all over the world for happiness without finding it. As Dr. James D. T. Bugental says, authentic living is characterized by getting rid of the idea of happiness as a goal in itself. The person who is vitally alive is busy finding expression for his talents and abilities in the fields he has chosen. He seldom stops to assess his happiness. It seems to be only the neurotic and unhappy who spend their concern directly on their happiness.

How do happy and unhappy people differ in the things they worry about?

Studies show that the happier people tend to focus their concern on controllable problems of their lives: the things they can do something about. The less happy are inclined to fret over things about which they can do nothing.

Would you be happier if all your wishes came true?

No, you wouldn't. It is lucky you don't have an Aladdin's lamp, because we do not know that's really best for us. Psychological studies attest to the truth of the old proverb: "If a man could have half his wishes, he would double his troubles." Make the best of what you have, and you will not have to seek happiness. It will come looking for you.

SECRET OF FRIENDSHIP
It Is The Order And Security We Live By

The nature of friendship has long been left to poets and philosophers. Now the psychologists have made it their business. Here they give answers which can help us lead happier lives.

Is it harder to make friends as we grow older?

No. Though the older person is most often pictured as being friendless, it is the young person who is most likely to be lonely.

Psychologist George V. Coelho, of the National Institute of Mental Health, has found that friendships are not only more numerous as age increases, but also more stable and enduring.

How do you make a real friend?

Everybody has sought the answer to this question, and found it elusive. Studies show how a person's ability to make deep and lasting friendships tends to go hand in hand with his ability to pick the right marriage partner, that is, the right person for *him*.

Friends (like marriage partners) are discovered rather than made. In both instances it is more important to find the right person. Friendship grows and ripens just as love does — but first there has to be a mutual response from both persons.

Finding friends is incredibly simple, but many people never discover the secret. Friendship grows out of acquaintanceship. You have to make casual contacts with fellow human beings. Sooner or later you will find a friend, and you'll know it because he will be looking for you, too.

Is it possible to blueprint a formula for friendship?

After an extensive study, Florida University's psychologist Sidney M. Jourard finds that a good friendship includes the following:

1. Each person has carefully sized up the other, has an accurate idea of his personality, and likes more than he dislikes. 2. Each feels concern for the happiness and growth of the other. 3. Each can communicate honestly his thoughts, feelings, wants, memories, beliefs. Neither partner is on the defensive, afraid to say what he thinks. Each wants to be known by the other, and actively strives to make himself understood.

What is the difference between love and friendship?

The two have much in common, yet are as different as afternoon and twilight. Friendship has been described as love without its wings. It has also been observed that friendship always benefits, while love sometimes injures. And Samuel Johnson found a delightful way to describe the differences. "The feeling of friendship is like that of being comfortably filled with roast beef; love, like being enlivened with champagne."

Are some people incapable of friendship?

Yes, some people are actually allergic to it. Sometimes, observes psychologist Jourard, a person will become panicky when someone shows signs of liking him. This anxiety usually stems from some unhappy past relationship.

On the other hand, there are some people who bend over backward to be liked, who mask or suppress their own feelings and desires, and pretend to be the type of person they feel would be most acceptable to the other. The result is ironic. How does a man profit from affection and regard gained for someone he pretends to be?

Can you have too many friends?

You frequently hear people say, "You can't have too many

friends." Psychiatrist Martin Grotjahn says, "My studies have convinced me that the average person does not have room for any more than three or four real friends — after they become acquaintances. If he tries to spread himself too thin, he cannot do justice to the friendship he already has."

Why do we need friends?

So we won't be lonely is an obvious answer. What else? After study, psychologists Robert S. Albert and Thomas R. Brigante conclude: "We need interested reliable friends in order to live satisfying lives. Friendship not only offers a rewarding basis for living, but friends help us to place on solid ground our thoughts, feelings, opinions, and attitudes about ourselves and our world. The support we gain from friendship becomes the order and security we live by."

'HOW WELL DO YOU KNOW HIM?'
Research Scientists Offer Some Hints On
Getting Next To People

Scientists are just as interested as you are in discovering what people are really like, and why they behave as they do. Universities and research centers are continually exploring the many facets of human personality. Here are some of their recent findings.

Do opposites attract, or does like attract like?

Psychologists at Boston University found that for some persons the like-attracts-like principle proves out, but with others the opposite is true.

For couples who believe in equality of the sexes, like attracts like. But for those who believe that the man should be head of the house, opposites attract, which is just as well, since such couples have complementary needs.

What does your sense of humor tell about you?

It is a good indication of your intelligence, creativity, and ability to achieve your ambitions. University of Southern California psychologists gave students a standard personality test which included sense-of-humor, intelligence, and creativity tests, and a test designed to measure achievement potential. Students who made high sense-of-humor scores also scored high on intelligence, creativity, and achievement. Those with low sense-of-humor scores also averaged low scores on the other tests. The study indicated that sense of humor is most strongly associated with high creativity "when the style of humor is original, playful, emotional, or expressive"; and is most strongly linked with intelligence when the person displays "a wry, conforming, controlled drollness."

What makes a person interesting?

At Cornell University, researchers sought the things which make one person interesting to another, why we find some people dull and others stimulating. They discovered that the people others find most interesting are those they have some difficulty in immediately understanding and who therefore provide a challenge. They also found that character traits in themselves had little to do with how interesting or uninteresting a person was thought to be.

How can you tell if you are good at sizing up others?

Research scientists at Colorado State University made a study of the characteristics of good and poor judges of human nature. Poor judges of others tended to be worrisome, complaining, intolerant, and lacking in self-control. Good judges of human nature, those whose judgments of others averaged the greatest accuracy, tended to minimize their own complaints and worries, were tolerant of others, relatively well-adjusted, and had good self-control.

Some persons think they can remember things that happened to them when they were one or two years old. Are they kidding themselves, or are they confusing fantasies with memory?

Studies made at the University of Wichita show that many "first memories" are indeed unreliable, being based on dreams, imaginings, or things told the person as a small child. But they found that people often do have accurate memories of events which took place before they were two years old. The study

151

also showed that introverts have far better memories for such things than extroverts do.

When a person is angry what is the best way to cool him off?

Tell him a funny story. At the University of Rochester, investigators conducted an experiment using undergraduate students as subjects. First they got each student good and mad by having each write a brief biographical sketch, and then subjecting both it and the writer to a barrage of insulting comments. This was sustained until each subject was thoroughly infuriated.

Immediately after, two thirds of the students listened briefly to tape recordings of jokes. The remaining third of the students were used as a control group. They listened to musical recordings.

Next, all students were given psychological tests to measure anger and hostility. The students who had listened to the jokes showed a significant decrease in anger-hostility scores; but the control group who had listened to music were still extremely angry.

Similar studies of the effect of humor on anger have been made at Duke University, and all forms of humor were found to be highly effective. The investigators also found that when a person's temper passed the boiling point, the kind of humor that most quickly reduced his anger was either hostile or sarcastic, the kind that carries a bite.

CONVERSATIONAL PITFALLS
Five Gambits Up With Which You Need Not Put

You will be a better conversationalist if you avoid being an Over-Talker, an Under-Talker, or a Verbal Pouncer.

Stanford University's Prof. John Eisenson has made a study of good, bad, and indifferent conversationalists. His findings show how conversational traits reveal personality. They also show you how to protect yourself from that social scourge, the Tangential Speaker, who specializes in undercutting your ego and sabotaging your efforts to carry on a conversation.

Are you an Under-Talker?

These people, Professor Eisenson finds, seem to be good conversationalists because they know when to punctuate another speaker's remarks with "Uh-huh's" or lengthy "Mm's." Sometimes they are merely maintaining contact by their sound signals, thus leading the other person to think he has a listener. Many persons (particularly those who are looking *only* for a listener) actually enjoy conversing with them.

There is nothing wrong with saying "Uh-huh" or "You don't say?" when the situation calls for it. But something is wrong when the sounds are used in situations which call for more specific responses. It may indicate: 1. A wish to avoid becoming involved in true communication. 2. Unwillingness to pay attention. 3. Innate shyness. 4. A wish to escape from the possible consequences of one's words; a desire to avoid committing one's self. Underlying the Under-Talker's verbal behavior is a feeling of inadequacy. He is afraid to stick his neck out.

What about the Over-Talker?

We all know persons who talk too much. Often the more they talk the less they say. The Over-Talker often ranks among the deadliest bores. Why does he keep on? Usually because he is afraid to stop. When he is not talking, he feels ill at ease. He talks to cover up this nervousness. Sometimes overtalking is intended to cover up a rationally indefensible position.

Are all talkative people Over-Talkers?

By no means. There are many talkative people who wish to

share freely their thoughts and feelings. If they do not intrude with, "This isn't the way I heard it," or feel the need to top another fellow's stories, there is no reason to equate overtalking with apprehension. Above all, if they are able to listen and then to respond in terms of what someone else has said, we may assume that the overtalking is a form of giving.

Do you worry about breaking a sudden silence?

"Most of us," says Eisenson, "have been in social gatherings when, after considerable chatter, a silence fell. Among hosts who measure the success of their parties by the length and loudness of the chatter, silence must be avoided. Hostesses have been known to run in panic from their kitchens to find out what was wrong because they became aware of a moment of disquieting silence.

"Some guests become as uncomfortable as their hosts. They twitch, redden, move in their chairs, and not infrequently assume the responsibility of breaking the silence by saying something, almost anything, to fill the void."

There are some persons who admit to memorizing "void fillers" so that they will not have to contend with silent periods at social gatherings. These persons tend to be apprehensive about life in general, and feel inadequate to cope with it.

The more self-confident a person is, the less he is bothered by a sudden silence. He is inclined to regard with secret amusement the intimidating effect it may have on others.

Are you a Verbal Pouncer?

He is the one who listens not to what is being said, but for a chance to break in. What he says may have little relationship with either the topic or the trend of the conversation. Any measurable silence entitles him to come forward with his topic.

Professor Eisenson is not certain of what motivates Verbal Pouncers. "We conjecture," he says, "that they must feel insecure and somehow need to say something rather than be a listener." They have no interest in what someone else has to say. Their own voice is music to their ears, and that is the music they march to. What would happen if one were to lock two of these persons in the same room?

Are you a Tangential Speaker?

He is one who must protect his sense of superiority. He must put down the initial speaker or take control of the conversation through the use of irrelevant wit.

You have just made what you consider an impressive point in a group discussion, and he chooses this moment to call attention to the Band-aid on your finger. "What did you do to your hand?" he asks. While you are trying to decide whether to ignore him or fumble for a reply, he snatches the conversation ball.

Or he may try to disconcert you with a dubious variety of left-handed wit. Suppose someone in the group has made a remark which reminds you of an anecdote you want to tell. "That reminds me," you say, clearing your throat and preparing to tell your story. This is the Tangential Speaker's clue to give you a searching look and say, "You know, you remind me of someone I've never met." If he doesn't get a laugh at your expense he at least spoils your story.

What is the secret of being a good conversationalist?

Be yourself. Almost anyone can be interesting if he is completely at ease. Only then can a person's natural charm find full expression. Remember this the next time you are expecting guests to drop in for the evening. If you are tense, your state of mind will quickly communicate itself to your guests, who will become tense in turn.

TELL A FUNNY STORY
But Know Your Audience

A good sense of humor is an asset. How well developed is your sense of humor? Recent studies have shown that where you rate on a test scale reveals a great deal about your character and personality, your creativity, insight, emotional stability, and ability to be realistic. Science can even tell you how to get the most mileage out of a funny story.

Do men and women differ in their appreciation of humor?

Studies at the University of Texas tested the reactions of men and women students to various types of humor. The most significant differences: the men preferred hostile wit (humor of the Charles Addams type, with overtones of violence or aggression) to a far greater extent than women did.

Women appreciated nonsense wit (such as a play on words) to a much greater degree than did the men.

Both sexes are equally fond of whimsical humor. Example: A fellow was pushing a wheelbarrow full of sand down a crowded thoroughfare, stopping every ten yards or so to sprinkle large handfuls of the sand on the pavement. "What's going on?" demanded a policeman. "I have to do this," said the man, "because it keeps away the crocodiles." "But," said the policeman, "there aren't any crocodiles around here." "I know," rejoined the sand sprinkler. "Wonderful stuff, isn't it?"

Does a sense of humor help you know yourself better?

Yes. Psychologists at the University of Massachusetts found that persons who make the best scores on sense-of-humor tests had the best insight into their own personalities, being more sensitively aware of their innermost feelings, wishes, and desires. Their greater ability to look at themselves objectively may come from their ability to laugh at their own short-comings. The man who can't laugh at his own imperfections doesn't like to look too closely at himself, for he is afraid of what he may find.

Can you be happy without a sense of humor?

Think of the people you know who have little or no sense

of humor, and you will recall that they seldom seem very happy. Researchers at Texas University and Michigan State show that people who have a well-developed capacity for the appreciation of humor are far happier than those who don't. It was found that persons who lacked in a sense of humor also were short of emotional stability, sense of well-being, self-confidence, and the ability to endure stress. Persons who had the greatest appreciation of humor also had the best contact with reality, and were the least likely to pretend to be what they are not.

How can you get the most mileage out of a funny story?

At a social gathering you let somebody else tell a story or two first. This simple device will make your story seem much funnier. No matter how funny your anecdote is, your audience will laugh more if other jokes precede it.

This interesting finding resulted from a humor-reaction study made on students at the University of Kentucky. Psychologists exposed students to various types of cartoons and jokes.

Each person tested was shown or told two at a time, in succession, first one, then the other. There was a marked tendency for the students to judge the second cartoon or joke as funnier than the first, and the third funnier than the second. The principle seems to be that our response to humor is sensitized by the playful mood or atmosphere engendered by previous laughs. Comedians save their best jokes till last, when their audience has been suitably warmed up.

Do wit and creativity go together?

Yes. Studies sponsored by the Air Force show that witty persons are much more creative than those without a sense of humor. A successful witticism itself is a creative act. A researcher observed that "clowning or humor is one of several effective techniques which the creative person uses to remain in groups, and to fend off group pressures toward conformity." A creative person can gain acceptance without conforming, using wit and humor as a passport. He is accepted because he is funny; and his would-be detractors restrain their impulses out of respect for his wit.

Does humor help us to cope with fears?

Yes. Psychologist Charles Winick has made a study of the ways in which witticisms can be used to allay our apprehensions. Dr. Winick says that one way of coping with the space age is to make fun of the unusual appearance of possible space visitors to the earth. When reports of flying saucers were more prevalent, Dr. Winick collected a total of 944 space-visitor jokes.

Example: A man from the moon asked a bartender for a screwdriver. The bartender served him a drink. "That's nice of you," said the moon man. "Now give me a screwdriver. My head's loose."

YOUR SPEECH IS YOU
What You Say Is Less Important Than How You Say It

Psychological studies show that the way you sound says more about you than anything you are likely to say. You can use your own voice to find out what kind of person you really are.

Can you tell from how a person speaks whether he is an introvert or extrovert?

Yes. If an introvert and an extrovert are sitting near you in a restaurant, you can identify each without even glancing in their direction, just by listening to their speech.

In an experiment at the London Institute of Psychiatry, investigators studied the relation between speech and personality. The subjects were given standard personality tests, then the speech of each person was recorded in various circumstances.

The researchers found that speech consists of short bursts of sound interspersed with silence. The introvert gives short bursts of speech and long pauses, extroverts give long bursts of speech and short pauses. The pauses are used for thinking, reflection, and other forms of mental activity. And it has long been known that the introvert is more inclined to thought and reflection than the more outgoing, action-minded extrovert.

What does your speech reveal about your personality?

The more pleasing your voice is and the better you express yourself, the more likely you are to have an emotionally stable personality. In studies conducted at the Boston University School of Education, students were divided according to those who were judged good speakers and poor speakers.

Personality tests were then given to both groups. The good speakers were found to have "a significantly higher degree of self-satisfaction, self-acceptance, independence, emotional control, and personality integration than the poor speakers."

What happens when you hear your own voice?

It is usually a shock. For your voice is you. It reflects the various aspects of your character and personality; the positive qualities and the negative qualities. And when you listen to a playback of your own speech, you hear yourself as others hear you. Listening to a recording of your own voice can help you know yourself better.

Studies show that persons who are on good terms with themselves may be surprised when they first hear their voice, but find the sound agreeable. But one who is dissatisfied with himself is likely to dislike the sound of his voice.

Psychiatrists at the Menninger Foundation found that many persons were perturbed at the sound of their own voice, that is, at the difference between their expectation of how their voice would sound and how it did sound.

Subjects of the study were selected from a Midwest city of 125,000. The investigators would say to each person, "We would like you to make a tape recording of your own voice. Would you please tell me about your first job?" Each person was allowed to continue talking until he indicated that he had finished. The investigator then said, "Now I'd like you to listen to this recording."

The reaction to hearing their own voices came very quickly. The comments ranged from thoughtful interest and pleasurable surprise to chagrin and disapproval. Some responded, "Oh, no! That's not me! Shut it off!"; or in amazement, "Man! I don't sound anything like I sound to me!" "It's so high pitched, so nasal and complaininglike." "It sounds so self-effacing." "I sound just like my mother! Yes, I *am* like her. I never realized it before, but I really am!" "Hmmm. It sounds affected, doesn't it?" "It has a funny tone; a childlike quality." Some persons smiled slightly indicating they were both pleased and interested in the way their own voices sounded. Others' feelings were mixed: "There's a lot that I like and don't like about the way I sound." "I'd like to listen to that recording again. It tells me a lot about myself. Some of the things I'd like to keep and some of the things I'd like to change."

Is it true that how we sound to another person is more important than what we say?

Yes. We use many nuances of speech and modulation to express our feelings and we not only use such inflections ourselves, but we also make judgments about others' feelings, attitudes, and character on the basis of how they sound to us.

Dr. Horace G. Rahskopf, professor of speech at the University of Washington, says, "People judge us almost as quickly by our voices as they do by our appearance; sometimes even more quickly."

What makes your voice sound the way it does?

Professor Rahskopf points out that the sound of a person's voice is influenced by the muscular tension and coordination of the person, which are intimately related to his thinking and emotional attitudes. When a speaker is expressing something he feels deeply, he produces tones which arouse similar emotions in the listener. Vocal quality communicates the emotional overtones of a speaker's thought.

Everyone has a basic timbre of voice which is a distinctive part of him. Thus we recognize the voices of our friends even when we cannot see them or understand their words. Professor Rahskopf observes that persons who are emotionally well-balanced speak in mellow tones pleasant to the ear. For many of us, however, the stresses, strains, and conflicts of everyday living are reflected in our voices, causing them to develop harsh, discordant, or otherwise unpleasing qualities. This happens so gradually that we may not realize it. Notice the vast differences in a friend's voice when he is happy, sad, calm, excited, suspicious.

Professor Rahskopf points out that most of these changes in voice quality are spontaneous, arising directly out of emotional attitudes of the speaker. This subtle overtone cannot be imitated or assumed. If you do not feel the emotion but are only pretending, your voice will proclaim the pretense. Ham actors, declaimers, and bombastic politicians are instantly recognized by discerning listeners.

Professor Rahskopf suggests that you make recordings of your speech and listen to them objectively.

THE POWER OF A SMILE
Change Your Face To Change Your Mood

Science has found that the expression on your face affects your general outlook, and that to change your mood you need change only the expression on your face.

We are used to thinking of our mood as affecting our facial expressions, and of course it does. But the reverse is also true. When you assume any specific facial expression, it generates the feelings which match that expression.

Here is an example of how the process works. A young matron consulted a psychologist. "I think my personality must be changing," she said. "For the last week I have been feeling as though my I.Q. had dropped 20 points. I've been feeling stupid. This morning my husband said that I even looked stupid."

The psychologist looked closely at her. She did not seem very alert; he noticed that her mouth was not quite closed, giving her a slack-jawed look, suggesting dullness and apathy. "Are you having trouble breathing through your nose?" he asked.

"Why, yes," she said. "I've had a cold for the last few days."

"Then you've been breathing through your mouth for the last week?"

161

"Right, more or less."

"And you have been feeling rather stupid during this time, sort of below par mentally?"

The lady nodded.

"All right," the specialist said. "Now take a deep breath so that you won't need to breathe for a little while, and close your mouth tightly. Now do you still feel stupid?"

The girl did as he directed, then stared at him unbelievingly. After a moment she smiled. "No," she said. "I certainly don't. I feel myself again!"

The psychologist smiled. "Your condition has made it necessary for you to breathe through your mouth. This causes the mouth to remain slightly open. This expression not only makes you feel dull and slow-witted; it makes you look that way. And the reaction you get from another person confirms your own feeling about yourself."

"I really thought that I was getting prematurely senile or something," the young woman said. "Is everyone affected that way?"

"Most people are. Ask any of your friends to let his mouth hang slightly open, to let his jaw become relaxed, and see if he doesn't immediately begin to feel stupid."

The expression on your face not only mirrors your feelings and emotions, but can cause an emotion. It is all but impossible to let your mouth turn down at the corners for even a few moments without feeling a "down-at-the-mouth" state of mind. And it is almost as difficult to let your mouth curve upward without immediately feeling cheerful.

Try this experiment: let your mouth hang slightly open long enough to feel utterly stupid (a few seconds is enough). Now try to feel intelligent without closing your mouth. You will find that it is like trying to make a car go forward when it is in reverse.

The dial-a-mood principle may affect emotions, but it is up to you to sustain them. But you can set the stage for just about any emotion or state of mind, depending on the facial expression you "dial."

Here are a few dial-a-mood settings. Want to sharpen your

powers of observation, increase your sensitivity to another person and what he is saying? Dial setting No. 1. Want to calm down? Try setting No. 3.

FACIAL SETTINGS

1. Open your eyes as wide as possible and let your face relax.

Result: You will feel receptive, accepting, and alertly impressionable. (To feel this way is part of the art of being a good listener.)

2. Scowl.

Result: Almost instantly you will begin to feel cross, irritable, and disapproving.

3. Straighten out your face: mentally smooth out all the lines and wrinkles.

Result: You feel your unpleasant emotions disappear as though erased from a blackboard. A fine way to ease nervous tensions.

Dial-a-mood can make for a good party game. ("Look, narrow your eyes, and see if you don't feel crafty and suspicious." "*Roll* your eyes — doesn't that make you feel gay and roguish?" "Purse your lips, and see if you don't feel pensive and thoughtful.") Some expressions work with some persons and not with others, but some for everyone.

DO YOU KNOW AS MUCH AS THE EXPERTS?
Sometimes Yes, Sometimes No

Many things that you think are true are not. This quiz will enable you to check your own knowledge against the experts.

1. The happier you are, the less likely you will be to catch cold. True____. False____.

2. Noise does not interfere with sleep if it is not loud enough to waken you. True____. False____.

3. An apple a day keeps the doctor away. True____. False____.

4. Women worry much more than men do about having a nervous breakdown. True____. False____.

5. Money is the underlying cause of most strife between husband and wife, either resentment because the husband does not make more, or disagreement over how it is spent. True____. False____.

6. If a person grinds his teeth in his sleep, it is a sign of deep-seated conflicts and emotional problems. True____. False____.

7. Reading in dim light will ruin your eyes. True____. False____.

8. Some things may not shock women more than men, but electricity does. True____. False____.

9. It makes for the best marriage if both partners do all they can to help each other. True____. False____.

10. Despite the progress civilization has made with medicine, primitive peoples who live out-of-doors, breathe fresh air, and get plenty of exercise are much healthier and happier than people are today. True____. False____.

ANSWERS

1. *True.* Research at the State University of New York has shown that a depressed state of mind lowers physical resistance and makes the body more susceptible to colds. In a majority of the persons studied, "depressed feelings in the subject invariably preceded the onset of a cold."

2. *False.* Studies conducted by Canada's National Research

Council have shown that even low sounds which never awaken the sleeper (a radio turned down for example) have a disturbing effect on sleep. Minor noises move the sleeper from a deep, healthful sleep to a shallow and less-beneficial one.

3. *True.* All evidence indicates that apples do contribute to a man's health and longevity in a way that you would probably never suspect. Research conducted at Rutgers University by Dr. Hans Fisher and Paul Griminger shows that an apple a day provides pectin, a carbohydrate, which limits the amount of cholesterol the body can absorb, reducing risk of strokes and heart attacks.

4. *False.* Almost everyone worries at times that he may crack up, but studies of men and women at Rutgers University show that nearly twice as many men as women were afraid of it. It may be because men are more exposed to the stresses of making a living in a competitive world, and most women are more sheltered. Other studies have shown that though women are more easily upset by little things, they are less likely to break down in a real crisis than men are.

5. *False.* Says Dr. Paul Popenoe, director of the American Institute of Family Relations, "Although many couples fight about money more than anything else, it is generally agreed that quarrels over finances are only symptoms."

6. *False.* In recent research at the University of Chicago, 40 tooth grinders were given psychological tests. Contrary to popular assumption, grinders did not have any more emotional problems than nongrinders. No one knows why some people grind their teeth in their sleep.

7. *False.* Dr. Robert L. Tour, eye specialist at the University of California's San Francisco Medical Center, found that reading in a dim light will not hurt the eyes. Though prolonged exposure to high intensity of light may cause eye damage, there is, says Dr. Tour, "no evidence that dim illumination will do the same." While it is true that prolonged reading in poor light may tire the eyes temporarily, he says, the symptoms are largely psychological or due to eye-muscle fatigue, neither of which causes permanent injury.

8. *True.* In studies sponsored by the National Science

Foundation, men and women psychology students at San Diego State College were tested for their sensitivity to electrical shock. Subjects were given harmless jolts of electricity of gradually increasing intensity. The amount of current passing through each person was measured at three levels: 1. "feeling the shock sensation"; 2. "feeling actual pain"; 3. "can't stand it." The average man's ability to stand the shocks without discomfort was about twice as great as the average woman's.

9. *False.* After a two-year study of 100 couples, half of whom were happily married, the other half not, Dr. Irwin H. Cohen, Veterans' Administration psychologist, said, "If one partner is the type who likes to give help, the other should be the kind who likes to receive. Two helpers are likely to frustrate each other, while two receivers leave each other dissatisfied."

10. *False.* Medical scientists of the University Medical Center, Cleveland, excavated hundreds of skeletons of early American Indians in primitive burial grounds in Ohio and found the people to be small (average height 5'3"), short-lived, and sickly. Many had arthritis in its most painful form and abscesses from bad teeth.

THE PROS AND CONS OF BEING SMART
Intelligence Has Its Advantages,
But It Is Easy To Overrate Them

Here are some new things science has found out about intelligence. See whether you think the following statements are true or false.

The more intelligent a person is, the easier he is to get along with.

False. Psychologists at San Jose State College studied men and women whose I.Q. scores indicated they were exceptionally bright. Personality tests showed them to be more impulsive, more outspoken, more independent, more excitable, more irritable, and more easily angered than others.

A high I.Q. assures success in life.

False. Studies at the University of Southern California examined the relationship between I.Q. and success in life, and found that a high I.Q. has been vastly overrated. Of greater significance, the investigators found, is a high S.Q., the Social-Intelligence Quotient." Research associate Maureen O'Sullivan says, "A high intelligence quotient, or I.Q., may be important for getting good grades and winning degrees, or for working in a laboratory, or living alone in an ivory tower, but for making one's way in the world it is the S.Q. that counts most. The socially intelligent person is able to get along with other people, and that is what helps a person get and hold a good job. Social intelligence, the ability to understand others is not measured by I.Q. tests."

Creative persons are usually neat and methodical, and lead well-ordered lives.

False. The opposite has been found to be true. A University of California professor of psychology, Dr. Donald W. Mackinnon, after a 20-year study of highly creative men and women, found that the creative person's desk, office, or dwelling place is likely to be in gross disorder. He admits to disorder in his life, doesn't mind it, enjoys the richness of it. He doesn't mind the disarray around him because he finds order on a higher level.

You can tell when a person is thinking deeply by watching

his eyes.

True. The pupils get larger when one is thinking intensely. Researchers at the Harvard Center for Cognitive Studies have shown that the more intense the mental effort, the more difficult the problem the person is given to solve, the more his pupils dilate.

The smarter you are, the longer you are likely to live.

True. Studies conducted by a life-insurance company have shown that men who have distinguished themselves by their mental ability "lived on the average distinctly longer than men in the general population."

You can think better on certain days of the week.

True. Studies show that you cannot think as clearly on days when you feel even slightly depressed. Since people are more likely to feel let down on Mondays, than on any other day in the week that day is not the best time for work involving hard decisions.

When doing mental work under frustrating conditions, a person of high I.Q. is likely to do better than a person of average intelligence.

False. In studies at Hunter College, students were separated into two groups: those with high I.Q.'s and those of average intelligence. Each group was given mental tasks to perform.

Under normal conditions, the students in the high-intelligence group showed superior mental ability. But when influences calculated to cause frustration were introduced by the psychologists, the mental performance of the high-I.Q. group fell to below the average performance of the other group. The performance of the students of lower I.Q. was scarcely affected by frustration.

The higher your I.Q. the easier it is for you to solve problems.

False. The University of Michigan Bureau of Industrial Relations found that the best problem solvers are likely to have only average intelligence scores. "The high-I.Q. person's sheer brain power may often be a hindrance to effective problem solving," the study suggested. The investigators point out that a person of high intelligence may see many more of the complicating factors surrounding a problem, and will probably make the mistake of trying to deal with them all, partly because he enjoys the exercise of mental gymnastics. Instead of concentrating on the essential factors which bear directly on the solution to the problem, he may succeed in complicating things by toying excessively with ideas.

WHAT IT TAKES TO BE LUCKY
A Self-Generated Syndrome

What makes you lucky? How much of our luck do we create ourselves? Is bad luck caused by the same things that make a person accident prone? Science has been finding out as much as possible.

What makes you lucky or unlucky?

All psychological studies indicate that a person's "luck," the good or bad fortune which comes to him, is influenced to a very large extent by his state of mind. Tests show, for example, that a negative or "beat" state of mind attracts bad luck. A negative attitude slows your reflexes and dulls your perception, causing you to misjudge situations and overlook opportunities. It also has a wet-blanket effect on your personality, making you less attractive to others and making it more difficult for you to engage their interest or enlist their help.

A pessimistic outlook will cut down your chances of succeeding in anything you attempt. In any undertaking, if you expect success, your efforts are far more likely to succeed. In a series of experiments at Harvard University subjects were assigned special tasks. Half of the subjects were led to expect that the odds were against their being able to complete the task successfully. Psychologists led the other half to anticipate that fortune favored their chances.

It was found that the mental attitude of the students distinctly influenced their success in performing the tasks. The report says that when a person expects to do poorly on a task, he "will take steps to make errors or oversights designed to re-affirm his negative performance expectancy." They were saying in effect, "You see, I didn't think I'd be able to do it, and, you see, I was right." Results of the study suggest that people sometimes fail in an understanding merely to vindicate their judgment that they were bound to fail.

Subjects in the study who expected to perform poorly, but performed well in spite of it, showed disappointment.

Is bad luck caused by the same things which make a person accident prone?

Yes, very frequently. Psychiatrist Karl Menninger has shown that accident proneness results from a state of mind which reflects the unconscious wish to inflict self-punishment to ease a sense of guilt arising from some real or fancied transgression. A man behaves in some situations in a way that he cannot reconcile with his conscience. He may express these feelings by "accidentally" bumping his shin, slamming the door on his finger, or, if he feels more self-punitive, suffering some more serious mishap.

Bad luck resulting from accident proneness involves only physical mishaps. But psychiatrists agree that a person can extend his bad luck to cover any part of his life, if he feels consciously or unconsciously that he deserves rebuke or punishment for thoughts or actions of which he doesn't approve.

Research at the University of Kentucky has also shown that there is a marked tendency for "unluck" things to happen to a person during periods, when he is not happy with himself.

How much of our luck do we create ourselves?

The extent to which good or bad luck is self-created has yet to be fully explored, but a psychiatrist, Sandor S. Feldman, has made a clinical study of it at the University of Rochester Medical Center.

"Man is born into this world with strong drives which subject him to more frustrations than gratifications," he says. "Some people, particularly those with neurotic tendencies, are inclined to dwell unduly on their frustrations (or "bad luck") and take their gratifications (or good fortune) for

170

granted." It is easy for any such person to convince himself that he is unlucky, and his negative attitude serves to further inhibit his chances of good fortune.

Says Dr. Feldman, "When a nonneurotic person takes a shower and the soap slips from his hand, he will calmly retrieve it. When this happens to a person who has convinced himself that he is unlucky, he becomes agitated and thrashes around, which only makes it more difficult to retrieve the soap, and perhaps causes him to slip and hurt himself in the process."

A person may complain that he always hits his head when he gets into his car. This irritates him tremendously, especially if he is wearing a hat and it is knocked off. He should be more aware of the size of the car, of his own size, and of the fact that he has a hat on his head. But he ignores all these things because he wants life to be good to him without his having to plan ahead. Thus he creates his bad luck.

Do poor judgment and bad luck go together?

Very often, according to Dr. Feldman. A person may try to carry four things at once to save an extra trip from kitchen to dining table. But he is very likely to drop one, and, in attempting to retrieve it, drop two more. He will probably decide that inanimate things have a grudge against him. But the episode was simply a case of poor judgment.

Do some people court bad luck?

Some people, Dr. Feldman finds, not only court bad luck, but derive a perverse kind of pleasure from it. The hard-luck-story artists who complain of their troubles and misfortunes whenever they can capture a willing listener are termed "psychic masochists."

Such a person will complain of how bad luck frustrates him on every hand, even in little things. He soils his necktie during meals, manages to tear his new suit the first time he wears it; his cigarette falls and burns a hole in the carpet; his new car is scratched by some unknown driver the first time he drives it. And, notes Dr. Feldman, as he recounts all these things, one is struck by the expression of pleasure on his face.

Does a person's luck tend to mirror his attitude and general outlook on life?

171

There are exceptions, but sociological studies conducted at the University of Santa Clara show that a man's luck tends to reflect his life style, and that a person who is inclined to attract good luck in one part of his life is likely to attract good fortune in others. This tendency toward consistency was found also to obtain with the losers, those who for one reason or another always seem to have an uphill pull.

Is there such a thing as a "run of luck"?

There are times when everything you touch seems to "turn to gold." And there are other times when, if you knock on wood, you are likely to get a splinter in your finger.

Science has not been able to analyze all the variables involved but studies at the University of Oregon show that for most people good luck or bad tends to go in cycles lasting for a given period, and then changing. In tabulating the results of various games of chance, for example, it was found that subjects who were lucky tended to remain lucky for a given period of time. On the other hand, unlucky subjects tended to continue that way over a protracted period of time, until their ill luck "ran out."

How often have you heard people say, "This is one of my lucky days! I had a hundred things to do, but everything seemed to fall into place perfectly."

All evidence is that "luck" is to a large extent self-generated. If you want to change your luck change your attitude.

IV.

MIND AND BODY

The popular folk-medicine diagnosis, "It's all in your head," can be true but seldom is true. The complex relationships between our mental and physical faculties have piqued the interest of the greatest doctors and psychologists who ever lived. They have found out more than the ordinary person has time to learn, but there is a body of facts the ordinary person can acquaint himself with and by knowing them understand other people and himself better. How healthy you are and even what diseases you get can depend a lot on how much control your mind has over your body and if you know enough about your condition you can sometimes keep physical illness from affecting your mental balance.

WHY YOU FEEL THE WAY YOU DO
Complex Explanations For Complicated Sensations

You feel the way you do as a result of a complex interaction of your mind, your emotions, and your body. Latest findings include discoveries which answer questions most of us have pondered.

Do psychosomatic ailments — those resulting from mental or emotional attitudes — often protect us against more serious diseases?

Yes. Recent British medical studies show that psychosomatic ailments "can protect a person from more serious disorder." For instance, an ulcer can be an effective brake on excessive drinking. A "nervous" digestion may force a person to be careful about his eating habits, causing him to avoid overindulgence that might shorten his life. Other emotionally based ailments can, and often do, prolong a person's life by causing him to take better care of himself, avoiding physical exertions which place undue strain on vital organs such as the

175

heart.

If you are a housewife and you are not happy with your job, is that likely to be reflected in your blood pressure?

Yes. In a recent University of Michigan study, 500 women between the ages of 25 and 65 were asked about their attitudes toward housework. The answers were compared with each woman's blood pressure (average of three readings). Findings: housewives who weren't happy with their role, who said "housework is often a strain," and that they "hadn't done very well in running the house," showed a definite tendency to have higher blood pressure than those who took satisfaction in housework.

Is it true that people who move frequently, whose lives are filled with dramatic and exciting changes, tend to be healthier and less disposed to illness?

No. Psychiatric studies made at the University of Washington show that dramatic changes in a person's habit patterns, occupation, personal relationships, or general life style tend to predispose him to illness. The investigators concluded that "The greater the magnitude of life change, the greater the probability that the life change would be associated with disease onset."

Why should this be? The investigators suggested that efforts of the human organism to adapt to life's changes serve to "lower bodily resistance and enhance the probability of disease."

Sometimes when you cope with one symptom, another appears to take its place. Why?

Specialists call this "symptom substitution." A number of medical studies indicate that when a physical symptom is eliminated without its basic cause having been removed, another symptom is likely to take its place. Sometimes the substitute symptom may be far more unwelcome than the original one. So it's a good idea to find out what's causing your symptoms, and then deal with that. Investigations have shown that many of the ills which plague us — backache, headache, stomache, chronic fatigue, skin trouble — originate from emotional stress. It's important to take this into consideration in determining what is really affecting you. It could be any stressful aspect

176

of your life, ranging from your job to various in-law or relative problems.

Are varicose veins related to life style?

Intensive studies recently completed by Dr. Colin James Alexander of Auckland Medical School offer evidence relating to the underlying cause of varicose veins, and indicate that the disease may be preventable. His findings strongly suggest that sitting in chairs may be the main cause. "I have found nowhere in the world a clinically important prevalance of varicose veins in a non-chair-sitting community. Conversely, I have found no example of a chair-sitting community in which the disease is not common," he says. The findings of the study "are consistent with the relative or almost absolute freedom from varicose veins of Eastern and primitive peoples."

If continuing studies bear out these indications, perhaps this distressing affliction can be eliminated simply by spending less of our lives sitting on chairs.

What is the time of greatest mental and emotional stress in most people's lives?

Adolescence is popularly thought of as the period of greatest emotional stress. But Dr. Eugene Peterman of the University of California, who has made a study of the subject, says that an equivalent period of stress occurs in middle age. This, he points out is not usually recognized. "Most of us get out of adolescence and grow into adults with the feeling that now, at last, we know what life is all about. It comes as a shock when, years later, we find ourselves again experiencing self-doubt and confusion, feeling restless and unhappy, and wondering why, and what to do about it."

This turmoil, Dr. Peterman says, can be the first step in a process which leads, if properly lived out, to a heightened sense of self, of the satisfaction of being alive, of a sense of individuality and purpose."

WHY SOME PEOPLE GET SICK AND OTHERS DON'T
Illness May Not Be "All In Your Head"
But It Is Affected By The Way You Feel About It

We all know people who look frail but are hardly ever sick. We know others who look robust but who catch everything that is going around. And many of us will develop a headache, digestive upset, or sinus pain when faced with going somewhere we don't want to go or doing something we dislike.

In universities and research foundations, scientists have been putting such illness under the clinical microscope. They have found that the person who comes down with every cold or virus differs in attitude from the person who rarely gets sick. Psychologist Horace Stewart of Augusta College studied the health records of hundreds of student nurses and divided them into two groups: those who were the most susceptible to illness, and those who were least susceptible to illness.

Those who were rarely ill were much more self-confident, more at peace with themselves, more composed, more concerned with the welfare of others. They were more realistic about life, and were much easier to get along with. They also differed from the other group in tending to be trustful of others rather than watchful or suspicious.

The University of Rochester School of Medicine studied a cross section of hospital patients suffering from many ailments. After medical diagnosis, each patient had a psychiatric interview. Some 97% of the patients, shortly before the onset of illness, had had a depressing emotional experience which left them with a feeling of helplessness. The experience ranged through marital separation, broken engagement, parental disownment, the loss of a close friend. And 74% of the patients developed their illness within one week of the depressing experience. In 38%, the disease began within 24 hours.

The researchers say that feelings of helplessness or hopelessness may be related to "increased biological vulnerability" to infection.

Scientists at Cornell Medical Center made a study of a group of people with similar family backgrounds of health and longevity. Each person's lifetime experiences were similar in most respects; all had faced many difficult life situations. The subjects were divided into two groups; those who had a medical history indicating a high susceptibility to illness; and those who were rarely ill.

Psychiatric interviews showed that the more frequently ill viewed their lives as difficult, demanding, and unsatisfactory; the less-frequently ill viewed their lives as interesting, varied, and relatively satisfying. Conclusion of the investigators: it is not the size of problems, disappointments or frustrations which life brings that determines the effect on our physical well-being. It is the way we face up to them or fail to do so. The seldom-ill group took misadventures in their stride. But the other group were inclined to view their life experiences as more threatening.

"There are," says Dr. Isabelle V. Kendig, in citing the findings of a study at the National Institute of Public Health, "people who appear confident of continued health, who make light of illnesses that do befall them; and there are people who fear the worst however minor the hazard: drafts, wet feet, unaccustomed foods." The institute's study showed that people in the first group were much healthier than those in the second.

Even when they became sick, cheerful persons recover from disease much faster than gloomy ones. Dr. Robert Roessler, of the University of Wisconsin Medical Center, cites studies showing that in illnesses ranging from Asian flu to infectious mononucleosis, the more cheerful the patient's outlook the faster the recovery. So a doctor's bedside manner may mean the difference between no recovery, slow recovery, or a swift one.

Cultivating an optimistic outlook on life is one of the best health investments you can make. For it pays double dividends: you will get a lot more out of living, and you will spend less time being sick.

'IS IT SERIOUS, DOCTOR?'
His Answer Will Often Surprise You

If you are like most people, you are often needlessly concerned about some common ailments, and not worried enough about others.

Medical specialists from the University of Washington School of Medicine looked into the matter in a study sponsored by the U.S. Public Health Service and the Institute of Mental Health. First they asked a representative cross section of men and women to rank a list of common afflictions in the order of seriousness. The list ranged from dandruff to diabetes, hiccups to heart attack, hay fever to hepatitis.

Next the investigators asked 100 practicing physicians to rate each ailment as to its seriousness. The physicians took a much more serious view of many of the diseases than the lay group did, and the laymen rated quite a few afflictions as a great deal more serious than the doctors did. For example, the physicians considered the common cold to be less consequential than did laymen, but they rated sore throat as almost 100% more serious than the other group.

The lay group thought nosebleed to be twice as serious as the doctors did. The reverse was true with heartburn; doctors rated it almost three times as high as the other group did. Among other findings: The average person thinks low blood pressure far more serious than it actually is, considering it to be on a par with relatively serious afflictions. The physicians ranked it somewhere between common headache and chicken pox.

The doctors' professional judgments indicate that the person without a medical background is likely to underestimate the seriousness of hay fever, eczema, high blood pressure, depression, overweight, migraine, sinus infection, and shingles. Indispositions which the laymen tended to regard as appreciably more serious than doctors do included mononucleosis, measles, hernia, heatstroke, laryngitis, mumps, and sunburn.

Here is a quiz which gives you a chance to check your judgment against that of 100 practicing physicians. Consider each ailment listed and check whether you think *a* or *b* is the more serious. Then compare your answers with those of the doctors.

1. (a) Sunburn ____.   (b) Heartburn ____.
2. (a) Bronchitis ____.   (b) Bursitis ____.
3. (a) Tonsilitis ____.   (b) Chicken pox ____.
4. (a) Frostbite ____.   (b) Heatstroke ____.
5. (a) Asthma ____.   (b) Arthritis ____.
6. (a) Farsightedness ____.   (b) Nearsightedness ____.
7. (a) Dandruff ____.   (b) Warts ____.
8. (a) Measles ____.   (b) Whopping cough ____.
9. (a) Nosebleed ____.   (b) A sty ____.
10. (a) Peptic ulcer ____.   (b) High blood pressure ____.
11. (a) Corn ____.   (b) A cold sore ____.
12. (a) Snakebite ____.   (b) Appendicitis ____.

Ranking by the Doctors

1. The physicians gave heartburn an appreciably higher rating. Sunburn can be extremely painful, and even temporarily disabling, but heartburn can be a symptom of a more serious condition.

2. Bronchitis scored only slightly higher on the scale, so you need not fault yourself if you checked bursitis.

3. If you picked chicken pox as the more serious, you shared the majority medical opinion.

4. Both of these are serious, but heatstroke was ranked as the more critical.

5. Arthritis scored higher on the doctors' scale.

6. The doctors' vote here indicated that farsightedness was considered less of a handicap than nearsightedness. There are more things to see farther away.

7. Though dandruff can be annoying, it was accorded the least status of any complaint, being ranked as the least serious of all the common afflictions on the list. Warts were regarded as somewhat more serious, but not much.

8. Whooping cough gave the doctors considerably more concern than measles.

9. A sty scored a higher rating here, but it beat nosebleed only by a nose. Both were ranked as minor afflictions, about

as serious as the common cold.

10. Both of these stress ailments were given a comparatively high ranking, but high blood pressure was deemed the more serious.

11. Corns can ruin a person's disposition, and be considerably more painful than their ranking indicates. But the doctors did score them as more serious than cold sores, and more deserving of sympathy than either dandruff or warts.

12. The medical opinion was that appendicitis involves fewer hazards than snakebite.

EIGHT WAYS TO STAY HEALTHY
Research Workers Have Decided That Sensible Living And A Full Life Are The Important Factors In Keeping Fit

Health, most will agree, is the priceless asset, and today's medical researchers are discovering that it is far easier to show a man how to stay healthy than to help him regain his health after it has been lost.

For this reason, researchers have concentrated on preventive therapy — in other words, locking the barn before the horse is stolen.

To this end, scientists have been burning the midnight oil in universities, clinics, and research foundations, seeking to discover the most effective means of staying healthy. Their findings make it clearer than ever that, when it comes to health, an ounce of prevention is worth a pound of cure.

Altogether, their words to the wise on what contributes to good health add up to a most effective — and economical — form of insurance for you and your family. Here are some of the most significant things they've discovered:

1. How much exercise, and what kind, do you need to stay healthy?

It is a well-known fact that a certain amount of exercise is necessary to good health, and it is also well-established that too much or too violent exercise can be worse than not enough. Most people — particularly sedentary workers — don't get either enough physical activity or enough of the right kind.

Desk-workers tend to fall into one or the other of two categories: Those who seldom take any exercise at all (they drive to work, drive home, eat, sit and watch TV or bury themselves in a book or magazine, or drive to a movie where they sit and watch the picture, and on a weekend they'll probably take a Sunday drive).

In the second category are those who sit five days a week at a desk and then crowd the weekend with such a round of strenuous and unaccustomed exercise that they overtax themselves, building up cumulative fatigue that lowers physical resistance and actually leaves them less fit than when they left the office.

To find out just how much and what kind of exercise a person needs to keep healthy, Dr. Laurence E. Morehouse, Professor of Physical Education, has conducted an extensive study. His findings show that two 10-minute sessions a week of the proper exercise can keep the average adult in good physical condition.

He emphasizes, however, that this does not mean 20 minutes a week of toe-touching, knee-bends, arm-waving, and other traditional setting-up exercises. Bending over and touching the toes, he points out, actually does more harm than good. This is because such exercise stretches the back muscles, already stretched to flabbiness by sitting down.

Here is a home-exercise program that Dr. Morehouse's studies show to be most effective:

● Vigorous warm-up exercise for several minutes, such as running in place. This will build up endurance.

● Stretching exercise for neck and back of neck.

● Abdominal-toning exercise, such as slow leg-raising from a supine position.

● Arm and shoulder exercise, such as push-ups from floor, wall, or table.

2. How much sleep do you need?

Although some people can get along on less, the average person will be healthier and longer-lived if he gets his full eight hours. In a wide-scale survey investigators asked thousands of men and women who had lived to a hale and hearty old-age about their mode of living.

The examiners found that "sleep was the most common denominator. Some drank, others never touched alcohol. Some smoked, others didn't. Some worked hard all their lives, others took it easier. But all saw to it that they got enough sleep, usually the traditional eight hours, all through life."

"Enough" sleep for you will depend to a large extent on what you do for a living. For example, mental workers require appreciably more sleep than the man who earns his living with his muscles. This is because it takes a longer time to replenish the energy expended by brainwork.

And tests showed that we recuperate quickest from fatigue that is purely physical. Chronic worriers, on the other hand, are likely to wake up tired no matter how much sleep they get, for they squander mental and nervous energies faster than any amount of sleep can restore it.

3. What is the best diet?

The best way to stay healthy is to eat a well-rounded diet that is high in meat, fish, or other protein. Nutritional investigations have shown that a high-protein diet pays the biggest dividends in physical fitness and general health.

4. What is the most important meal of the day so far as your general health and well-being are concerned?

The one that you eat when you get up in the morning. Studies have shown that a skimpy breakfast can sabotage your health, ruin your disposition, and seriously impair your daily efficiency. Indeed, to do a half-day's work on an almost empty stomach puts two marks against you so far as physical fitness is concerned; this practice lowers body resistance and renders you much more subject to deficiency diseases. Besides, studies show that you can't make up for an inadequate breakfast by eating extra at lunch and dinner.

A substantial breakfast lays the basis for health. This should be followed by a light lunch and a leisurely dinner.

5. What about mental hygiene?

This is far more important than most people realize. For authorities estimate that well over 50% of physical complaints are emotionally induced. Investigators made a 15-year study of this matter. Their findings may surprise you. Here is a list of some of the common symptoms of which people complain. The percentages of times physicians found the complaint to be emotionally induced are:

Pain in the back of neck, 75%; ulcer-like pain, 50%; gall-bladder-like pain, 50%; dizziness, 80%; constipation, 70%; tiredness, 90%.

6. What part does worry play in health?

Studies show conclusively that nothing saps health and physical resistance more than worry. You can eliminate most groundless worries — particularly about the state of your health. If you suspect something is physically wrong with you, arrange for a medical check-up at once. The odds are better than even that your fears of this are groundless.

Millions of persons have worried themselves sick over fancied ailments, which a simple examination would have shown they did not have.

So far as your other worries and anxieties are concerned, a university study has shown that 40% of them are over things that never happen, 30% over things in the past, 22% over petty trifles — leaving only 8% of any consequence. Take a careful inventory of the things you worry about. Jot each one down on a separate piece of paper and sort them into the above categories. If you're like most people, you'll find that more than 90% of your worries have no justification.

7. What is the best way to deal with the emotional tensions, frustrations, and guilt feelings that make us feel under par?

One of the most effective formulas ever devised was developed by Dr. E. J. Kepler, of the Mayo Clinic. Dr. Kepler observed the effects of various forms of therapy on hundreds of patients who, though they had nothing organically wrong with them, suffered from various aches and pains, felt chronically fatigued, and had lost the zest for life.

Diagnosis showed that each of the sufferers without physical cause was leading an unbalanced life. The prescription: Each patient was instructed to adjust his personal life carefully so that it was equally influenced by four things — work, play, love, worship (devotion to something greater than oneself).

Each of these influences was to be equally dominant. Where this rule was followed, case histories show no instance where chronic symptoms failed to disappear completely. Also, Dr. Kepler's records show no case where a chronic-fatigue sufferer's life was not decidedly lacking in balance. More often than not, at least one of the four factors was almost entirely absent from the lives of the chronically fatigued.

8. Is it important to keep busy?

Extensive studies show that people who keep the busiest are the ones who stay the healthiest. Indeed, psychologists have found that the individual who doesn't keep busy, who has too much time on his hands, tends to deteriorate fastest — mentally as well as physically.

His resistance to disease is lower. If he doesn't develop actual physical ailments, he's likely to imagine that he does — and suffer the aches and pains and general "poor health" of the hypochondriac. Why? It's simply a matter of morale. Doctors agree that morale is a key factor in health — and nothing saps it faster than idleness or nonproductive activity.

Says Dr. David H. Fink, psychiatrist: "Evidence all up and down the line bears out the fact that leading an active and busy life is one of the best forms of health insurance. It is often said that a machine will rust quicker than it will wear out. This is even truer of a man."

WHAT DO YOU LIKE TO EAT?
Check Your Food Tastes With The Preferences
Of Other Americans

Do you think the fellow who invented parsnips should be shot — or get a prize? What dessert do you like best: apple pie or strawberry shortcake? Or are you a lemon-cream pie man? Here's a chance to compare your food tastes with those of other Americans.

Long ago the U. S. Army decided that pleasing soldiers' palates pays off in morale. It has found out as much as possible about what foods Americans like and don't like to eat. In a continuing study, it has polled representative samples of thousands of enlisted men selected from every area in the country and representing every age group from the late teens through middle age.

Field investigators from Maine to California had each subject fill out a questionnaire indicating how much he liked or disliked just about everything you'll ever find on a dinner table. Preference ratings were obtained for 400 foods, and each was carefully scored on a scale from zero to 100.

First, the results of the dessert derby. Top favorite was strawberry shortcake, which outdistanced the field with a rating of 99. Banana-cream led all the pies with a high score of 96. Lemon-cream came in second with 94. Biggest upset was apple pie, long touted as the American favorite, which trailed in third place with a 92. Next highest-ranking fruit pies were peach and cherry.

Banana cake finished second in the cake division (after strawberry shortcake), scoring 93, followed closely by peach short-cake and pineapple upside-down cake. The big surprise here is that chocolate cake — always regarded as an American favorite — came in 5th.

Ice cream came very close to nosing out strawberry short-cake for first place in the general dessert race, with a score of 98. But puddings in general made comparatively poor show-ings.

Favorite fruits, listed in order of preference, were peaches, watermelon, cantaloupe, apples, and oranges.

Vegetables as a class were the least-liked foods. The study showed that adults aren't much more enthusiastic about them than kids are. Every food on the "least preferred" list compiled by the investigators turned out to be a vegetable. High on the "least preferred" list were parsnips, cauliflower, squash, turnips, asparagus, and broccoli.

Despite the generally poor showing made by vegetables, two were extremely well-liked. They got higher preference ratings than most desserts. They were fresh corn on the cob, with a score of 96 (4 points higher than apple pie); and fresh tomatoes with a rating of 94. Besides these two standouts, there are only three other vegetables that scored about 50 on the preference scale. These were green beans, lima beans, and green peas.

There were of course, regional preferences for certain vegetables. Turnip greens, like black-eyed peas and hominy, scored high in the South, particularly in rural areas.

Hot soft rolls and hot biscuits both scored top in their category with a score of 99. Muffins and hard rolls made a far less-creditable showing, in the low 60's. And white bread had a comfortable 30-point lead over whole wheat. Hot cornbread, which made more mouths water in Southern states than anywhere else, was still sufficiently popular throughout the rest of the country to earn a rating of 69. Rye bread, on the other hand, scarcely got off the ground in the South, but scored very high in the Midwestern and Eastern states. Generally speaking, people from the smallest towns liked cornbread best. Rye bread was most popular with soldiers who came from the largest cities.

Potatoes ranked higher in popularity than anything else that grows out of the ground. French fries were the favorite, with a preference rating of 97 — far higher than most desserts! Mashed potatoes scored 93; the next, potato chips (83). Least liked: potatoes boiled in their skins (22). Sweet potatoes did well below the Mason-Dixon line, but made only a fair-to-middling showing elsewhere.

Most popular meat was steak — which equaled strawberry shortcake's high score of 99. Fried chicken came close behind with 98. Roast beef and roast turkey were also in the high 90's. Pork chops, with a 93, took a comfortable lead over roast pork and baked ham, which tied at 90. Breaded cutlets scored highest (87) of the veal dishes. Roast veal fell considerably behind with 79.

Lamb, which proved most popular among New Englanders, and was given its highest preference rating by people from large cities, did less well in the smaller towns and rural areas.

Other findings follow. Young people were most inclined to like dessert. Older ones showed the greatest preference for "hot," highly seasoned dishes. People from the Southwest had the fewest food dislikes, and New Englanders had the most. All over the nation, simple, uncomplicated dishes scored a decisive victory over fancy varieties. People with higher-than-average education and I.Q. showed the greatest preference for celery and olives. Likewise, intellectual attainment and a marked liking for grapefruit tended to go hand in hand.

When a woman feels like going out of her way to please the man in her life, she may ask him what he'd most like for dinner. Even though studies show that men enjoy eating far more than women do, the question is likely to throw him for a loss. He'll scratch his head, shrug, and mumble something like, "Fix whatever you think will be good." A wife may likewise feel stymied when she has guests coming for dinner and wonders what on earth she can serve that will please everyone.

The answer, of course, is simple: American's favorite dinner. Serve a menu composed exclusively of foods that scored the highest-preference rating in the survey.

ALL-AMERICAN
MENU
Steak
French Fried Potatoes
Corn-on-the-Cob
Sliced Tomatoes
Hot Rolls or Biscuits
Strawberry Shortcake

GRAB-AND-RUN BREAKFAST IS NO GOOD
As The Most Important Meal Of The Day,
It Should Be Adequate

Swallowing a cup of coffee and a slice of toast, Mary rushes off to the office. She has a hard morning's work ahead of her, but a glance at the clock tells her there just isn't time for anything else — and besides, she's trying to reduce.

Mary's breakfast may sound skimpy, but surveys show it's a hearty repast compared with the breakfasts of thousands of office workers who either skip the meal altogether, or compromise on the calories to be found in a hastily gulped cup of coffee. The meal which, according to leading doctors and nutrition authorities, should be the most substantial and nourishing one of the day has become for millions a grab-and-run ritual without enough vitamins to nourish a gnat. Let's look in on a typical family breakfast.

Father, who has put off getting up until the very last minute, has just time to gulp some orange juice and wash down a couple of pieces of toast with his coffee before he sprints for the 8:15. Mother, who has been trying to get breakfast on the table with one hand and the children dressed and off to school with the other, is too nervous and harried by the time she has a chance to sit down at the table to want much breakfast.

The children — picking at their food with one eye on the clock — haven't much appetite either. And small wonder!

It's a well-known fact that the emotional stress caused by hurry and excitement actually paralyses the flow of digestive juices.

Therefore, even if Mum is successful in getting the children to finish a full-sized breakfast, it's likely to do them as much harm as good — for doctors agree that one of the prime causes of indigestion, and resultant stomach disorders, is eating under conditions of hurry and excitement.

Studies in America have shown that one-third of undernourished children owe their deficiencies to the fact that they do not start the day with an adequate breakfast.

In addition, tests have repeatedly demonstrated that so far

as maintaining physical health and well-being is concerned, breakfast is by far the most important meal of the day. And it's also been proved that you can't make up for an inadequate breakfast by eating extra amounts at dinner and supper.

Leading authorities agree that to do half a day's work on a virtually empty stomach not only tends to seriously undermine physical resistance, but has a crippling effect on mental and physical efficiency.

Surveys show that industrial and office workers who skimp on breakfast make more errors; and students who slight their morning meal average poorer grades and are much more subject to deficiency diseases than are their well-breakfasted fellows.

The Mayo Clinic's Dr. Russell M. Wilder finds that the reason most persons are chronically fatigued during mid-morning and mid-afternoon is directly due to the fact that they don't start the day with a substantial breakfast. Breakfast, Dr. Wilder's studies show, should include either whole wheat bread or whole grain cereal; milk, to supply the necessary calcium; fat, in the form of butter or margarine; and protein, such as egg or meat.

Not so long ago the American city of Hartford, Connecticut, took official cognizance of the fact that skimpy breakfasts were impairing the health, happiness, and efficiency of its citizens. Exhaustive surveys and clinical studies convinced them that school-children's inability to concentrate, office workers' inefficiency, businessmen's midmorning and afternoon fatigue, etc., were largely due to the fact that its citizens didn't eat enough breakfast.

Accordingly they launched a "better breakfast" campaign. Citizens were made aware of the importance of breakfast through the mediums of newspapers, billboard, and radio. Mountains of leaflets were distributed hammering home the point that a substantial breakfast is just as important as a good night's sleep.

The campaign was successful. Overnight Hartford became breakfast conscious. Typists, clerks, and businessmen who had formerly gulped down a morsel of toast and a swallow of coffee now took time to enjoy fruit, cereal, bacon or eggs – with all the trimmings.

The effect was immediate. Business firms reported a much higher morale among workers. Clerical mistakes took a sharp drop. Employees ceased complaining of that "all gone" feeling in the middle of the morning.

Shoppers found salespeople more cheerful and efficient; and clerks in turn found customers more affable and easier to wait on. Teachers reported that children, now fortified with a well-balanced breakfast, no longer found it difficult to concentrate on their studies.

Ask the confirmed breakfast skimpers why they elect to start the day with two strikes on themselves, and you'll usually get one of two answers. "Why," they'll tell you, "there simply isn't time! What with the mad scramble of getting the family up and dressed and off to school and the office on time, we're lucky to have time for even a makeshift breakfast." Or they may say, "But I simply have no appetite at breakfast time. All I want is coffee."

If reason Number One is your favorite excuse, the answer to your problem is simple. First, bear in mind that to receive anything approaching maximum benefit from your breakfast, it must be eaten leisurely.

To make breakfast a really pleasant meal, you should have time to linger over that second cup of coffee. And in order to achieve this luxury, you must school yourself to get up a half-hour sooner! That extra half-hour's shut-eye won't benefit you anywhere nearly as much as a good breakfast, and anyway you can always go to bed a few minutes earlier.

Problem Number Two seems more difficult to solve, but actually it isn't. You complain that you haven't any appetite at breakfast time. Do you know why? Mental and physical tension are undoubtedly to blame. You've probably allowed yourself so little time for completing the routine morning preparations that the hurry and flurry of rushing around has tightened you up like a violin string.

By the time you are ready to catch your breath and face a cup of coffee, you've no appetite for much else.

And small wonder, for — as I've pointed out — hurry, worry, or anxiety stop the flow of digestive juices and put the damper on your appetite quicker than anything else. The most appetizing breakfast in the world wouldn't tempt you when you're in such a state — and if you did eat much of anything, you'd get little good out of it anyway.

It isn't the breakfast you have no appetite for. You'd have no desire for any meal of the day if a similar state of tension accompanied it.

The answer to your problem is the same as the previous one — just get up a few minutes earlier. And instead of rushing around — which you'll probably do at first from force of habit — take it easy. Allow yourself plenty of time to relax and enjoy a tempting and nourishing breakfast.

If you need to sell yourself on this plan, just remember that when you get up you've been 12 hours or so without any food at all. You're facing the day with a stomach that is completely empty, and your store of energy needs to be replenished.

If it weren't for the tension that you build up each morning racing against the hands of the clock, you'd feel the hunger that actually exists. And the tantalizing smell of bacon and eggs sizzling in the pan would whet your appetite to the point where you'd not only put away a king-sized breakfast, but you'd really enjoy it.

Don't, however, expect full results the first morning you allow yourself plenty of time for breakfast. Years of fighting the clock before breakfast have built up a conditioned reflex of tension which it will take you a little while to break completely.

You've become so accustomed to feeling rushed and harried before breakfast that you'll continue to feel that way for a few days automatically, even though you have all the time you need.

When you finally let go, however, you'll be able to savor the full enjoyment of sitting down to a delectable and well-balanced breakfast — one you can linger over leisurely.

Remember, science has found that you'll be healthier, have more energy, and function better mentally and physically if you'll stop skimping on that all-important first meal of the day. And besides, breakfast can be the pleasantest meal of the day — if you'll take time to relax and enjoy it!

FACTS AND FICTION ABOUT DRINKING
Scientific Research Explodes Some Popular Theories, But Supports Others

Many things that people believe about alcohol are just not so, and many things commonly thought to be fallacies are true. In studies, surveys, and clinical research, scientists have been separating fact from fiction.

Alcohol always makes a person less cautious, more inclined to take risks. (True____. False____.)

False. Studies show that people who have been drinking become *more* cautious when confronted with new or unfamiliar situations. But in familiar circumstances, the reverse is true; they are inclined to take greater risks than they ordinarily would

If you are feeling low, having several drinks will make you feel better. (True____. False____.)

False. Harvard University studies show that having *one or two* drinks can provide a lift which may reduce feelings of anxiety or depression, but drinking more than that can reverse the effect. Most people, after several drinks, feel *increased* anxiety and depression. Taking even moderate amounts of liquor to relieve fears or anxieties can be hazardous, for whenever one uses alcohol as a crutch, he risks becoming dependent upon it.

Drinking increases aggressiveness. (True____. False____.)

False. Scientists at Rutgers University tested subjects who were sober and others who were drunk, The experiment demonstrated that, contrary to widely held belief, there is little relationship between alcohol and feelings of aggression. The investigators concluded that if alcohol stimulates aggression at all, it is merely because it "can function as a cue for behavior that would otherwise be unacceptable." Some people feel that they can behave badly when drinking because their unruly behavior will be excused on the grounds that they were not responsible.

Neither black coffee nor fresh air will help a person who has had too much to drink. (True____. False____.)

True. Here is an extremely popular notion that scientists

call a fallacy. Studies in medicinal chemistry made by specialists at Georgetown University indicate that neither of these
time-worn prescriptions is effective. Letting a person "sleep
it off" was found to be the best remedy. Coffee or fresh air
can cause a sleepy person to become wide awake, but being
wide awake is not the same as being sober.

Medical studies made in Britain have exploded another old
myth: that you can sober a person up by walking him around
the block. The experiments showed that exercise has no
significant effect on the "sobering-up" rate. Several forms of
exercise were tried, including walking, swimming, and running
for extended periods.

*Taking even one or two drinks will increase the likelihood
of an automobile accident for most drivers.* (True_____.
False_____.)

False. Studies conducted at the Center of Alcohol Studies
at Rutgers University show that for most drivers, those aged
from 25 to 54, small quantities of liquor do *not* increase the
chances of accident. But the same investigation showed that
younger and older drivers were more affected by alcohol, and
more likely to have an accident after having even one drink.

There are more abstainers than heavy drinkers in the U.S.
(True_____. False_____.)

True. People who seldom or never take a drink number
almost four times as many as those who drink more than is
good for them, according to a nationwide survey conducted
by George Washington University's social-research group.
The findings: 47% drink rarely or not at all, and 12% are
heavy drinkers.

*A person is more ready to gamble if he has had one or two
drinks.* (True_____. False_____.)

True, if he has had only one or two drinks. But if he drinks
appreciably more, he is *less* inclined to bet on games of chance.
A recent psychological study has shown that "a large amount
of alcohol decreased the willingness to gamble, but a small
amount was found to enhance the willingness."

Alcohol plays tricks on your sense of time. (True_____.
False_____.)

195

True. Studies show that it makes time go much faster for the first half hour or so; after that it makes time appear to pass much more slowly than it does.

Alcohol decreases a driver's ability to see a pedestrian at night. (True_____. False_____.)

True. Studies at the University of Indiana's Division of Optometry show that the more a driver has to drink, the less he is able to see a person crossing in the dark ahead of him. Drinking drivers found it particularly difficult to see pedestrians dressed in gray or black clothing. Pedestrians clothed in white were safely visible for a driver traveling up to a speed of 50 miles an hour. But at speeds greater than that, only reflectorized clothing was safely visible.

Many persons who are inclined to have "one drink too many" would not take so much if they could see themselves as others see them. (True_____. False_____.)

True. Studies conducted at Jefferson Medical College, Philadelphia, demonstrated that people with an alcohol problem can often be cured simply by taking candid movies of them when they have had too much to drink, and then letting them view them when sober.

A SCIENTIFIC LOOK AT TOBACCO
Your Use Depends On Your Personality

Do smokers and non-smokers have different personality characteristics?

A study conducted at Tufts University showed that smokers tended to be restless, energetic, self-reliant, and given to acting on impulse. Non-smokers, on the other hand, had less-colorful personalities, but were inclined to be more steady, dependable, and hard-working than the others. They were more uncommunicative and had greater difficulty in expressing themselves. These personality differences were most marked when non-smokers were compared with heavy smokers.

A study of 2,360 subjects directed by psychologist H. J. Eysenck and a team of researchers showed smokers to be far more extroverted than non-smokers. Pipe smokers, however, were found to be quite different personality-wise from cigarette smokers, and tended to be even more introverted than non-smokers.

Another study of 1,806 persons has shown that smokers change jobs more frequently. But this is hardly unexpectable in view of the findings of the Tufts University investigation showing smokers to be more restless and impulsive.

Who smokes the most?

In their investigation of the psychological aspects of smoking, Profs. George Saslow and Joseph D. Matarazzo of the University of Oregon Medical School cite the findings of leading studies and surveys which show: 1. that bachelors and spinsters smoke the least, 2. that the incidence of smoking is the highest among persons who are widowed or divorced, 3. that farmers smoke less than any other occupations group.

Do fat men smoke more than lean men?

No. Dr. Albert Damon, professor at Harvard School of Public Health, made a careful study of this question. The results of his investigation showed a significant tendency for lean men to smoke more than stout men.

Do smokers and non-smokers have different food preferences?

Yes. Studies conducted by Dr. B. Bronte-Stewart, Monica J. Perrin, and L. H. Krut (reported in the *British Medical Journal)* show that smokers tend to have a strong preference for food that is salty, spiced, or well-seasoned. But non-smokers, for the most part, preferred bland foods.

The investigation also showed that non-smokers are the most "dessert happy," and eat appreciably more sweets — cakes, candies, and particularly chocolate — than smokers.

Does smoking have the same effect on women that it does on men?

In many cases it does not. Wide-scale studies, conducted by the American Cancer Society, show that women tend to inhale to a lesser degree than men do.

When a person stops smoking, how does it affect his weight?

To find out the answer to this question, Profs. Joseph Brozek and Ancel Keys, of the Laboratory of Physiological Hygiene at the University of Minnesota, made a five-year study using 300 business and professional men as subjects. The "experimental" subjects were men who voluntarily stopped smoking. A control group was obtained by selecting men who did not stop smoking, and who matched the other subjects in age and relative body weight. Both groups represented healthy men, whose weight was close to their age standard. For those who stopped smoking there was an average weight gain of 8.2 pounds in two years. For the control group which continued to smoke there was no really significant change in body weight.

What makes a heavy smoker?

Dr. Leo H. Bartemeier, medical director of Seton Psychiatric Institute, Baltimore, has made a special study of this matter. Oversmoking, overeating, and overdrinking, he finds, all stem from the basic emotional need to obtain satisfaction, relieve tension, protect against anxiety. The food, the cigarette, the alcohol is a sedative. Where one is used to excess and it is taken away, the individual usually turns to some other form of self-indulgence.

Some people, he observes, indulge in excessive smoking to obtain the satisfaction which their work does not provide them. They are like some students who insist they can study better while listening to soft radio music. Smoking, like drinking or eating, has many different meanings for different people, and there are many who depend upon excessive indulgence in one form or another to avoid anxiety, to be able to work and to be friendly or sociable with others.

Should you stop smoking?

This is a matter for personal decision. The findings of countless medical studies evaluating the effects of smoking on physical health have been too widely publicized to require further mention here. It is the privilege of each individual to make up his own mind.

For people who decide to stop smoking, the advice of Dr. George William Ware is both helpful and realistic. Concludes

Doctor Ware in a treatise summing up results of his findings and conclusions: No one stops smoking because of newspaper articles, requests by the wife, or half-hearted intentions concerning next week. When he becomes convinced personally, he *can* stop. Most smokers cannot "cut down." A voluntary restriction of cigarettes is likely to last only a few days. They must be stopped completely, not even one per day permitted. The person who can stop at any given moment is rare. The usual smoker is better to pick a target date, such as a weekend away from smoking associates. He should publicly state his intentions to stop on this day.

On D-Day, the patient should realize that the first eight hours are the most important. Gum and candy are helpful substitutes. Cooperation of the spouse must be obtained, since she will bear the brunt of the patient's irritation. The hardest step will be to abstain when in the company of smoking friends, when the desire for cigarettes is greatest. Hence it is important that the smoker inform his friends that he is about to stop — and then do so.

Are there some people who can't stop smoking?

This is a moot question. But there are a great many who feel they can't — particularly among heavy smokers. It's axiomatic that the more a person smokes the harder it is to quit — and vice-versa. But many heavy cigarette smokers, who felt they should quit, but couldn't bring themselves to break off completely, have compromised by stopping cigarettes completely and making the process easier by smoking a cigar now and then. They point out that it's a lot easier for the heavy smoker to trade his two-pack-or-so-a-day habit for the occasional cigar (which you don't inhale), than to trade it for nothing at all.

A SURE-FIRE WAY TO BREAK YOUR BAD HABITS
It's Called Aversion Therapy

Do you want to stop smoking? Quit compulsive gambling? Eliminate overeating?

Science now has come up with a fascinating formula to help you break your bad habits. Called "aversion therapy," its basic principle is this: if you have an unpleasant experience while doing something, you will stop *wanting* to do it.

Studies at the University of California prove that aversion therapy really works — if administered under professional supervision. In the experiments, subjects carried a small battery-powered device in their pockets and whenever they felt the urge to indulge in an undesirable habit, they gave the device a squeeze. Immediately a mild-to-moderate shock was administered.

This method of "punishing" the habit was highly successful in the case of nail-biters, and with smokers, a vastly tougher breed, the technique recorded a 50% success rate.

Dr. Malcolm Kushner of the Institute for Research in Clinical Psychology cites an interesting case history involving aversion therapy. A 17 year-old girl had been afflicted with chronic fits of sneezing. She underwent a complete series of examinations, tried a variety of medications, and even resorted to hypnosis and sleep therapy — all to no avail.

Doctor Kushner's treatment involved placing a microphone around the girl's neck, connected to an amplifier and a shock source. Electrodes were taped to her arm, and every time she sneezed, the amplified sound triggered a mild shock. After several treatments, the sneeze frequency diminished gradually and finally stopped.

While not all cases are as serious as this, Doctor Kushner feels that aversion therapy is the answer to equally persistent bad habits, such as nail biting, smoking, and overeating.

The technique was equally valuable in curing a compulsive gambler. Two British psychiatrists, Dr. J. C. Barker and Dr. Mabel Miller, were called in to help a man who was losing his weekly earnings. The two doctors made films of him at a gambling establishment and at home. Seating him in a dark room, the films were shown to him and each time the gambling-hall film was run, he was given mild shocks. The homelife film was accompanied by the soothing voice of his wife.

Doctor Barker later announced, "The patient has not been near a gambling establishment in more than two months."

Not all forms of aversion therapy require the shock technique, though. A Beverly Hills psychiatrist tells of a case involving a movie star with compulsive eating habits. The man, as a matter of habit, would make midnight raids on the refrigerator, and his wife sought professional help.

The doctor recommended that she get a picture of a grossly fat man, enlarge it to life-size, and superimpose the head of her husband on it. She stood the figure in front of the refrigerator each night and before long her husband's midnight forays ceased.

Authorities feel that aversion therapy may play its most important role in coping with surface habits and should not be used in cases where the habit is caused by a deep-seated neurosis.

In any case, professional recommendation and approval should be sought before applying aversion therapy because, as with any form of therapy, *when* and *how* it should be used is best left to the judgment of a trained professional.

THE SECRET OF SLEEP
A Late Snack, A Warm Bath
And A Mind Freed From The Cares Of The Day
Are The Best Formula For It

The average person of 60 has slept as long as Rip Van Winkle — 20 years. When it comes to sustaining human life, sleeping plays an even more important part than eating.

We can live three or four times as long without food as we can without sleep. Exactly what sleep is and what causes it, nobody knows — though science has diligently sought the answer since ancient times.

Science does, however, know practically everything else about the subject. The intensive studies of foremost scientific authorities, including millions of hours of research and laboratory tests provide the answers to a number of interesting questions.

Eight hours' sleep is the average requirement. The quality of sleep however, is more important than the quantity. Tests have repeatedly demonstrated that six hours of deep sleep is more beneficial than eight hours of shallow slumber.

Persons of achievement do not require less sleep than others. A poll of the world's leading men revealed that their sleep requirements ranged from five hours a night to 12 hours.

Those who averaged less than eight hours generally possessed the ability to drop off into a sound slumber at a moment's notice. Some napped regularly during the morning or afternoon; others catnapped at various intervals throughout the day.

Strangely enough, people who perform heavy physical labor do not require more sleep than mental workers. Exhaustive studies directed by Dr. Donald A. Laird have proven that brain-workers require considerably more sleep. It was found, for example, that while timber-cutters could perform their duties satisfactorily with as little as four or five hours' sleep, mental workers required a full eight hours to function at top efficiency.

Laboratory tests showed that while four hours' sleep served to replenish physical energies to a large extent, four additional hours were required to effectively complete recuperation of the mental faculties.

It has been scientifically established that the first two or three hours of sleep do by far the most good. Actually the deepest level of sleep is reached about one hour after sleep begins. After that the recuperative powers to be gained from sleep taper off. Therefore, if you sleep six hours at night and another hour in the afternoon, you will actually receive greater benefit than if you slept eight hours straight through.

As a matter of fact, scientific findings indicate that sleeping two hours, getting up for several hours, then sleeping two hours more, will theoretically provide the equivalent of eight hours' slumber.

A number of persons have adopted this sleeping regime and report that it works splendidly for them. Nevertheless, this system has not been sufficiently tested to warrant recommendation.

The type of bed you sleep on makes a great deal of difference. Spring and mattress should allow maximum body relaxation and at the same time provide adequate support. Tests have shown that a medium-soft mattress used with a coil spring of medium stiffness is best.

Authorities find that women require more sleep than men. They also sleep more soundly. It is interesting to note in this connection that, though lacking men's muscular strength, women have more resistance and staying power.

You need more sleep if you work in a noisy place than you would if your surroundings were quiet. Research at a leading university has established that you will be 19% more fatigued at the end of each day in a noisy office than in a quiet one. Also, noise will disturb your sleep even if you are sleeping too soundly to hear it. Even relatively slight noises which do not awaken you have a profoundly disturbing effect on sleep. A light tapping on the wall, for example, will cause your blood pressure to jump 10 or 15 points. Really sound sleep requires absolute quiet.

Strangely enough, it isn't difficult to go to sleep when you aren't the slightest bit tired. An average person, with no trace of fatigue, will almost invariably go to sleep in a few minutes if he lies down with eyes closed in a quiet, darkened room.

Extensive studies have shown that most people sleep better after eating a light, easily digested snack. However, heavy foods consumed before bedtime have been found to interfere with restful sleep.

The light snack delays the hunger contractions which set in as soon as the stomach is empty. Heavy foods at bedtime are bad because their digestion is more difficult.

Alcohol aids sleep during the first three or four hours, hampers it for the rest of the night.

Professor Walter Miles, in a special study, found it is perfectly possible for persons to sleep with their eyes wide open. It is difficult, however, and the subjects studied were able to accomplish this feat only under conditions of extreme fatigue. Dr. Miles' studies proved that a person cannot stay awake merely by keeping his eyes open.

When a mental worker loses two hours' sleep, he will have to expend more than double the energy to do the same amount of work next day and thus will be more than twice as tired at the end of the day.

The most positive and effective way to stay awake is to keep the muscles tense. If you must stay awake, just tighten up, and your chances of dozing off will be minimized.

The five senses are lost progressively, one by one, as sleep deepens. The first sense to go is vision, next taste, then smell, then hearing and finally, touch. That is why a person unless he is sleeping very soundly, will awaken immediately if you touch him. It also explains why none but the lightest sleepers are awakened by the smell of smoke.

Insomniacs always believe that they get much less sleep than they do. In unconscious and semi-conscious states the same time sense is distorted to such an extent that 30 minutes of sleeplessness may seem like several hours. Laboratory tests have shown that most insomniacs actually get five or six times as much sleep as they think they do.

Sufficient bed covering is vital to sleep because during sleep the circulation is reduced, rendering the body highly sensitive to cold. When the skin is chilled, sleep is impossible.

If you have difficulty getting to sleep, something can be done about it. Leading authorities recommend a 10-minute or 15-minute bath at body temperature. It relaxes mental and physical tensions and also improves circulation.

If you're hungry, eat a light snack. And remember that sound sleep is impossible unless your mind, body and emotions are relaxed. Learn to shed your cares along with your clothes and you'll sleep like a log.

TALK IN YOUR SLEEP?
New Scientific Discoveries About An Age-Old Puzzle

If you talk in your sleep, you will be interested to know that science has been looking into this kind of talk and has made some intriguing findings.

Some people talk in their sleep regularly, almost every night; others even when they nap in the daytime; and some only occasionally. And, of course, there are those who never utter a word during their sleeping hours.

Some sleep talk is slurred and poorly articulated, with only fragments of uncompleted sentences, difficult to understand. Other people speak in barely audible whispers, and some chatter merrily in a kind of unintelligible gibberish. But for many, sleep speech is as clear as waking speech.

It is usually difficult for people to be convinced that they talk in their sleep, even when it is confirmed by other members of the family. Unlike dreams, sleep talk is not usually registered by the conscious memory. Sometimes the only way to convince a person that he talks in his sleep is to make a tape and play it back for him next day.

Sometimes a bilingual person will use one language in his waking hours and another when he talks in his sleep. And one wife reported the case of an extremely taciturn husband who was much more voluble in his sleeping hours than when he was awake.

For sleep talking, psychologists now have a special word, *somniloquy*. Their studies explode the myth that there is anything odd, abnormal, or neurotic about talking in one's sleep, or as one team of researchers put it, "It is evident that somniloquy is widespread among the 'normal' population."

Contrary to what many people believe, most sleep speech occurs when the person is *not* dreaming. One study has shown that 75% of sleep talking has nothing to do with dreams, but is associated with other mental activity which takes place during sleep. It might even be described as a subconscious "thinking out loud."

Some studies have reported that women talk more in their sleep than men do. This finding is hardly surprising, since women have also been found to be more talkative when they are awake, too.

Dr. Alfred Adler long ago noted that sleep talking bears out the life style of the sleeper. People who stutter in their waking hours sometimes stutter when they talk in their sleep. And sleep talking is often an expression of innermost feelings which may never be in evidence when the person is *awake*.

It is easy to tell when a person is talking in his sleep whether he is dreaming or not. Studies show that if his eyes may be seen moving under his eyelids, he is dreaming — he is "watching the action." If there is no such eye movement, then the sleep talk is likely to have nothing to do with dream life.

In one study the content of 166 sleep speeches uttered by 28 habitual sleep talkers was studied in a psychological laboratory. The sleepers were awakened during and after sleep talking and asked to describe what had been passing through their minds while asleep. Most often reports on being awakened were in accord with the thoughts and ideas the persons expressed in their sleep talk, though in a few instances, they had little or no recall.

Can you hold a conversation with a person who is talking in his sleep? Can you obtain rational answers to questions, for instance? Several researchers have found that it is indeed possible if certain rules are followed. One investigator found when asking questions of a sleep talker that "questions must harmonize with the inner mood of the person. Thus if the questioning is adroit, if the interrogator is *en rapport* with the sleeper, then sleep talkers can be induced to talk of many things. He further noted that the sleeper will often respond to some people and consistently refuse to respond to others.

All evidence indicates that when it is possible to hold a conversation with a sleep talker, it can often promote deeper understanding in any relationship with another (spouse, offspring, relative, close friend). One wife observed, "I never knew exactly what was troubling my husband, why he acted so tense and withdrawn at times. When I'd ask him what was the matter, he would just shrug and change the subject. I suppose he didn't want to burden me with his problems. One night when he was talking in his sleep, he hinted vaguely about something that seemed to be worrying him greatly. I gently questioned him, encouraging him to tell me what was bothering him. He did. And once I understood what the trouble was, we were able to deal with the problem together and finally resolve it."

To what extent sleep talking can be put to useful purpose has yet to be determined. One writer of popular fiction used to ramble on in his sleep about plots, stories, and dialogue. His wife could understand only part of it, and when she would wake him he would have difficulty in piecing his thoughts together. Now he sleeps with a tape recorder at his bedside. Sometimes, by playing the tape back slowly, he can understand the gist of most of his ideas. Many of them provide a nucleus for characterizations and fiction sequences.

A composer who not only talks lucidly in his sleep, but sometimes hums as well, occasionally awakes with original melodies and arrangements. When this happens, his wife, who is awakened by the musical notes issuing from under the covers, turns on the bedside tape recorder. "I get some of my best ideas while I'm asleep," he says. "Insomnia could ruin my career."

SLEEP LIKE A BABY?
You Don't Really Want To — Almost All Children
Lead A Troubled Night Life

The better you understand your child's "night life," those significant hours between bedtime and mornings, the better you will cope with behavior problems which crop up during the day. He spends more than a third of his childhood in bed, either sleeping, dreaming, or tossing restlessly.

These hours which he spends alone, during sleep and half-sleep, being amazed, mystified, happy, and somewhat intimidated with what he finds, plays as important a part in his development as anything that happens in the daytime hours. The results of careful studies provide practical answers to many of your questions in dealing with problems.

Suppose your child hates to go to bed, gets up after you put him there, or often sleeps fitfully, getting up at all hours? One big reason why a child may not look forward to bedtime, and why his sleep may often be troubled, is that much of his night life, particularly when he's small, takes place in that submerged part of his consciousness where nightmares are common. Dr. John E. Mack, of Harvard Medical School, who has made an extensive study of the subject, cites nightmares as one of the most intense forms of terror that a child can experience. "Anyone who has observed small children during the night, who has tended them when they awake in terror, or who has chosen to be attentive to their reports of monsters, witches, and harrowing chases, will readily acknowledge that children rarely sleep 'like logs'," he says.

If a parent were to trade places and experience some of the episodes in the child's night life, he would sleep just as fitfully as the child sometimes does, and he would not always look forward to going to bed. If parents keep this in mind, they will readily understand why a child will sometimes need the added security of a night light or the protection of a cuddly teddy bear. Dr. Mack cites studies showing that children's dreams, particularly those of younger children, tend to be nightmares.

At what age are a child's dreams the most troubled?
Dr. Louise Bates Ames, of the Gesell Institute of Child
Development, finds from the institute studies that the peak
period for children's nightmares tend to occur between five
and seven years. After the seventh birthday, there are fewer
dreams of all varieties, and nightmares occur only occasionally.
Unpleasant dreams were found to occur less frequently up to
the approach of the tenth year, when there was a recurrence
of nightmares, with bad dreams outnumbering pleasant ones.
More than a third of the ten-year-olds studied reported sleep
disturbed by nightmares, and these ranged from being menaced
by fire-eating dragons, robbers, cutthroats, and brigands to
fates too fearsome for the child to mention.

Nightmares tapered off in the 11th year, with good dreams
predominating more and more with each successive year. For
the 16th year, the study observed, "Nearly all dreams reported
now are good. They are about friends, sports, 'places I've
seen.' "

How much sleep does your child need? This question
troubles most parents, particularly during the period just
before and during the early teens, when a great many children
"simply hate to go to bed," and do all possible to circumvent
parental efforts to get them settled at bedtime. Parents need
to realize that sleep requirements of children vary just as
widely as adult needs. And there is a very good chance that
your child doesn't need any more sleep than he thinks he does.
Imposing an early bedtime may cause him to sleep more hours
than he requires. And sleep researchers have found that too
much sleep can be just as bad as too little.

Dr. Wilse B. Webb, a University of Florida psychologist,
points to studies of "long sleepers" and "short sleepers" in a
school-age population of 100 boys and girls selected at random.
Nearly 10% slept less than six hours a night on the average.
But there were nearly that many who habitually slept well
over ten hours. No significant differences could be found
between the two groupings, either in their school achievement
or in their psychological characteristics.

"If a child is showing no behavioral effects, such as sleepiness in school, I would suggest that he is probably better off with less sleep, and less conflict. If you try to impose sleep on a short sleeper, you are going to have difficulty," Dr. Webb says.

Dr. Ames observes, "Our investigations show that it is wrong to assume that the normal child will go right to bed, right to sleep, and will sleep right through the night." She notes how markedly children of the same age vary in the amount of sleep they require, how readily they go to sleep, whether they are easy or difficult to awaken in the morning. The child's body build, which other psychological studies show to be closely related to temperament and personality, has a direct bearing on how well he sleeps and how much sleep he requires.

The ectomorph, or tall, slender person who tends to be introverted, nervous, sensitive, highstrung, who is easily fatigued and finds it difficult to relax, is the most difficult child to get to sleep. Paradoxically, he needs more sleep than other children to restore his physical and nervous energies.

The child with an athletic body build (mesomorph), which tests show to be the most extroverted, can go to sleep readily, sleeps soundly, and requires the least sleep.

The type of child who has been found to enjoy sleeping the most, who may even look forward to bedtime, is the endomorph (inclined to short and chubby). He enjoys sleeping so much that it's often extremely difficult to get him up in the morning.

What if your child walks in his sleep? Drs. Allan Jacobson, Joyce D. Kales, and Anthony Kales of the University of California conclude from their studies that "at least 15% of all children between the ages of five and 12 years have had at least one sleepwalking incident." In almost all instances, they find, the child's tendency to talk in his sleep is soon outgrown. Their advice to parents: take simple precautions to minimize the possibility of the child injuring himself. This includes removal of obvious hazards from the path of the sleepwalker. Locking doors and securing windows is also strongly advised.

What if your child talks or makes strange noises in his sleep? It's nothing to worry about. All sleep studies show that it is not uncommon, and occurs occasionally with most children, as with many adults.

When you wish to tell your child something you want him to remember, should you tell him just before he goes to sleep? Yes. Psychological tests show that the closer it is to his bedtime, the more clearly and completely he will recall the things you've told him.

In studies conducted by psychologist Bruce Ekstrand, University of Colorado, one group of students was given materials to commit to memory just before going to sleep; another group was given the material several hours before going to sleep. Tests the following day showed students in the first group remembered far more, and with greater accuracy, than the others. The students who remained awake after being exposed to the materials forgot more than twice as much as the students who went to sleep directly afterward.

Sleep apparently allows the memory impression more time to crystallize without being disturbed by the constant flow of thoughts and activities which occur in daytime hours.

If your child is a chronic forgetter, you can use this principle to your advantage. And when he is preparing for school exams, he will do much better if his study time is followed immediately by sleep.

DREAMING WITH A DIFFERENCE
What You See Tells How Creative You Are

If you think you have what it takes to be an artist, designer, or writer you can get an idea of how good you are by answering seven questions about your dreams. Psychologist Joseph Adelson and his associates at the University of Michigan suspected that the dreams of creative people differed from those of non-creative persons. So they put the matter to a clinical test.

The subjects of the study were college students divided into two groups; those who showed high creative ability and those who did not. Each morning the students recorded their dreams of the night before. Each one was then questioned in detail about them, asked to clarify obscure parts, to identify the dream figures, and such. It was found that dreams of the creative people differed markedly from the dreams of the others.

Here is a seven-question test, based on the findings of the study. Answer each question honestly, then check the analysis which follows.

1. Do you ever dream comic dreams? 2. Do your dreams generally take place in a local, familiar place, or in some unusual or foreign setting, such as Hong Kong, the South Seas, or Africa? 3. Could most of your dreams happen in real life, or are many of them physically impossible (walking on air, lying on a cloud)? 4. Do you generally appear in your dreams as yourself, or as an intrepid explorer, a football hero, a glamorous society figure, an exotic princess, or a beautiful bride? 5. When you dream, does the setting shift from place to place, from scene to scene, or does it usually take place in one setting, such as a house, field, boat? 6. Are the people in your dreams usually hazy, or do you have a clear impression of them? 7. Do you usually participate in the action of a dream, or are you just an observer?

1. One of the most significant differences between the two groups was the presence or absence of comic situations in dreams. The creative students had something funny happen

in 17% of their dreams. But nothing amusing happened in any of the dreams of the noncreative students.

2. The dreams of the noncreative students were always tied to the local and the familiar, to the here and now. But the dreams of the creative subjects might take place anywhere: in Paris, in a mosque, or in a tropical jungle; a setting completely foreign to them. In 20% of the creative student's dreams, there was an exotic dream figure: a king or queen, or a Roman soldier. Such figures almost never occurred in the dreams of the noncreative students.

3. The creative group frequently had bizarre, outlandish, and physically impossible dreams; the other subjects seldom had them.

4. The study showed that the noncreative students dreamed of themselves just as they were in real life. The creative students (about 23% of the time) dreamed of themselves being married to someone they were in love with, or being a celebrated personage. Also, the creative subjects might, for example, turn a friend into a dentist, a mother into an employee, and so on. There was not a single transformation of this kind in the dreams of the noncreative subjects.

5. Professor Adelson says, "We find that with the creative subjects there are many different settings within a single dream; we see a continual transformation of scene, a constant shifting of locale. On the other hand, the majority of the dreams of the noncreative persons take place against a single background, with no change of scene."

6. The creative ones tended to see other persons much more clearly in their dreams than the other group did.

7. In 20% of the dreams of the creative subjects, the dreamer at one point or another did not participate in the action of the dream, but was completely detached from it. On the other hand, the noncreative dreamers were always personally involved in the events of the dream. Psychologist Adelson suggests that "the ability to stand apart from reality is a necessary first condition for transforming it imaginatively. To do this, we must be able to have a detached awareness of it, so that we can know it, reflect on it, and judge it."

SLEEP'S DARKEST MYSTERY
The Subconscious Mind Of Man Holds The Deep Secrets And The Intricate Causes Of A Strange Human Malady — Sleepwalking

At midnight on a lonely country road, two schoolteachers driving home from a party saw what looked like a ghost, gliding along the road. The figure, shrouded in white, suddenly turned and, with outstretched arms, vanished across a field.

The frightened teachers sped to the nearest phone and informed the police. Officers in a patrol car finally spotted the apparition on an adjacent road. As they cautiously closed in, their flashlights revealed a comely woman in a flimsy nightgown — fast asleep. Her smooth, effortless stride seemed to keep perfect time to the sound of her breathing. Later they learned that the lady's nocturnal stroll had taken her two miles from home.

Occurrences like this are not as rare as you might think. Millions of people walk in their sleep. In addition, the somnambulists read books, write letters, engage in workaday activities, embark on a train or bus or even drive a car. They have also robbed houses, committed murder and taken their own lives while sleepwalking.

Though science has discovered much about sleep's darkest mystery, certain phases of somnambulism still baffle experts. One fact is certain: the sleepwalker's body is controlled by his subconscious mind. This deep reservoir of our hopes, fears, problems and frustrations takes direct control not only of the sleepwalker's limbs and muscles but borrows some of the faculties of the conscious mind itself. It uses them, often fantastically, in the physical expression of subconscious desires.

Take the somnambulist who has a persistent urge towards kleptomania. During waking hours he may fight the urge to steal; but at night he's likely to arise in his sleep and lift his roommate's wallet.

Army psychiatrists, who made an intensive study of somnambulists at Camp Lee, reported many strange cases. One soldier, for instance, suffered from an acute sense of insecurity.

An orphan in his youth, he had never enjoyed parental love and affection. He had been reared by an uncle, who had given him real sympathy and understanding, but after reaching maturity he had lost trace of him.

Drafted into the Army, the soldier's feeling of insecurity became intensified; he began to rise in his sleep and spend the night in sleepwalking jaunts across country, looking for his uncle. To Army psychiatrists the answer was simple. Subconsciously the uncle symbolised security. And the soldier's subconscious mind simply used his body to implement the search.

A common form of sleepwalking is motivated by a subconscious urge to escape from reality or from a disagreeable situation. In his desire, for example, to get out of a house, the sleepwalker may use a door, window or even a fire escape.

Because the subconscious usually employs only a fraction of the intelligence possessed by the conscious mind, it often causes the sleepwalker to commit highly irrational acts. A typical case concerns a noted novelist, who awoke one night to find himself perched perilously on a window ledge outside his hotel room. Alarmed, he secured himself in bed the next night by means of a small chain locked around his ankle. The key he hid under a carpet.

But he awoke again to find himself on the ledge. Even in his sleep he was able to find the key. On succeeding nights he tried hiding the key in different places, but the result was always the same.

Not infrequently the somnambulist's subconscious will completely dominate the conscious mind, employing all its faculties and senses. When this occurs, the sleepwalker's actions are just as rational as during waking hours. In fact, the somnambulist's sensory powers often become abnormally acute, making it possible for him to accomplish feats which normally would be impossible for him.

The *British Medical Journal* reports a typical case — a woman who would arise from bed and, in almost total darkness, write letters and perform the most intricate type of crochet work. When medical investigators awakened the woman and asked her to repeat these feats, she found it impossible to do so.

In the more common forms of sleepwalking, somnambulism usually occurs about two hours after retiring — when sleep reaches its greatest depth. How long the state lasts depends upon the individual and his personality. It may last a few minutes, a few hours, or several months. The somnambulist may journey to a distant town, get a job, establish residence, and even marry. Hence, some authorities believe that most of the amnesia cases we hear about may actually involve somnambulism.

The French psychologist, Dr. Pierre Janet, cites numerous case histories which typify the behavior of persons whose sleepwalking extends over long periods. Mr. X left his home in Nancy on February 3rd to keep a luncheon engagement at a friend's house. En route he noticed a slight headache. Next thing he remembered was waking up in a meadow, famished and exhausted, and covered with snow. With difficulty he managed to walk to the nearest town, found that he was in Belgium and that the date was February 12th. Of the preceding nine days he remembered nothing.

Investigation revealed that he had spent this time in a headlong flight from his home town. Finally without funds for food or lodging, he collapsed outside Brussels. When the somnambulistic state was broken, he remembered only that he was due at his friend's for lunch.

Inquiry revealed X's life involved problems from which he wanted to escape, but this urge was repressed. Finally, when it became too strong to be contained, his subconscious mind took over — and through the medium of sleepwalking translated the old desire into physical action.

Though sleepwalking in any form is a definite abnormality, authorities reassuringly point out that it neither leads to insanity nor bears any relation to it. To cure it, the physician must first discover the underlying cause, then take steps to remove it. This, of course, involves psychotherapy.

Some forms of somnambulism yield easily to treatment, others prove extremely difficult, for the processes which

activate a sleepwalker's personality are intricate and involved.
Science doesn't begin to understand them all, and perhaps
never will — until it discovers the mystery of sleep itself.

YOUR SHAPE AND YOU
Handsome Does As Handsome Is

In an office high above the traffic, the company psychologist
and the personnel manager were discussing three persons sitting
in an adjacent room, plainly visible through a glass partition.

"The president of the company cannot decide which of these
applicants is best qualified for that new post," the personnel
man said. "And for that matter, neither can I. But he has put
it up to me, and I can't afford to make a wrong decision.
Perhaps you can help me. They are all well-qualified by background and experience."

The psychologist surveyed the three candidates through the
window. Each looked poised, alert, capable. One was short
and a little overweight. Another was well-proportioned and
about average height. The third was tall and slender. "Well,"
the psychologist said, "other factors being equal, there's no
question about it. The tall, slender man is your best choice."

Was the psychologist making a snap decision? Or can science
really predict a person's behavior on the job just by noting if
he or she is tall, short, thin, or plump? Ever since Harvard
University began the first research, other universities have
made studies which show that the way people look does, indeed,
provide a clue to their character, general personality, and outlook on life.

At Georgetown University, psychologists John B. Cortes and
Florence M. Gatti divided students into the three classic physical
types: 1. those with a short, heavy-set body build; 2. the
medium-proportioned, medium-height; 3. the tall and slender.
Each student was asked to rate himself on a personality scale.

217

Each of the three body types were found to have distinct personality characteristics. To check the findings, the investigators conducted two additional studies on groups of people from various walks of life and of various ages, and got the same results.

Try the test yourself. Here it is, reproduced (by permission) in the exact form used in the study.

Complete the following statements about yourself. For example, in statement No. 1 fill in the blanks with three words selected from the list immediately below. Select the words that seem to fit you most closely. Follow the same procedure with the rest of the statements in the test.

1. I feel most of the time _____ , _____ , and _____.

calm	relaxed	complacent
anxious	confident	reticent
cheerful	tense	energetic
contented	impetuous	self-conscious

2. When I study or work, I seem to be _____ , _____ , and _____.

efficient	sluggish	precise
enthusiastic	competitive	determined
reflective	leisurely	thoughtful
placid	meticulous	cooperative

3. Socially, I am _____ , _____ , and _____.

outgoing	considerate	argumentative
affable	awkward	shy
tolerant	affected	talkative
gentle-tempered	soft-tempered	hot-tempered

4. I am rather _____ , _____ , and _____.

active	forgiving	sympathetic
warm	courageous	serious
domineering	suspicious	soft-hearted
introspective	cool	enterprising

5. Other people consider me rather _____,
_____, and _____.

generous	optimistic	sensitive
adventurous	affectionate	kind
withdrawn	reckless	cautious
dominant	detached	dependent

6. Underline the *one* word out of the three which most closely describes the way you are.

a. assertive, relaxed, tense
b. hot-tempered, cool, warm
c. withdrawn, sociable, active
d. confident, tactful, kind
e. dependent, dominant, detached
f. enterprising, affable, anxious

The three body types rated themselves in entirely different ways. People in the short, heavy-set group tended to choose these words as most accurately describing their character and personality: calm, relaxed, complacent, contented, placid, leisurely, dependent, cooperative, affable, tolerant, warm, forgiving, sympathetic, soft-hearted, generous, affectionate, kind, social, soft-tempered.

The medium-proportioned, medium-height ones described themselves as dominant, cheerful, confident, energetic, impetuous, efficient, enthusiastic, competitive, determined, outgoing, argumentative, talkative, active, domineering, courageous, enterprising, adventurous, reckless, assertive, optimistic, hot-tempered.

The tall and slender people chose these words as most truly self-descriptive: detached, tense, anxious, reticent, self-conscious, meticulous, reflective, precise, thoughtful, considerate, shy, awkward, cool, suspicious, introspective, serious, tactful, sensitive, withdrawn, gentle-tempered.

See how your own self-description and body type compares with the subjects in the studies. If you do not quite fit in any one of the three groups of body types but merge into another one you can expect your personality traits to behave in the same way.

Why do people with specific body builds tend to have

personality characteristics in common? Researchers Cortes and Gatti do not know for sure. They do not know how physique influences temperament, but their studies demonstrate that the two are closely related. They conclude that body build predisposes a person to certain temperamental traits, and that the total physique as represented by the organs of the body, glandular secretions, and the particular body chemistry limits the range of temperament traits and thus inclines a person towards some traits more than others.

The investigation also found that when a person alters his own physique, either by gaining or losing weight, or even by growing a mustache or changing his hair color or style, he not only looks different and feels different, but his outlook on life is likely to be different.

WHAT YOUR HANDS TELL ABOUT YOU
Long, Short, Broad, Slender:
They Often Speak More Plainly Than Words

Science has discovered that your hands give clues to your I.Q., personality, and outlook on life. They can even tell how healthy you are.

Does the way you use your hands indicate how smart you are?

Yes. The fellow who is skillful with his hands, whether he is a brain surgeon or an artist, is likely to have a high I.Q. Nimble fingers tend to go with better-than-average mental ability. Studies at Columbia University show a high correlation between intelligence and manual dexterity.

Can your hands show how healthy you are?

They tell a doctor a great deal. Instead of saying, "Stick out your tongue," doctors might well be saying, "Stick out your hand." Dr. Harold F. Falls of the University of Michigan, in reporting findings to the International Congress of Human

Genetics, cited 80 afflictions which can be detected from a person's hands. Disorders which show up range from gout to sickle-cell anemia, indicated by tubular enlargement of the fingers.

Is one hand more sensitive to pain than the other?

Yes. Research at New York University Medical Center has shown that if you hit your left hand with a hammer it will hurt more than if it was your right hand. But if you are left-handed, your right hand will be more sensitive. So either way, the hand you are more likely to hit or cut is the one which will hurt the more.

What makes a person left-handed?

Nobody knows. Scientists have advanced many theories, but in their recent study, University of Kansas psychologists Charles Neuringer and Jane A. Finn concluded that "a satisfactory explanation for left-handedness has not yet been proffered." So if you are a leftie and wonder why, you have company.

Do right and left-handed persons differ in other respects?

In the University of Kansas study, those who were right-handed and those who were left-handed were each given a personality test. The left-handed students differed from the right-handed in their attitude toward others and their general outlook on life. They were much more likely to be independent-minded than the right-handed students. They were less inclined to "go along with the crowd" and had a greater dislike for being told what to do. They were more involved in social and political controversies, and tended to take the side of the minority group. The left-handed person, in an election, would have a greater tendency to vote against one candidate than for another.

The authors of the study suggest that "a left-handed child may feel frustrated in a right-handed world, and the frustration may foster oppositional tendencies." They point out that it is startling to left-handed persons to learn that most implements, appliances, and household items are manufactured for the right hand. It is as difficult for a boy to find a left-handed baseball glove as it is for an adult to find left-handed golf clubs.

Even books are placed on library shelves for the convenience of right-handed people.

The left-handed person may feel discriminated against by inconveniences foisted upon him by the majority group, the right-handers.

Does the shape of your hands tell anything about you?

Studies have shown broad hands to be associated with extrovert tendencies. They are likely to belong to persons who are gregarious and action-minded rather than contemplative; and who are more concerned with concrete thinking than philosophizing.

Slender hands, bony hands, and small hands are linked with introvert qualities; a tendency to be reflective, imaginative, idea-minded, and possessing a greater sense of self-awareness.

Do some persons think with their hands?

Many people gesticulate so continuously when they are talking that their thought processes would be inhibited if they could not use their hands. A University of Rochester study indicates that hand gestures often serve as a definite adjunct to the mental processes. Other investigators have concluded, "The hand's relation to the intellect is so strong that it becomes a part of it." A hand gesture can often be far more expressive than words.

THE EMOTIONAL SIDE OF EYE TROUBLE
No Matter How Perfect Your Eyes May Be,
Fears And Worries Can Upset Your Seeing Mechanism

There are a great many people who can't see more than two feet in front of them, and yet they have nothing wrong with their eyes. And many whose eyes are perfect are almost blind. Also, there are countless thousands suffering from eye afflictions without any *physical* cause.

Vision, far from being just a physical function, is a psychological process as well. Fifty per cent of the process of seeing is accomplished by the brain. The act of seeing merely *begins* in the eye. It is completed in the visual cortex area of the brain. If, for any reason, this cortex isn't functioning precisely as it should, your vision will be affected — no matter how perfect your eyes are.

The function of the "seeing" areas of your brain can be affected by your mental outlook, by inner conflicts, by extreme anger, worry, or chronic anxiety.

A typical case, cited by Dr. Edward Hartmann, leading New York ophthalmologist, concerns an extremely farsighted woman who became nearsighted during a period when she feared losing her son through his marriage. The doctor fitted her with a new set of glasses, but advised her to hold on to the old pair. Soon the woman's son *did* marry, and she became reconciled to the fact. Almost immediately she complained to the doctor that she could no longer see with her new glasses. The doctor tested her eyes, smiled, and said, "I told you to keep your old glasses. Go home and put them on. You'll find they fit perfectly."

Many people see things a great deal larger than they are — a condition called macropsia. This is often caused when a person seeks subconsciously to escape reality by returning to childhood. If this desire is strong enough, it may affect the visual area of the brain, causing the perspective to revert to that of an infant.

When micropsia — the opposite condition — results, the whole visual field appears contracted and reduced, conforming

223

to the restrictions of the individual's mental outlook. Persons whose vision thus causes them to live in a Lilliputian world usually suffer from a rather severe neurosis. Invariably when the neurosis has been cleared up, normal vision is restored.

A 17-year-old boy, afflicted with an extremely severe case of micropsia, was admitted to the famed Menninger Clinic for special observation and treatment. Like the heroine of *Alice in Wonderland,* he saw things around him getting smaller and smaller. Objects finally appeared so tiny that he was able to perform such simple functions as eating and dressing himself only with the greatest difficulty. Just before the boy was admitted for observation, his condition was further complicated by the fact that he even felt himself getting smaller.

After diagnosis, the clinic's Dr. Ernest Lewy explained that the boy saw things small as a defense mechanism against feeling small himself. The phenomenon occurred whenever the youth felt "low" − and was accompanied by a loss of the sense of reality, and a fear that his ego might shrink so small as to disintegrate altogether. Normal vision could be restored only if psychiatrists could deal with his mental condition.

As New York University's Dr. Otto Lowenstein points out, normal vision is affected by a physical process combined with a psychological attitude. One is as important as the other − and both functions must synchronize and perform as a perfectly integrated unit. The neurotic or emotionally unbalanced individual may impair his vision by disassociating the two processes involved.

Even in the case of well-balanced persons, a state of comparatively mild anxiety or excitement may result in temporarily impaired vision. Dr. Mark J. Schoenberg, noted eye authority, states that in numerous instances poor showings made during eye examinations are due to the fact that the patient has been nervous or over-anxious at the time.

Authorities have found mental conflict and emotional stress to be major factors in disturbances of vision. After exhaustive clinical studies, Dr. Schoenberg reports that even glaucoma may be caused by emotional states, by "disturbing the mechanism which maintains normal intro-ocular pressure."

Dr. Hartmann reports that mental stress and worry very often bring about a condition of nearsightedness. He also cites cases of cyclo-paralysis and hemorrhages of the retina due to the same causes. Dr. Smith Ely Jelliffe, the distinguished psychiatrist, finds that nearsightedness is due to a wide variety or combination of mental disturbances. His studies show that nearsightedness occurring at the time of puberty is not infrequently due to the patient's desire to exclude himself from the outside world.

Hysterical blindness, which results from *acute* emotional conflict, represents a paradoxical condition. The victim is physically capable of seeing, but not mentally conscious of the fact; thus the vision centres in his brain do not perform their function.

In this connection, it is interesting to mention a situation where this condition is completely reversed. Some individuals, though actually stone blind, fail to become mentally conscious of the fact. Though the physical process of vision has become defunct, this fact does not penetrate to the visual areas of the brain. Therefore, these areas continue to function as they normally would.

In describing the reactions of patients of this type, Dr. Emil A. Guntheil states: "They actually believe they see objects of which people around them are speaking. When asked how many fingers are placed in front of their eyes, they immediately respond with any number, even though no fingers at all are held up; or they 'read' a text supposedly shown to them which was never exposed. Patients of this type vehemently deny their blindness. It is not real to them because they simply cannot become conscious of it; and they act precisely as though their defect did not exist."

It is difficult to determine just what percentage of defective vision and eye disease is due solely to non-physical causes. However, an examination of 500 cases attending a leading British ophthalmic clinic, revealed that *over one-third of the eye afflictions were mental in origin.* In a high percentage of these cases the eye disorders were completely cured by psychotherapy.

Not only can a state of mind affect a person's ability to see, but it can even make it impossible for him to open his eyes. Dr. Alfred Kestenbaum, noted eye specialist, cites a particularly interesting instance of this kind. The patient was a middle-aged gentleman, employed as a clerk in a large office. During a brief recess from work, he had closed his eyes; then had been startled to find that he couldn't open them again.

Panic-stricken at first, he later decided that the condition would pass if he lay down for a bit. It didn't pass, so he was taken to the specialist. Examination revealed no trace of any-thing wrong — except, of course, the man's patent inability to open his eyes. Questioning the patient finally brought out that a large embezzlement had taken place where he was employed, which involved a number of his fellow workers. He, himself, the man emphasized, was completely innocent. He reiterated several times that he positively had seen nothing relating to the embezzlement.

The doctor remarked this fact, and presently suggested, "Isn't it just possible that you've been keeping your eyes closed in order not to see any of the dishonest goings-on? Isn't it possible that you've been keeping them closed *literally* as well as figuratively for that reason?"

The patient looked startled. After a minute he said hesitatingly, "You know, Doctor, I think . . . I think that you may be right." Beads of sweat stood out on his forehead, and presently he opened his eyes. "Doctor," he said, his voice choked with emotion, "I'll never forget what you've done for me." Generously overpaying the doctor's fee, he left the office.

Unfortunately the happy ending in this particular case was only temporary. The phenomenally quick cure was not permanent, for some years later the doctor ran across his patient again, and this time in a psychopathic ward, afflicted with further mental and optical symptoms.

Dr. Walter B. Lancaster, former president of the American Academy of Ophthalmology, and one of our foremost eye authorities, has this to say on the subject of vision: "Seeing is one-half physical; one-half mental. To improve the physical

226

part is the daily task of eye specialists. To improve the mental part requires training, exercises, and practice. Eye exercises have been successful in treating many eye conditions, and a great deal can be accomplished by them."

Dr. Lancaster points out that eye exercises do not necessarily result in an improvement of the eyes themselves, but that their potency lies in treating the mental side of seeing. "The notion," he says, "that eye exercises have value because they result in strengthening eye muscles is erroneous. The value lies in developing mental skills in ocular performance, and in building up a fund of relevant experience which permits the individual to make more accurate and effective *interpretations* of his visual sensations."

It has been repeatedly demonstrated that the mental side of vision can be made to function so effectively as to completely compensate for poor eye performance. The brain can actually make allowance for — and correct — distorted images which imperfect eyes relay to it.

Many people suppose that when they lose one eye, they have lost half their field of vision. Actually, they lose only about one-fifth. The vision centres of the brain make up for the difference by re-evaluating the visual sensations they receive. Thus, as the noted eye surgeon Dr. Phyllis Duke-Elder points out, in a very short time the one-eyed man is so little inconvenienced by his disability that he is unaware of it.

As we all know, when we look at something the image received by the eye's retina is always upside down. The optic nerve, which is an extension of the brain, turns the picture right side up.

To demonstrate the extent to which the brain can compensate for and correct faulty vision, Stanford University's Professor George Stratton performed this experiment. He designed an optical contrivance which resembled a pair of spectacles with short tubular extensions. When the device was secured to the eyes, specially adjusted lenses made everything appear upside down.

Confining himself to his laboratory, Professor Stratton put on this contrivance, and wore it during his waking hours for

227

a period of three days. At first, all images appeared inverted; the room and all in it appeared upside down. The second day it was still the same. But by the end of the third day the upside down world had completely righted itself, and everything appeared in its normal position. The brain had adjusted itself to the situation, and had ceased to turn over the pictures received by the eye. When Professor Stratton finally removed his vision-inverting spectacles, he expected the world would appear upside down again. But it didn't — the brain made instant readjustment and vision was perfectly normal.

Exactly how far the brain can go in compensating for faulty vision nobody knows. Science has determined, however, that it can go a very considerable distance. And you can paste it in your hat that your "mind's eye" is every bit as vital to vision as the pair of eyes that sit under your eyebrows.

THE MENTAL SIDE OF SEEING
Vision Is A Matter Of Eyes Plus Brain

It is a fairly well-known fact that 50% of the process of seeing is accomplished not by the eyes — but by the brain. Indeed, scientific studies have clearly demonstrated that the act of seeing merely begins in the eye — and is completed in the visual cortex areas of the brain.

Very few people realize, however, the extent to which the function of the "seeing" areas of the brain are affected by our mental attitude — by conflicts within our personality, by worry, anxiety, and other forms of emotional stress.

Consequently, it is difficult for most of us to appreciate how frequently and how seriously vision may be impaired — even when there is nothing wrong with our eyes. As a matter of fact, mental or emotional stress often is the sole cause of defective eyesight.

A survey of 500 patients attending a leading ophthalmic

clinic showed that more than one-third suffered from vision defects caused by mental states which impaired the function of the sight centres of the brain.

And numerous other studies show that nearsightedness, and many other forms of vision impairment are very frequently due entirely to mental disturbances. Even a state of comparatively mild anxiety or excitement can affect our vision. Dr. Mark J. Schoenberg, noted eye authority, has conducted exhaustive researches in this field.

He finds that often a poor showing made in an eye examination is due to the fact that the patient was nervous or over-anxious at the time. Thus a man who goes to have his eyes examined — fearful that he may be forced to wear glasses — may appear to need them, even though he actually doesn't require them at all.

Nearsightedness is merely one of the many afflictions which mental conflicts can produce. They can also result in complete loss of vision. This is termed hysterical blindness, and results when the victim is physically capable of seeing, but does not see because the visual centres of the brain fail to function.

The famed ophthalmologist, Dr. R. G. Gillespie, studied hundreds of cases where vision was seriously impaired — even though there was nothing wrong with the subjects' eyes. The afflictions ranged all the way from acute nearsightedness to total blindness.

Here are the factors which the specialist's study showed responsible for these conditions:

1. The wish not to see — whether conscious or subconscious. (Desire to shut out the world, to "get away from it all," to escape from a situation which the victim feels incapable of facing.)

2. Acute emotional tensions, arising principally from feelings of anxiety.

3. Unwarranted fear on the part of the subject that "something is wrong with my eyes."

In a recent report Dr. I. Irving Vics points out that the person who has become convinced that he is losing his sight is very likely to do just that. He cites numerous case histories, including that of an almost sightless woman who came to him for treatment.

Some years previously she had been examined and had been told that her condition would worsen, and eventual blindness would result. The patient accepted the prediction of ultimate blindness, reconciled herself to the fact — and gradually proceeded to become psychologically blind. That is to say, the seeing areas of her brain ceased to function.

After listening to her story, the specialist gave her the following treatment. She was fitted with telescopic spectacles, then subjected to mental therapy: "In place of the original hopelessness, a program of hopefulness and optimism was substituted, and a release obtained from her psychic trauma." Her vision began to return almost immediately. Soon her eyesight improved to the point where glasses were discarded!

A man's mental outlook can affect his vision in many other ways — some of them so bizarre as to be almost incredible.

Sometimes a situation occurs which is completely the *reverse* of psychological blindness. Just as there are people with good eyes who cannot see, there are others with *sightless eyes* whose mental seeing areas continue to function. Their brain simply refuses to acknowledge the fact that the physical side of seeing has ceased to function. Their eyes are defunct, but the visual cortex of the brain goes on functioning just as though nothing had happened. As a consequence, they fail to become mentally conscious of the fact that they cannot see.

The well-known authority, Dr. Emil A. Guntheil, who has made exhaustive studies of persons so affected, has yet to find one who would admit that he could not see. They vehemently deny their blindness, and strenuously resist all efforts to make them conscious of the fact.

Ask them to read from a paper, and they will effect to read — even though the paper be perfectly blank. Ask them to describe the view outside a window, and they will lucidly describe an outdoor scene — which may have nothing at all in common with the one they are "looking" at.

When the "mind's eye" is not functioning precisely as it should, a condition known as alexia, or "word blindness" may result. When this happens, the individual finds himself suddenly unable to read. He can perceive the *letters* in a given word, but the sight centres of the brain fail to relate these letters to each other. Thus if he is able to read at all, he does so very slowly and with extreme difficulty. This is not a rare phenomenon, but affects more persons than is commonly realized.

At Northwestern University, a study of 133 cases of alexia was made by Dr. George E. Park. Except for their reading difficulty, the majority of subjects had normal vision. Explains Dr. Park: "Since printed letters and words are abstract symbols, it is necessary that complete visual perception take place in order to apprehend their meanings when arranged in phrases and sentences." There are, he finds, many individuals of normal and superior intelligence, who are unable to understand printed words or signs, and therefore have to rely on oral instruction.

Mental attitudes which may result in word blindness include strong feelings of guilt, depression, anxiety, and the like. Here is one of several instances cited by investigators at Glasgow University.

Mr. "B" was a 63-year-old engineer. Until a few months before he came under clinical observation, he had always been in good health mentally and physically. Suddenly, however, he became extremely irritable and suspicious. Whether with justification or not, he accused his wife of being unfaithful to him and trying to rob him of his life savings. Soon afterwards he was shocked to find that he couldn't read his morning paper.

Clinical examination showed that single letters were usually recognized correctly — except those of an angular shape like *N* or *X*. And he could read very short words by slowly spelling them aloud to himself. But with longer words he would be forced to give up after reading two or three letters. Otherwise, except for a difficulty in recognizing colors, his vision was normal. (Note: psychiatrists were successful neither in restoring Mr. B's ability to read, nor in convincing him that his suspicions about his wife were unfounded.)

Word blindness can be caused by other things besides mental and emotional states. One young woman for example, recovering from her confusion after having been rescued from a burning building, found to her amazement that she couldn't read handwriting and could decipher printed words only with the greatest difficulty. Neurologists examined her and found that the carbon monoxide fumes to which she had been exposed had apparently damaged the visual perception areas of her brain.

After two years of persistent effort, the woman succeeded in overcoming her word blindness to an appreciable extent. Her condition improved to the point where she could actually read a novel — but it took her three months to do it. She still can't read handwriting, however — even her own.

Though admittedly difficult to cope with, word blindness does respond to treatment under favorable conditions.

Neurologist Alexander Adler points out that "far-reaching rehabilitation can be expected in patients who have sufficient intelligence and interest," provided brain damage is not too great.

The mind's eye can indeed play incredible tricks on our consciousness. It can, as has been pointed out, produce visual hallucinations that are just as convincingly real as anything we see with our physical eyes.

On the other hand it has been repeatedly demonstrated that the vision centres of the brain can function so effectively as to compensate for poor eyesight. The brain can actually correct distorted images which imperfect eyes relay to it.

That is why — as the noted eye specialist, Dr. Phyllis Duke-Elder points out — when we lose one eye we do not lose half of our field of vision. Actually we lose less than one-fifth. The visual cortex areas of the brain compensate for the difference — shortly after an eye is lost — by re-evaluating the visual sensation it receives. Thus the "mind's eye" makes it possible for a man with one blind eye to see practically as well as though he had two perfectly good ones.

Just what further feats the "mind's eye" may be capable of, no man can say. Science has only partially explored its potentialities. But when those hypersensitive sight centres of the brain are functioning at peak efficiency, they can go a long way toward compensating for poor eyesight — much farther, in fact, than most people dream.

Best way to keep them functioning at their best is to try to avoid emotional stresses that tend to throw their delicate mechanism out of order. Things most likely to play havoc with the sensitivity of these "hidden eyes" are prolonged periods of worry, anger, anxiety and related emotions.

WHAT 'SHIFTY EYES' CAN TELL YOU
It All Depends On The Direction In Which They Move

Science has made a discovery which enables you almost instantly to tell a great deal about another person. It even tells you something about the ailments he is most likely to have. The discovery resulted from studies of a cross section of men and women made by Veterans Administration psychologist Merle E. Day.

Dr. Day noted, in making routine psychological tests, that when you ask a person a question which requires reflective thought (such as, "How much of the time do you think most people are happy?" or, "What person do you most admire in the world today?") his eyes will immediately move either to the right or to the left. Repeated tests showed this reaction to be consistent, with some people's eyes moving automatically to the right, others to the left.

In a series of succeeding studies, right and left-eye movers were separated into two groups and given personality tests. Each group was found to have strikingly different characteristics.

The left-eye movers were far more introverted than the others. Tests showed they were more contemplative, possessed much greater self-awareness, and had better insight into their own feelings and desires. The right-eye movers shared more extro-vert qualities, were more action-minded, more concerned about doing than thinking. Their attention was focused outward, making them more keenly alert to situations around them. They were less aware of themselves than the left-eye movers, but they showed greater awareness of others, better insight into their personalities and were better judges of human nature.

Left-eye movers were quicker to learn new things and to absorb new ideas, as indicated by tests showing more alpha brain-wave activity. And, possibly because of their greater receptivity to new ideas, they were more easily hypnotized than the right-eye movers.

Right-eye movers scored consistently higher on reading-ability tests, and did better in all tasks requiring a high degree of visual attention. Left-eye movers were more responsive to music, more sensitive to the sounds around them, quicker to respond to a person's tone of voice or manner of speaking.

There were even great differences between the two groups in the use of language. Left-eye movers were more given to flowery adjectives; the speech of right-eye movers was more concise, assertive, matter of fact. Their language tended to be blunt, direct, and to the point; the left-eye movers favored speech which was more colorful, and more expressive of nuances of feeling and shadings of meaning.

The investigation showed that the two types even respond differently to fear and anxiety. Psychologists found that the right-eye movers feel anxiety as a free-floating panic deriving from some external threat, something which poses a real or imagined danger. The left mover tends to feel anxiety as coming from within, a tense, jittery, "butterfly stomach" sensation. He does not try to conceal his anxieties, but the right-eye mover does; he does not like to admit them even to himself and tries to repress them.

Previous research had shown that different personality types tend to be subject to certain specific afflictions so it is not surprising that this is also true of left and right-eye movers. Dr. Day says, "The right mover is more likely to have emphysema, duodenal ulcer, an hypotension (low blood pressure); the left mover tends toward asthma, gastric ulcer, and hypertension (high blood pressure)."

He further notes, "An exciting and unexpected finding of

the study is that husband and wife are almost always opposite eye movers. Close friendships are also usually formed between right and left-eye movers."

Other findings of the study:

1. The eye-movement phenomenon does not occur in children until the age of four.

2. It is not related to sex (56% of 237 men observed by the investigators were right movers and 58% of 284 women observed were left movers; the difference is negligible).

3. The eye-movement phenomenon is reduced when anxiety is extremely high, as when a deliberately anxiety-provoking question is asked.

4. It occurs even in persons who have been blind since birth, indicating that the spontaneous movement of the eyes consistently to either right or left is related to personality characteristics rather than to the visual function.

5. It is not related to eye dominance or right or left-handedness.

Just why should a little twitch of the brain relate systematically to differences in response pattern to a single stimulus? Dr. Day points out that the eye-movement phenomenon involves frontal-lobe brain centers close to those active in the rapid eye movement of dreaming, and to those involved in producing expressive speech.

Though a more complete explanation awaits further research, the study establishes this fascinating fact: that when you ask a person a question requiring reflection, the direction in which his eyes involuntarily move tells you a great deal about his character and personality.

YOUR EYES GIVE YOU AWAY
They Express How You Really Feel About Almost Anything

Little goes on in your mind that doesn't show in your eyes. Tests show that when a person looks at something or someone he likes, the pupils of his eyes grow larger. When it is something unpleasant, the pupils contract.

Dr. Eckhard H. Hess of the University of Chicago, who made the studies, says that the responses have nothing to do with the amount of light. They are not even controlled by the same part of the nervous system.

Though this phenomenon has only recently been scientifically tested, Dr. Hess says that some people have been aware of it for a long time. Magicians can tell which card in a deck a person is thinking of because his pupils will enlarge when the card is exposed. Chinese jade merchants gauge a buyer's interest, and how high a price he may be willing to pay, by watching his eyes.

Men have a much larger pupil while looking at pictures of women than when looking at pictures of men. Women have larger pupils when looking at men. Psychological studies at Michigan State University show that the pupils of the eye respond immediately to an emotional stimulus. In 95% of the subjects tested it was found that even emotionally charged words caused their pupils to enlarge; neutral words had no effect at all.

If you like someone, your pupils will tend to expand on meeting him. If your attitude is neutral, no pupillary action is likely. If you dislike the person, or he says something that affronts you, your pupils will contract. The pupil dilates with pleasure and constricts with displeasure. But, of course, sudden changes in light intensity must be taken into consideration in forming judgments from pupil responses.

The University of Chicago studies showed that even when we try to mask our true feelings, our pupils still range from extreme dilation to extreme constriction. Pupil responses show how people *really* feel about almost everything.

A pollster who asks a voter about political candidates would do well to watch the person's pupils as he mentions each nominee. We can adjust what we say to conform with what we feel like revealing, but we have no control over the way our pupils respond.

The discoveries could be important in consumer research: as each housewife is interviewed about her attitudes toward various products or services, an automatic camera might record the varying size of her eye pupils. A person's reply to an interviewer's question is often tempered by what he feels he is expected to say.

A poker player would do well to pay close attention to his opponent's pupil responses when he draws cards to fill out his hand. If his pupils grow larger, he probably got what he wanted. If he is disappointed, the pupils are likely to contract. If his response is neutral or bored, pupil size is likely to remain the same.

University of Chicago investigators showed a group of subjects two photographs of an attractive young woman. They were asked to choose the one with the greater appeal. One picture brought a far more enthusiastic response than the other, and was described by most subjects as being much more attractive in every way: a "nicer person to know," a "pleasanter and more sympathetic person." The pictures were identical in every respect except that the pupils in the first picture had been made larger by retouching, in the other picture they had been made smaller. The first picture drew the warm response.

Why do we find people more appealing when their pupils are dilated? As scientific tests have shown, when a person looks at you with dilated pupils, it's a sign he likes you. And people seem to have an instinctive awareness of it. When someone looks at us with dilated pupils, even in a photo, it suggests that he likes us, or would like us if we met him or her. We tend to like the people we feel will like us.

The University of Missouri made a similar study, using live people instead of pictures. Men and women college students were asked to choose a partner from two candidates who were dressed similarly and had been selected by a jury of 200 students who voted them equally attractive. Each student was advised to pick the candidate who he felt would be the more pleasant and easy to talk to, since the experimental task would require their working closely together. One of the candidates had his pupils dilated by eye drops. Three times as many subjects chose the partner with the dilated pupils. When asked why, the students said they were unable to explain or said that the one they chose seemed "more attractive," "friendly," "pleasant." Though not one person reported a choice based on pupil size, the evidence was clear.

SEEING RED, FEELING BLUE
Color Affects You Physically, Mentally, and Spiritually

Scientists are discovering new things about color. Did you know that the color of an automobile can mean the difference between life and death on the road? That the color in your living room affects how happy your marriage is? That your color preference may reveal what kind of person you are?

These are just a few of the things science has found out about the part color plays in your daily life, and the extent to which it affects your happiness and well-being. Here are more of their findings.

Do colors have a physical effect on us?

Yes, particularly red, green, and blue. Tests show that where red predominates in a room it does four things: 1. It increases your blood pressure. 2. It quickens your muscular reactions. 3. It excites your emotions. 4. It tends to produce a general feeling of restlessness. It can cause high-strung people to become even more excitable. So if you are the nervous type, you will be happier if you avoid red shades for home furnishings and clothing.

The effect of color on neurotic persons or those who are otherwise emotionally unstable is even more pronounced. A neurologist cites as an example an emotionally disturbed woman whose nervous symptoms so increased when she wore a red dress that she couldn't walk without stumbling or falling.

But green or blue dresses restored her equilibrium to the point where she appeared almost normal.

If you are doing something that requires a steady hand, don't do it in a red room. Investigations by the Veterans Administration have shown that though red surroundings have a stimulating effect on your physical activity, quicken your reflexes, and enable you to work faster, efficiency is impaired if the job requires careful judgment, precision, and good physical coordination.

It is easier to wake up in the morning if your bedroom has a lot of red in it. Experiments at the University of Canterbury in New Zealand have shown red to be the most "arousing" color. Its effects on our emotional responses were described by the investigation as "extremely stimulating," "exciting," "awakening," "attention-drawing," and "lively." So a rosy dawn can make us want to be up and doing, and the dull gray of an overcast sky tends to make us want to sleep a bit longer.

The same investigators found that green slows down muscular responses, has a calming effect on the nerves, and is conducive to reflective thinking. Blue was found to have a similarly soothing effect.

Can the color of your surroundings affect your mood, morale, and general feeling of well-being?

Yes. Studies have shown that the difference between a living room with drab, lackluster decor and one which is attractive, with pleasant colors, can mean the difference between a happy or unhappy home life. To be surrounded with colors which are depressing, irritating, or to which a person feels "allergic" can have a profound psychological effect.

In a series of studies by psychologists at Brandeis University, two experimental living rooms were constructed. One had dull gray walls; the other was filled with pleasant colors. Subjects who visited the first room reported feelings of monotony, fatigue, headache, discontent, irritability, and hostility. But the living room which was pleasantly and colorfully decorated caused the subjects to experience feelings of comfort, pleasure, enjoyment, importance, energy, and well-being.

Those who spent their time in the first room, when given

personality tests, tended to be critical, uncharitable, fault-finding, and argumentative. The other living room produced the opposite psychological effects.

Can the color of an automobile really mean the difference between life and death on the road?

Yes. Studies at the University of California at Los Angeles showed that the color of an approaching automobile influences a driver's judgment of speed and distance. Some colors make a car seem closer; others make it appear to be farther away. Judged from a distance of 200 feet, objects of some colors appeared to be as much as six feet closer than objects of other colors.

And the investigators had determined that under average traffic conditions, a distance of six feet in judging distance can mean the difference between a serious accident and no accident.

Of the various colors tested on 164 subjects, blue and yellow made distant objects seem closest, both by day and by night. Gray shades made objects appear to be farthest away.

So a two-toned car of blue and yellow would seem to be one of the safest car-color combinations: the blue safest in daylight and fog, and the yellow safest at night.

Does the temperature affect how you respond to color?

Yes. Tests show that a person's preferred colors change completely, depending on whether he's hot, cold, or just comfortable. Psychological studies show that the thermometer serves as a good barometer of the colors a person prefers.

Some 100 people selected at random were divided into three groups. The first group was asked to select their preferred color when the temperature was about 100°F. The favorite of most was blue. The second group was tested for their color preference when the thermometer was just a few degrees below freezing. Red was the over-all favorite by a great margin. Blue, the hot weather favorite, got the fewest votes of any color. The third group of subjects was similarly tested when the temperature range was in the 60's. Then red scored again with the most preference votes, with green second in preference.

If you prefer pure colors to tints, does this tell something about your personality?

At Hunter College in New York City, psychologists separated students into two different groups, those who showed a preference for pure colors, and those who preferred tints. Each group was then given several personality tests.

Those who liked tints best tended to be introverted, to live more in their own thoughts, and to adapt less readily to the outer world than the other group. They were more inclined toward introspection, and had a greater degree of self-awareness than the others. They were also much more discriminating in their tastes, more appreciative of subtleties and more likely to feel that their friends and acquaintances did not understand them. They differed markedly from the other group in that they tended to be much more given to thought than to direct action.

Those who preferred pure colors possessed all the qualities of the extrovert. They were seldom given to soul-searching or meditation; were far more materialistic than the other group, and showed much less interest in philosophical or esthetic matters. They were also more gregarious and less changeable in their opinions or attitudes.

What about people who say they don't like colors?

People who dislike color, or simply fail to respond to it, are, psychologists say, likely to be repressed, to keep a tight rein on their emotions, to be fearful of letting themselves go, or of departing from rigidly controlled reaction patterns. Failure to respond to color seldom goes with a well-adjusted personality.

Experiments at the Drexel Institute of Technology, Philadelphia, have shown that those who dress in a variety of colors tend to be much better balanced emotionally than persons whose clothing is drab.

Does even a small child associate certain colors with happiness or sadness?

Yes. At the University of California, nursery school children were separated into two groups. The first was told a happy, heart-warming story. The second group listened to a sad story. The children in both groups were then asked to color the dress of the heroine in the story. Each was given just the choice of using either a brown crayon or a yellow one. The majority of the first group chose yellow to color the girl's dress, and most children in the second group chose the brown crayon.

How do colors affect our moods?

It has been demonstrated that the colors around you can mean the difference between a sense of happiness or of depression. The most emotionally depressing colors are black and shades of grays. The most uplifting colors are those which predominate in nature. When these colors are shrouded or blacked out, when overcast or fog blots out the blue of the sky and darkens the colors of the landscape, people are inclined to feelings of depression. This was particularly so of women, who are known from earlier studies to be more affected by color than men are.

How can we get the best guidance as to the most effective use of color?

By studying the color combinations of nature, the blendings and shadings, its subtleties and the striking contrasts, No one has yet decorated a room that can compare in beauty to a lovely day outdoors.

SCIENCE LOOKS AT PAIN
It's "All In The Head," But It Really Is There

Happiness has been defined as feeling no pain, and most people would say that is not a bad definition. The most objectionable thing about pain is that it hurts, but there are some good things about it, too.

Is it true that pain hurts less if you have a well-balanced personality?

Yes. Studies at the University of London have shown that an emotionally stable person tends to have an appreciably higher pain threshold. He scarcely feels pains which might give another high distress. Other researches have demonstrated that neurosis is associated with less tolerance for stress "whether

242

it be physical, as in painful situations, or psychological, as in frustrating situations."

Is it true that you should never make an important decision when you have a headache?

Yes. Psychological tests have demonstrated that any kind of pain — headache, stomachache, backache — affects your ability to think, reason, or weigh facts carefully. If you have an important matter to decide, wait till that tooth stops hurting or that heartburn goes away.

Is it true that you can make any pain hurt less simply by relaxing?

Investigators made a series of psychological tests in which the varying intensities of pain felt by subjects was measured by a dolorimeter. When tension or anxiety were present, pain sensitivity increased significantly. But when the men and women subjects were induced to relax, their pain decreased. It is not always easy to relax when in pain, but it is well worth trying.

Can we sometimes be hurt without feeling pain at all?

Often we will suffer some injury which goes completely unnoticed until next day. Then we may find one shoulder to be so stiff we can hardly move it, or we find a big bruise on an ankle, or a mysterious sore spot which causes us to wince whenever we touch it. Usually it means that our brain has been too busy with other matters to pay attention to the impulses received from the pain nerves. Even a soldier in battle sometimes does not realize until after the engagement is over that he has been hurt.

One Johns Hopkins University study has shown that even being mildly preoccupied with some action or activity can reduce the amount of pain we feel by almost half.

Does not getting enough sleep make all kinds of pain hurt more?

Yes. Studies have demonstrated that the more sleep a person loses, the lower his pain threshold, thus causing a headache or a toothache to hurt more. Several investigations have shown that sensitivity to pain is very definitely affected by fatigue. Thus if you hit your thumb when you are tired, it will hurt more than when you are rested.

Wouldn't it be wonderful if we could lead a painless existence?

No. If we lacked the ability to feel pain, we could seriously injure ourselves without realizing it. If a hot stove caused no pain when we touched it, we could suffer critical burns. A tooth that never ached when it needed a dentist's attention would soon be beyond restoration. And then there are all of the other bodily pains which serve as warnings of a physical problem and which help a physician to diagnose an ailment. There are a few persons, as medical researchers show, who never feel the slightest pain, whose pain nerves simply do not function. But they find this far more of a liability than a blessing.

Is it true that some people literally "give you a pain"?

Yes. Clinical studies have shown that many of the pains we feel when we are around certain people for any length of time — headaches, stomaches, and so on — result simply from our emotional reaction to the person. So some people whom we consider "a pain in the neck" really are.

CAUSE AND CURE OF COMMON HEADACHE
It's Really "All In Your Head"

In terms of the number of people it afflicts, headache unquestionably deserves the title of Public Nuisance Number One. No other complaint ruins so many people's days, or sends so many of them scurrying to their doctors seeking relief. And the payoff — and medical studies attest to this fact — is that the overwhelming majority of these headaches are lacking in any physical cause whatsoever.

These "phantom" headaches — doctors call them psychogenic — afflict more people than all the other kinds of headaches put together. They are just as painful as the less prevalent varieties, and often more difficult to cure.

Medical scientists have spearheaded a wide-scale assault on this common enemy, tracked him down to his lair, found out how he operates, whom he afflicts, and why. Most encouraging of all, they've found out what you can do to avoid him.

Dr. Henry D. Ogden, clinical professor of medicine at Louisiana State University Medical School, and his colleagues spent months interviewing headache victims in every profession and calling, compiling exact data. They questioned housewives, lawyers, ditchdiggers, office workers, students, farmers, and people in just about every occupation they could think of. All were asked the same questions: "Do you have headaches?" "How often do you get them?" "When?" "Under what circumstances?" and so on.

After surveying a cross-section of 6,000 people of every age and description, the investigators were able to draw an accurate picture of who gets headaches and why. And their findings bear out the conclusions of other authorities that most headaches have no physical basis, but stem rather from mental and emotional causes.

The Louisiana State University survey showed that women have more headaches than men do. (Other studies show, incidentally, that women are far more emotional.) Single persons have many more headaches than married ones. Young people get them a good deal more often than older persons.

People in their early 20's have headaches almost three times as frequently as those in their 60's. That's because older people are generally calmer and more relaxed.

The study revealed that people whose work calls for mental effort are far more subject to headaches than those who earn their living with their muscles. And the better educated you are, the more frequently you are likely to be reaching for aspirin tablets. The survey showed for example, that headaches are almost twice as prevalent among college graduates as among those with less education.

It is well-known that the medical student undergoes one of the toughest mental grinds in the book. And significantly, he ranks at the very top of the list when it comes to having the most headaches. Only 2 executives out of 10 don't suffer from this complaint. Ranking only slightly lower are professional men, lawyers specifically. Housewives rate farther down, but even so they suffer more than either salesmen or clerical workers. Ranking almost at the bottom of the list is the manual laborer. But the man who has fewer headaches than anybody is the farmer. (Lest this start a back-to-the soil movement among headache sufferers, it might be pointed out that bad-crop years might alter this statistic appreciably.)

Medical scientists can tell you exactly the type of person that this psychogenic — or "tension" — headache most often afflicts. He is meticulous, overly conscientious, and inclined to be a perfectionist. He is also tense, and highly sensitive. If he is a businessman he is apt to be a demon for punctuality and neatness.

In the case of a housewife, she is apt to carry the matter of being a perfect housekeeper to the extreme. She is disturbed when anything is out of place, or when anything occurs to disrupt her household schedule. These are not the only types that the psychogenic headache strikes, but it does hit them hardest and most frequently.

Studies show that the typical "nervous" headache seldom occurs at regular intervals, that it is almost never present upon awakening in the morning. Most frequently it begins with a feeling of neck tension. It isn't really pain at first. In most cases there is an almost imperceptible tightness that begins at the back of the neck and creeps up over the skull — feeling at first like a gentle vise, gradually increasing its pressure until even the forehead feels taut. Then, just as gradually, the actual pain begins — a dull, heavy ache moving slowly upward from the base of the skull, sometimes settling in the temples, sometimes spreading over all parts of the head.

In short, as Cornell University's Dr. Harold G. Wolff points out, the common "nervous" headache is due to a sustained contraction of the muscles of the scalp and neck — resulting, not from any physical cause, but from emotional tension. What causes this emotional tension? Authorities agree that the chief factors are worry, anger, frustration, inner conflict, feelings of insecurity or guilt. The only effective cure for headaches of this kind lies in the domain of mental hygiene.

Findings of a study of 400 chronic-headache patients recently conducted by a group of New York doctors showed that sedative and pain-relieving drugs were effective in relieving the pain in an appreciable percentage of patients — but they found that plain sugar pills did practically as well, if the patient thought the sugar pills were a real drug, and if the doctor seemed interested and sympathetic.

When drugs potent enough to really cope with an excruciating headache are habitually used, a definite danger arises. The emotional tensions, denied the headache outlet, are likely to find expression in some far more serious form of nervous disorder. This fact has been established by research conducted at the University of Illinois College of Medicine. Says the university's Dr. Stuyvesant Butler: "We have had a number of patients with severe tension headaches to whom intravenous histamine has been given at their insistence, and have found that much relief was given. But we also found to our sorrow, that unless adequate psychotherapy was also given (to correct the *basic* cause), other nervous phenomea such as functional diarrhea, neuro-circulatory asthenia, and other syndromes replaced the headache."

Frequently, as Dr. Butler observes, the tension headache may represent a habit pattern formed over years as an escape from distressing situations. For example, Mrs. Smith does not want to see a certain person, or attend some function, so she says she has a headache. This excuse works so well, and is so socially acceptable, that she continues to employ it as a means of avoiding something she does not wish to do.

So what happens? Psychiatrists have found that pain that is repeatedly feigned can create pain that is actually real. "Never," says neuropsychiatrist David Harold Fink, "use a headache as an excuse to get out of an unpleasant social situation. If you do, before long you are likely to really get headaches when faced with anything you regard as distressing or unpleasant."

Next, the sufferer must fully convince himself — and this often takes a bit of doing — that his headaches are produced by his own mental attitudes. He should make an honest and sincere effort to resolve whatever emotional problems are upsetting him. Whether he can accomplish this sufficiently to alleviate his headaches, or whether he may require the help of a specialist to give him further insight into his problems, depends entirely upon the individual. Some people can do the trick unaided, and some cannot.

If mild sedatives afford the headache victim temporary relief while he is trying to remedy the underlying cause — that's fine. But he should regard them as a crutch, not a cure. Be the headache mild or severe, medical scientists agree that the only way to cure a person suffering from psychogenic headaches is to alter his emotional attitudes.

STUTTERING CAN BE CURED
Even If You Stammer In Your Sleep, There Is Hope For You

How successful you are, whether you are fulfilled or frustrated, happy or unhappy, depends to a large extent on your ability to express yourself verbally to others; to communicate your thoughts, your dreams and aspirations. In some persons this ability is innate, in others it must be cultivated. Without it, your talents will go unrecognized.

One of the greatest handicaps to self-expression is inability to articulate smoothly, the verbal static produced when our speech is punctuated by halting, stammering, or hesitancies which make both speaker and listener uncomfortable. Speech experts define the stutterer as a "person who shows, noticeably, any one of these symptoms: blockings, stickings, grimaces, forcings, repetitions, prolongations, or other rhythm breaks or interruptions in the flow of speech."

Stuttering, in that broad sense, is much like the common cold, in having many causes, some of which remain obscure. Just as medical science strives vainly to cope with the common cold, so speech therapists, psychiatrists, and other specialists are struggling to assist stutterers to gain fluency. Like a cold, a speech impediment may stubbornly resist all forms of therapy, then suddenly disappear.

Dr. Henry Freund, of the Veterans Administration Hygiene Clinic says that stuttering results from "a deep-seated feeling of anticipatory anxiety." The source is sometimes apparent; but often it is at least partially hidden. It is something like writer's cramp and stage fright. Always, the cause is associated with anxiety or fear of failure.

Most stuttering has been found due to extreme concern over the impression we are making on others. One study of 125 stutterers showed that the speech of well over half of the subjects had improved appreciably when they were alone. Some did not stutter at all when they were by themselves. The findings suggest that many persons with speech difficulty may resolve their problem simply by overcoming self-consciousness.

Do some persons stutter even when they talk in their sleep?

Yes. The extent varies with each person. Some stutter only in certain situations, or in the presence of specific persons (as someone they are very much in love with; or someone who makes them feel ill at ease, like the boss or a disapproving mother-in-law). Some stutter only when they go out in public. And some even stutter in their dreams when they talk in their sleep.

What are the chances of self-recovery from stuttering?

Very good, indeed! At the University of California a survey was made of 2,400 students. They were given a speech-screening examination and individual interview by four speech experts to discover whether each was: 1. a stutterer; 2. a normal speaker; or 3. a recovered stutterer. Of those who had a previous problem of stuttering, four out of five had recovered.

What was responsible for their recovery?

Since recovery from stuttering, especially that without therapy, is so often baffling, each student was questioned on what he attributed his recovery to and what advice he would give another stutterer.

For the most part, recovery was attributed to a specific change in mental attitude, slowing down and relaxing, speaking more, and putting oneself forward instead of trying to avoid challenging situations; developing a positive rather than negative attitude toward oneself. The importance of self-acceptance and self-esteem was emphasized. Columbia University studies show stutterers to be less self-accepting than nonstutterers

How can you overcome a fear of speaking in front of others?

Many persons who can express themselves fluently to another panic at the thought of speaking to even a small group. At San Diego State College, psychologist John M. Grossberg made a special study of this form of stage fright. His method of dealing with it is called "desensitization." It can be adapted to fit almost any speech problem.

Professor Grossberg cites the case of a 41-year-old woman who had returned to college to prepare herself for a career in a new field. When she learned that she would have to take a public-speaking course, the prospect terrified her. She dropped

250

out, abandoning the project. She tried tranquilizers and individual and group therapy, but her fear of speaking in front of others remained.

Professor Grossberg arranged for a series of desensitization sessions. First, she read aloud to the speech therapist in his office, next in an empty classroom. ("It doesn't bother you if no one else is present, does it?" No, it didn't.) Then she was asked to speak extemporaneously. Comparatively relaxed, and with some degree of confidence, since no others were there to cause panic, she was able to express herself with reasonable fluency. Then Professor Grossberg had her repeat the performance with one other person (a student) in the classroom. Rather to her surprise, the addition of an audience had no appreciable effect on her. With each session, another auditor was added until, in a comparatively short time, she was speaking to a number of people. She enrolled in the required public-speaking course and happily resumed her studies.

How can you express yourself best: by speaking or writing?

At the City University of New York, students were required to express themselves in both ways. Though some students preferred writing to speaking, tests showed that spoken expression produced far more ideas and elaborations of ideas, more expressive words, phrases, and sentences, than written expression.

Why should speaking one's mind be more productive and more expressive than writing it? First, it was found that the very act of writing tended to have an inhibiting effect on the flow of ideas, tending to make each person more circumspect. Writing is a more permanent form of expression, requiring more deliberation than speech.

Speaking utilizes the natural functions of the larynx; writing uses a learned mechanism of the fingers, wrist, and arm. Speaking begins while we are in the crib, but writing is an artificial function that begins (often against resistance) at about six years of age.

Even though you may feel, as many people do, that you can express your thoughts better on paper, these findings suggest that you might do better if you dictated, using your larynx instead of a pencil.

NOISE GET YOU DOWN?
Science Now Explains The Whys and Wherefores

How noise affects you depends on whether you are a man or a woman, an introvert or an extrovert, a child or an adult. Here are science's latest findings on the sound frequencies that are balm for some people, bedlam for others.

Can men stand noise better than women?

No. Studies show that women have what scientists term "a resistance to noise trauma," which means they can tolerate it with fewer ill effects than men can. That doesn't mean that women thrive on noise or that their hearing is not affected or their nerves frayed by continuous exposure to it — but they can take it better than men can. And, investigations show, so can children. Indeed, children *love* noise and like nothing better than to make it.

Does your memory work better when it's noisy?

Yes, according to studies conducted at the London Institute of Psychiatry. Tests on two groups of subjects, one under noisy conditions and the other in an atmosphere of quiet, showed that it is more difficult for a person to absorb new knowledge when it is noisy than when it is quiet. But the investigators also found that the group who learned in a noisy atmosphere remembered what they had learned the next day better than those who studied in quiet surroundings.

Can noise affect the body's metabolism?

Yes. University of California's Dr. Chauncey Leake, who has made an extensive study of noise, finds that noise affects the body's endocrine balance immediately. It was also found to cause a specific disturbance to thyroid function, and to upset the water and salt balance in the body. He also cited "the interference with mental processes that come from long or frequent exposure to noise. And among the effects on the cardiovascular system are increases in blood pressure." Much essential hypertension, he concludes, is caused by noise.

Is it true that the sounds you hear when eating or drinking affect your taste centers, and can make things taste good, bad, or indifferent?

Yes. Studies conducted by Dr. Kristian Holt-Hansen at Copenhagen University Psychological Laboratory have demonstrated that sensations in the mouth, tongue, palate, throat, and head are greatly affected by the sounds around us. The tests showed, for example, that a drink which subjects described as tasting "smooth and full-bodied" while an amplifier produced certain sounds, reported the same drink as tasting flat, insipid, or watery when the tone of the sounds was changed to a different pitch or frequency.

When the subjects in the study were tested on various brands of beer, it was found that each variety of brew tasted better when certain sounds were produced by a tone-generator. The "note of harmony" which gave each beverage its best taste differed with the type of drink. And a raising or lowering of the tone altered the taste of the drink and made it less pleasant. As one subject reported, "when the note of harmony moves upward, the beer seems bitter and does not taste good, and when the note of harmony moves downward, the taste grows thin, stale, and more watery.

The study suggests that what we eat and drink might taste a lot better with special background music harmonizing with the various cocktails, wines, and entrees. If science can develop the research to that point, eating and drinking should be more pleasurable than ever.

Is it true that if noise doesn't bother you — if you just don't notice it — it won't do you any harm?

No. Studies at the University of Wisconsin Medical School show that continual exposure to the sounds of a typical house-hold — noisy appliances, a blaring radio or record player, and people shouting to make themselves heard — is a major factor in the "tired-mother syndrome," nervous tension, gastro-intestinal upsets, severe headaches, and similar ailments. There may also be a gradual but progressive hearing loss. And the psychiatrists who conducted the study point out that this physical damage takes place even when a person becomes so accustomed to the noise that he pays no attention to it.

Is it true that what is unpleasant noise to one person can be a beautiful sound to another?

Yes. What constitutes noise depends on the person who is listening to it, whether he is young or old, what he is doing at the time, who is making the sounds. Noise has been defined as undesired sound. "A beautiful song may be more noise if it interferes with a task," he says. And one study has shown that one of the noises most objectionable to adults is that made by children.

Would we be better off if noise could be completely eliminated?

No. Many people find too much quiet as disturbing as too much noise. Studies show this applies particularly to extroverts. A big, new office building, air-conditioned, with efficient sound-proofing and sealed windows, proved so quiet that it made employees nervous, and caused many to complain that the silence was driving them crazy. So engineers developed a device which produces a "mild, watered-down" kind of noise, similar to the muted sounds of traffic and the distant murmur of people speaking in low, quiet tones, and this carefully edited "noise" is now piped to all the offices.

HOW TO BEAT FATIGUE
There Are Three Kinds Of Fatigue:
Physical, Mental and Emotional
Learn What Causes Your Tired Feeling,
And You Can Cope With It

Fatigue is one of man's worst enemies. Psychologists find it responsible for more unhappiness, more failures in marriage and business than any other single factor.

Scientists in leading universities and research organizations have been putting fatigue under the clinical microscope to find the cause and the cure.

Physical fatigue presents the least problem and is the easiest to cope with. The quickest way to banish physical tiredness, according to studies at the University of California, is to stand under a cold shower for a few minutes. Science hasn't discovered precisely why this has an instantaneous effect, but tests show that it works like a charm. Investigators have also found that the average man can do twice as much physical work and accumulate less fatigue at the end of the day if he takes short, frequent rest periods. And researchers at DePauw University discovered that physical fatigue is greatly reduced when a housewife, or anyone else for that matter, does her work to the rhythm of music. This is because work performed rhythmically requires much less energy.

Now we come to mental fatigue. Mental workers who want to avoid "that tired feeling" must realize that the man who works with his brain requires more sleep than the man who earns his living with his muscle. Experiments conducted at Colgate University have shown, for example, that while manual workers could accomplish their jobs efficiently on four-to-five hours' sleep a night, mental workers required an additional four hours to turn in a par performance.

Rest periods are even more important to the mental worker than to the physical worker. At the University of Cincinnati researchers have found that if your work is largely physical you will get the greatest benefit from hour rest periods by relaxing as completely as possible. However, the mental

255

worker, investigators found, should engage in some mildly stimulating activity because it "serves to maintain alertness at an optimum and at the same time to relieve cramped muscles and a jaded brain."

Incidentally, you won't tire nearly as easily if your office or place of work is kept at the right temperature. Scientific studies have definitely established that you'll do the best work, and will be the least fatigued by it, when the room temperature is kept at 68-70° F.

To perform mental work with a minimum of fatigue, it is highly essential that you have plenty of fresh air. At the University of Illinois, students were given intelligence tests while breathing air which contained a normal amount of oxygen. Then, with the oxygen content of the air artifically reduced, the tests were repeated. The students made much poorer scores.

Now we turn to the matter of nervous fatigue. This is the most common form of tiredness. It is not caused by work, and cannot be banished simply by rest. It is caused by worry, anxiety, frustration, boredom and similar emotional attitudes. Since these states of mind drain our energies much faster than rest can replenish them, they are responsible for the feeling of "perpetual tiredness" or chronic fatigue.

The noted neurologist, Dr. Walter Freeman, finds that additional rest actually worsens the victim's condition and makes him more tired than before. His studies show that patients respond quickest to a regime of rigorous physical activity. Exercise, he points out, provides a release for the pent-up emotional tensions. Another way to keep emotions from sapping your energies to the point where you're always tired is to keep busy.

What about boredom? Does it exhaust us and literally "make us tired"? It does, indeed. A half hour of acute boredom can burn up more nervous energy than a whole day's work. Psychological tests have shown that boredom is always accompanied by extreme physical and emotional tension. And this, of course, is debilitating.

So, if boredom is draining your nervous energies and making you feel chronically tired, you need to snap yourself out of it by cultivating new interests and broadening your horizons.

CAN YOU REALLY THINK FASTER ON YOUR FEET?
Yes, But Other Kinds Of Cerebration
Go Better When Sitting Or Lying Down

Position in life may not be everything, but science has found that your body position — whether you are sitting, standing, or lying down — affects your ability to think, your memory, your mood, and even your ability to hear or judge distance.

Can you think faster standing up?

Yes. Psychologist Hugo Beigel of Long Island University first demonstrated the influence of body position on mental processes. Men and women were given various mental tests while standing, sitting, and lying down. The results showed that each of the three positions increases a person's ability for specific types of thinking.

The standing position favored faster thinking, with the entire mental set being much more action-related. But the disadvantage was that subjects tended to draw hasty conclusions.

The reclining position has precisely the opposite effect, inhibiting action-minded thinking, but promoting contemplative thinking, and deliberation.

The sitting position was found best for all-purpose thinking: not as quick on the mental trigger as the standing position, nor as creative as the reclining position, but a good combination of both.

Can you hear better when you are lying down?

Yes. In studies at Pennsylvania State University, students were first screened for normal hearing, then given hearing tests in the three principal body positions. It was found that different positions had a significant effect in raising or lowering the hearing threshold. Hearing was most acute in the reclining position.

How does your posture affect your ability to judge distance?

Studies show that when you are not sitting or standing erect, your visual perception is affected in such a way that you have difficulty in estimating distance, with a strong tendency to see objects as farther away than they are.

Does your imagination work better when you are lying down?

Yes. In studies at New York University, students were given

creative-imagination tests while standing, sitting, and reclining. Best scores were made when the subjects were lying down. Next best showings were made in sitting positions, and the poorest while standing.

Are you more susceptible to persuasion when you are standing up?

No. Psychological studies at Florida State University show that a person is most receptive to ideas when he is lying down. Other investigations indicate that a man has the most sales resistance when he is standing up, less when sitting down, and the least when lying down.

Does your memory work better when you are sitting up?

No. Research at Michigan State University has shown that memory functions best when you are lying down. This position made it possible for subjects in the study to recall memories which completely escaped them when they were standing or sitting upright. This was found especially true of things which had happened a long time ago.

Does your posture affect your state of mind?

Your posture can affect your entire outlook. Just as our mood influences our posture (when we feel blue, our shoulders slump and we tend to drag out feet), our posture has a direct effect on our state of mind. You can change a negative mood into a positive one: sit erect instead of slumping, and trade that shambling gait for a brisk stride.

HOW GOOD A DRIVER ARE YOU?
Many Factors — Personality, Attitudes, Emotions, Age, I.Q., Even a Spat With Boss or Spouse — Influence Your Capability in Handling Horsepower

How good a driver you are depends on more things than you've probably ever imagined. There are more important things than speedy reflexes and the ability to judge distance down to the fraction of an inch. And there are considerations of greater consequence than how smoothly you can tool a car through traffic or ease effortlessly into a cramped parking space. Actually, how happily married you are or how well you get along with your boss can be far more important in determining how you rate as a driver.

Your I.Q. is important too, as you'd naturally expect. But there may be a surprise for you in that department.

Many of us assume that if people had more brains there would be fewer accidents; that the more intelligent a man is, the better able he is to cope with the problems of driving an automobile. Not so. Wide-scale studies at Iowa State University's Driving Research Laboratory show that people with the most brainpower are *not* the most capable when it comes to handling horsepower.

It is the person of about *average* intelligence who makes the best driver. People who tend to have accidents are those who are 20% or more below normal in the I.Q. department, and those who are 20% or more *above* normal. The below-normal group aren't attentive enough at times. Let their attention lapse and they can get into trouble.

Those who are above normal also get into trouble because of inattentiveness, but for a different reason. Just jockeying a car around doesn't provide sufficient challenge to give their higher I.Q. much of a workout; so they tend to become bored, restless, and impatient. This results in carelessness, chance-taking, and, of course, higher accident hazard.

A frequently argued question is the age at which man's driving ability begins to deteriorate. Actually, it depends on the individual. Some people are competent and capable drivers even

259

after they pass the century mark. For example, a survey conducted by the American Automobile Association cites the case of a 102-year-old judge who still drives to work six days a week, rain or shine, enjoys driving despite rush-hour traffic — and has never had an accident. Dr. Morris Fishbein, who has evaluated findings of leading studies on the senior citizen behind the steering wheel, points out, however, that the accident rate increases sharply for both men and women after 60. (Though they still have fewer accidents than drivers under 21.)

Handicaps in vision and hearing are chief factors militating against the competence of the aging automobile pilot. Other things which tend to diminish are ability to judge distance, reaction time, and glare-resistance.

Since marked deficiency in any of these departments can convert a carefree driver into a statistic in a fraction of a second, one leading authority makes the following recommendation for all drivers past 60: Take a reaction-time test and other driver tests in order to find out how you rate, and what to do to offset any point on which your rating is not tops. Also test your night vision and glare resistance.

Personality plays an even bigger role than intelligence in determining how good a driver you are. For example, extroverts run more stop lights than introverts, make more illegal turns, show more reckless disregard for other motorists, bash more fenders, have more collisions of every type and variety, and collect more citations for major and minor offenses. At the University of Minnesota, psychologists administered personality tests to nearly 1000 subjects, separating those who had predominantly introverted or extroverted tendencies. The driving record of each of the subjects was made available to the investigators by the Minnesota State Highway Department.

The extroverts not only had far more accidents and traffic violations to their credit, but in summing up the findings of the study, psychologist Bernard J. Fine observes that if more data on the causes of the accidents were available, there is reason to suspect that a great many of the accidents in which introverts were involved were actually caused by extroverts.

What kind of drivers do people with ulcers make? One might expect them to make excellent drivers. For, as authorities point out, the personality characteristics of the typical ulcer man — conscientiousness, striving for perfection, and willingness to assume responsibilities — appear conducive to careful, accident-free driving. However, a leading research foundation recently studied the accident rates of drivers with ulcers and found that they had significantly *more* accidents per capita than the general driving population.

Why should this be the case? One psychologist suggests a very simple explanation: "Ulcer people" are so pressured by inner conflicts that they simply fail to properly perceive and react to dangerous situations — which they might otherwise have handled with ease.

People with the pleasantest personalities have the fewest accidents. Extensive studies reported by Michigan State University's Safety Highway Center have shown that "faulty personality traits and attitudes are contributing causes in 80-85% of all traffic accidents." For example, there is the aggressive driver whose pent-up hostilities and emotional frustrations are expressed by cutting in on other motorists, speeding, running red lights, refusing to let others pass, and driving in a generally hazardous and belligerent manner.

Other forms of neurotic behavior include the "show-off," who feels insecure and seeks to impress others by fast, tire-spinning starts, cornering at excessive speeds, and taking deliberate driving risks with a "Look, Ma, no hands!" attitude. Investigators point out that though this is commonest with young drivers, adults are by no means immune from it.

Even a man with a normal, well-adjusted personality may get into trouble driving while emotionally upset. When the horsepower under the hood is triggered by a man seething with anger, or moody and depressed, his alertness and perception are blunted and he becomes one of the most serious hazards on the highways. The experts strongly advise: If you have a fight with your wife or a run-in with your boss, take a breather and don't get behind the steering wheel until you've had time to cool off.

Some researchers suspect that the suicide-prone driver may constitute a substantial menace on the highway. Prof. Frederick L. McGuire, head of the Division of Psychology, University of Mississippi Medical School, reports in an issue of the *Mississippi State Medical Journal* on one accident in which a 30-year-old California male seemed bent on self-destruction. Having broken up with his girl friend, he tried to sideswipe another car and then yelled at the driver: "What's the matter, are you afraid to die?" He then drove onto a boulevard, veered into the left lane, scattered approaching motorists, and finally collided head-on with another car, killing the driver. He survived, and while in the hospital with his broken jaw wired shut, he scribbled on the scratch pad, "Let me die!" Many cases, of course, are far less clear-cut and require careful investigation before suicidal intent can be assumed.

Says psychologist McGuire in reviewing the findings of his studies: A disturbing facet of this problem of suicidal impulses on the highway is that the motor vehicle is so *readily* accessible. When a person contemplates suicide by firearms or poison, for example, he must usually contrive to possess the necessary equipment. Often a suicidal impulse of this sort is thwarted by the fact that he cannot obtain a gun or a bottle of poison at the propitious moment.

The motor vehicle is not only right at hand, but when a person is speeding along the highway he often is separated from violence and possible death by only a few inches, or by a slight twist of the steering wheel. Should a destructive impulse strike him at such a moment, he could react with disastrous results.

In spite of educational efforts to convince the public, the motor vehicle is not popularly identified as an instrument of hostility or death. If a person finds himself carelessly playing with a loaded gun, he is more likely to sense a disturbing emotion, either in terms of being reminded of death and injury by the very nature of the weapon, or by being reprimanded or restrained by other people. But if he suddenly finds himself speeding on the highway, taking a corner too fast, following the car ahead too closely, or crowding the white line, he is not apt to associate this lapse of judgment with violence. Thus the automobile encourages the release of destructive urges in people who otherwise might maintain control of such impulses.

Concludes the university psychologist: Motor vehicles do not drive themselves and accidents are not produced by concrete roads or cloudy skies. They are produced by people — people made up of fears, hopes, impulses, and inhibitions. Only through understanding of how these forces affect a person's driving performance can we ever hope to control our mounting epidemic of death and injury on the highway.

V.

WORRY, FEAR AND FRUSTRATION

WORRY, FEAR AND FRUSTRATION

*It's been said so often that most persons lead lives
of quiet desperation, that it would be a research
project in itself to determine who said it first. Coping
with mental anxieties is the chief preoccupation of a
good many of us. Just as real psychotic difficulties
can often be helped by dragging memories from the
subconscious to the conscious mind, being able to
account for our moods, depressions and mental
states in general ordinarily relieves some of the
mental pain. To cope with life on this less-serious
level requires, shall we say, a heavy smattering of
knowledge of the sources of your disquieting feelings,
the interrelated reactions of your mind, emotions
and body.*

WHAT'S WORRYING YOU?
Science Can Now Tell You How To Cope With Anxiety

Life is frightening to most of us, for we all have fears and
anxieties. Researchers have been taking a hard look at what
gives us that uneasy feeling in the pit of the stomach. They
are now able to help a little.

Who is the most fearful?

Often it is the person you would least suspect. Psychologists
have found that the seemingly carefree person is often most
plagued by fears. He adopts his flamboyant manner to conceal
his anxiety from himself and others. His doubts about his
ability drive him to flirt with danger in a constant effort to
prove himself.

What are most people afraid of?

Rutgers psychologists made a study of the most common
fears of both sexes. Men had three chief fears.

1. *Fear of failure:* I just hope I can handle that new job.
If I don't pass that examination, I'm sunk. Everything depends
on landing this contract.

2. *Fear of being rejected by others:* I would like to get acquainted with them, but I am not going to take a chance on getting snubbed. It is safer not to stick your neck out. I am always so nervous when we have them to dinner. I never know what to say that will be of interest to them.

3. *Fear of being rejected by a girl:* I am afraid to ask her for a date. I do not know what I would do if she turned me down. I think she is attracted to me, but I could be wrong, and maybe there's someone else. I am afraid to let myself like her until I know how she feels about me.

Women also had the same fears. But they were less fearful of being rejected by a man, much more fearful of rejection by others, and less afraid of being a failure. But they had many more intense fears than the men did, including fears of appearing foolish or ridiculous, the prospect of a surgical operation, fear of men, fear of dead bodies. The findings do not mean that women are more fearful than men. The investigators concluded that women either are more upset by various situations or that women are more honest in reporting their feelings. Perhaps they are more honest because it is more socially acceptable for women to have such fears.

Is it true that good men have the fewest fears?

It has been observed that "fear is the tax that conscience pays to guilt." Psychologists agree that a man who is on good terms with himself and who feels he is doing his best is far less subject to anxieties than the man filled with self-doubts and inner conflicts. Fears do spring from many other sources, but often how confident or how fearful you are depends on how harmonious your relationship is with yourself.

Does anxiety dull your wits or sharpen them?

It depends on the person. One person will find his perception dulled, his reflexes slowed; and his ability to reason impaired. But on some people anxiety has the opposite effect. At Duke University, psychological tests showed that anxiety sharpened the wits of superior students, but dulled the mental faculties of those with only average ability.

What is the A.Q. (anxiety quotient)?

Here is a check list to measure the amount of anxiety you

268

feel at any given time, based on psychological studies conducted at Stanford University. The more you find applicable, the higher your anxiety level.

Are you tense and ill at ease in conversation?

Do you frequently scowl and wrinkle your forehead?

Are the palms of your hands frequently moist?

Do you have trouble concentrating?

Are you jittery and easily startled?

Do you sigh frequently?

Are you easily fatigued?

Is your voice plaintive? (You must check with a friend on this one.)

Do you have any nervous mannerisms, such as repeatedly pulling at your hair, rubbing your chin, tapping your feet?

Do people who are socially and financially secure have fewer fears and anxieties than those who are not?

University of California investigators interviewed a cross section of the adult population of the entire Los Angeles metropolitan area. Every part of the socioeconomic ladder was represented, from dowagers to ditchdiggers. The findings: people who have plenty of money and high social status have just as many fears and anxieties as those who have to struggle to get by. The socially and financially secure may not have to be concerned about money or status, but they find many other things to be worried about.

Is moving from place to place a good way to relieve anxiety?

No. But it can be a good way to cause it. Surveys conducted by the University of Arizona show that people who have changed their residence frequently tend to become more fearful than those who have moved only a few times. It would seem that most of us thrive best and feel most secure when we put our roots down.

How can you fight worry?

1. Do you live in the past or the future? One is dead, the other is not yet born. Live in the present. Do the best you can now. Do not speculate about tomorrow; wait until it becomes today, then it belongs to you and you can do something about it.

2. Remember that hurry increases worry. To restore a feeling of poise, try to arrange your schedule so you don't have to rush. Allow time for the things you want to do. Anything that will not fit without crowding, do tomorrow. Do all you can to plan your day so you will not have to worry about hurrying.

3. Do not think of problems as justifications for anxiety. Think of them as opportunities for action.

YOUR ANXIETIES ARE SHOWING
But Don't Try To Hide Them; It Is Better To Face Them Out

Anxious people live in their own special unreal world. Psychologists have made many studies to find out more about anxiety, why it affects us the way it does, and how we can best cope with it.

Is anxiety the same as fear?

We react to known dangers, which are immediately present, with fear. We react to remote or uncertain dangers with anxiety. Dr. Raymond B. Cattell, a psychologist, finds that even our physical reaction to anxiety is quite different from our reaction to fear. Fear releases adrenalin; anxiety does not. Fear makes the mouth dry; anxiety increases saliva flow.

Do anxious people feel threatened by almost everyone, even their friends?

Yes, to a marked degree. Columbia University studies show that people with a relatively high degree of anxiety were far more likely to speak of others (even persons they liked) as "arrogant," "belligerent," "disapproves of me," "dislikes me," "frustrates me," "hurts me," "is prejudiced against me," "treats me as an inferior." Regardless of the other person's attitude, an anxious person is constantly watchful, ready to interpret something the other says or does as a slight upon himself.

If you are an anxious person, is your voice likely to betray the fact?

At the University of Kentucky, psychologists grouped men and women into four basic types according to the sounds of their voices: 1. normal, 2. harsh, 3. nasal, 4. hoarse-breathy. Personality tests were then given each group. People with hoarse-breathy voices were found to be the most anxious. People with the least anxiety were those with normal or harsh voices.

Does an anxious person's speech give him away?

Studies sponsored by the National Institute of Mental Health have shown that the more a person is plagued by anxieties, the more he uses "nonverbal sounds," such as gestures, laughs, coughs, throat clearings, deep breaths. Another speech mannerism which the investigators noted in many high-anxiety people: "The speaker seems to procrastinate, to delay getting on to his next point. He uses delaying sounds (such as 'ah', 'um') or prolonged vowels, or words (such as 'well'), or phrases ('How shall I say?'); sometimes even 'I don't know.' "

Do anxious persons have more problems to cope with than others?

At the University of Georgia, psychologists administered a battery of personality tests to students. They found that those who made high-anxiety scores had a great many more personal problems, both big and small, than those who had low scores on anxiety tests. These problems were of much the same pattern: "disappointment in a love affair," "parents expect too much of me," "acute financial difficulties," "health and physical-development problems," "finding friends." This raises the question of whether high-anxiety people tend to be problem-prone, or whether the presence of many pressures provides a favorable climate for anxieties.

Will your anxieties increase or decrease as you grow older?

Some will; others not. There are two forms of anxiety: overt and covert. Covert anxieties are those which the person does not wish to recognize. He pushes them out of his mind, permitting them to sleep fitfully below the level of consciousness. Overt anxieties, those which the person frankly admits to himself and is fully conscious of, are more common.

271

Studies conducted at the University of Pittsburgh show that overt anxieties tend to decrease as we grow older. Not so with the covert anxieties; they increase with age.

What can you do to cope with your anxieties?

The first step is to face them, admit them to yourself and bring them to the surface, where you can look at them objectively. When you try to silence anxiety by pretending it is not there, you only increase its power to disturb you.

It is frequently a great help to have a good friend with whom you can talk out your worries. Often the very act of talking them out brings answers to real problems, shows up the fallacies of half-hidden ones, and causes those which are groundless to vanish.

If there is no one to whom you can talk freely, take a pencil and paper and try to write down all of your concerns and apprehensions. Let what you have written stand a day or two, then read it over. You will find yourself looking at them with far greater insight, and you will find them diminishing year by year.

WHAT ARE YOU AFRAID OF?
Science Offers Good Advice On How To Cope With Anxiety

Fear can range from mild apprehension to pure panic. It is one of the most basic of all emotions. Some of us are more subject to it than others, but most of us know it in various forms and guises.

What do people fear most?

The National Institute of Mental Health sponsored a survey of persons from various walks of life, ranging in age from 13 to 85 years. Results of the study show that people's chief fears ran a wide range, from having something happen to a loved one, fear of failure, being hurt or crippled by accident or affliction, to fear of being rejected by others or of speaking in public. Among the top ones was fear of drowning, and it seemed not to matter greatly whether the person lived near water or not.

What are the most common "irrational" fears?

Studies at the University of British Columbia have shown that the most common of this type is extreme fear of snakes and spiders. Such fright was found to be about seven times as prevalent among women as among men.

At what ages do people have the most fears?

The same study showed that the groups expressing the most fears were the adolescents (13 to 18) and the older people (60 to 85). The finding "suggests that individuals experience increased stress at the ages immediately preceding and following the period in life accompanied by the greatest responsibility and productivity. Adolescents and older people in our society are typically somewhat insecure and subject to conflicts with regard to independence-dependence," say the authors of the study.

Other investigations have shown that this feeling of insecurity and fearfulness is *not* shared by older people who continue to be productive in their work or profession. Many describe these years as the happiest and most fruitful of their entire lives.

Which sex is the most fearful?

All studies indicate that women's fears tend to be more numerous and more intense than men's. But one investigation has shown that men's fears tend to increase with age more than women's do. Older men may undergo a greater period of change, and the fact that older men, more than women, face a difficult time in adjusting to the change in life style occasioned by retirement might account for the difference.

Are people who readily admit their fears the most fearful?

No. Psychological studies have shown that people who are the most reticent are the most fear-ridden; those who freely admit their fears tend to have the fewest.

Do smokers have more anxieties than nonsmokers?

Yes. Studies were made at the University of California, where hundreds of men and women of various ages were interviewed as to their smoking habits, and then given psychological tests. Smokers averaged significantly higher anxiety scores than nonsmokers. The majority of smokers said they smoked more when they were under stress.

Does fear affect a person's appetite?

Yes, and the effect depends on whether he is overweight or not. Columbia University experiments have shown that people of normal weight ate much less when frightened. But the over-weight subjects ate just as much whether they were frightened or not. Another finding: unlike people of normal weight, over-weight persons ate about the same amounts of food under *all* experimental conditions, whether their stomachs were full or empty.

What about phobias?

Phobias are *intense* fears. The common ones are acrophobia (fear of heights), mysophobia (fear of dirt and germs, compulsior to wash hands often), agoraphobia (fear of open spaces), aquaphobia (fear of water), claustrophobia (fear of closed places), nyctophobia (fear of dark), pyrophobia (fear of fire). This is only a partial list, for there are almost as many kinds of phobias as there are kinds of people.

A noted Britist psychiatrist, Dr. Isaac M. Marks, observes that fear sufficiently intense to be called a phobia occurs only in a small proportion of adults. The commonest phobia, he finds, is the fear of open spaces. Women are more subject to phobias in general than men are, but men have been found equally susceptible to what are termed "social phobias"; acutely painful feelings of self-consciousness in the presence of others, particularly strangers; and to "isolated" phobias such as darkness, heights, thunder, or accidents.

What can you do to cope with your fears?

First, realize that there is nothing abnormal about feeling anxious. Fear is a natural reaction when faced with some hazard that threatens your physical or mental well-being. Whenever your fears are really justified, don't try to ignore them. They warn you of potential danger. Paying them heed can save you from foolhardy action. Both men and animals *need* to feel fear and act on its prompting. Without it, many living things would have been extinct long ago.

Irrational fears are another matter. They can ruin your life. They represent the negative, destructive side of fear. The thing is to differentiate your legitimate fears from phantom fears, the imposters which can cloud your mind. You will need to view your fears in perspective, so *write them all down*. Then take the list to one or more close friends, who know you well, and let them help put your fears in the right columns.

Such a fear-inventory, if done conscientiously, will help you to see things in their true perspective. If you are a fearful person, you are likely to find after this inventory that you have far less cause for concern than you ever suspected.

Next, separate your legitimate fears into two groups: those you will just have to learn to live with, and those you can do something about. You will find most, if not all, in the second group.

Everyone has problems in his life. If a person faces up to them, they never become more than challenges. But for the person who does not go into action, problems soon become fears. And the more he hesitates, the more fear is generated. So if you have been playing it this way, the time has come to tackle your fears head on.

HOW TO HANDLE YOUR FEARS
Science Can Tell You How To Cope

Most people are afraid of something, and some people are afraid of almost everything. Whether you are capable of facing hazards without turning a hair, or spend most of your time anxious and worried about things that never happen (or somewhere in between), you will be interested in the latest discoveries about fear.

Does fear make pain hurt worse?

Yes. University students were examined under the influence of various emotional states by means of an algesimeter, which measures pain thresholds. The research showed that fear lowered the threshold significantly, increasing sensitivity to injury and causing pain to hurt appreciably more.

Is it true that if you simply avoid the people, things, objects, or places which frighten you, phobias will disappear?

No. The opposite is true. Hiding from that which frightens you only enables your fears to get a stronger grip. All psychological research indicates that one effective means of eliminating fears, or at least cutting them down to size, is by a gradual or graded exposure to whatever fear you wish to overcome. And a Stanford University study makes it evident that if you can relax when you do this, it usually will work even better.

But do not expose yourself to objects, places or persons you fear if any real hazard is involved. Such encounters should be undertaken only under the supervision of a qualified specialist.

Do many people have such a fear of success that they try either to avoid it or minimize their chances of achievement?

Yes. University studies show that people of low self-esteem are, in the words of the researchers, "allergic" to success, and "are made uncomfortable by success because of its inconsistency with their low self-appraisal." And the prospect of success induced only anxiety and discomfort in low self-esteem subjects when the success was due to their own skill and effort. Success was more acceptable to them when it was largely due to luck.

Is it true that the more a person enjoys life, the less he fears death?

Yes. Psychological studies at Vanderbilt University have shown that the more a person is getting out of life, the more rewarding his pursuits, the more purposeful his existence, the less he fears death. Conversely, it was found that people whose lives were lacking in meaning and purpose, who were, in effect, getting the least out of life, had the greatest fear of death.

Is a truly brave person fearless?

No. If a person is fearless, it may well be because he is either too foolhardy or too insensitive to fully appreciate potential dangers in a given situation. ("Fools rush in where angels fear to tread.") Besides, if the person feels no fear, he doesn't require courage to proceed. The bravest man is the one who must summon up the greatest courage to overcome his fears and go ahead in spite of his misgivings. Bravery has been defined as "getting up in the morning and facing life."

Is it true that one of the best ways to achieve mastery over fears is to learn to laugh at them?

Yes. Psychiatric studies show that the more you can learn to laugh at your fears, the more you remove their power to frighten you. Humor provides an effective way of sharing your concerns and anxieties with another person. If you do this as though you were telling a joke on yourself, you will find both you and your confidant being amused, often laughing together over something which you previously found frightening. Your friend may then be inclined to tell you about some of the things which scare him. Humor not only serves to restore perspective, but, as studies have demonstrated, it is a good way of breaking down social barriers and mastering many of our anxieties.

WHAT MAKES YOU BLOW YOUR TOP?
You May Be Surprised To Learn What Makes People Angry.
It's Other People

Only saints and goldfish never lose their tempers. Ordinary people can be ruffled by almost anything from a circling mosquito to a nervous cough. No doubt you have your own list of things that burn you up, but it's fun to see how your peeves compare with everybody else's. Here's your chance — a question-answer breakdown of science's findings on what makes people blow their tops and why:

Q. What does the average American find most irritating of all?

A. An inconsiderate fellow-American, according to the American Institute of Public Opinion.

An exhaustive study made by the late psychologist, Professor Hulsey Cason, reveals, however, that it's not what you *are* that irritates, it's what you *do*. Professor Cason collected over 21,000 of the most common annoyances from men and women of all ages in many different occupations. Then he classified them according to their capacity to irritate. Front-rank offenders turned out to be:

The person who cheats at cards, or, for that matter, any game.
Fresh or disobedient children.
High-pressure salesmen.
Show-offs.
The constant talker (especially the one who chatters through a movie, concert or lecture) and the "have you heard about my operation?" type.
The sneezer and cougher.
The teeth-picker.
The nail-biter.
The gum-chewer.
The grown woman who talks baby talk.
Couples making love in public.
The man at the next table slurping his soup.
The woman next to him with the overpowering perfume.
The perfect stranger — store clerk or waitress — who croons

"dearie" or "honey."

The hostess who insists you have a second helping.

Q. How do most of us react to such annoying characters as the above?

A. We swallow our irritation, according to British psychologist Peter McKellar, who made a study of over a hundred angry people. A few will blurt out their feelings, and about one in a hundred will respond with a violent left to the jaw.

Q. Can you be annoyed by yourself?

A. Definitely. One nationwide survey shows that you could be all alone on a desert island and still grind your teeth. The trait people found most exasperating in themselves was bad temper. Its opposite came second: being too easy-going. Other popular self-irritants were impatience, extravagance, unnecessary worry, laziness, lack of self-confidence, too much talking, too much drinking, selfishness, inability to get along well with others, stubbornness.

Q. What other major irritants are there?

A. Noise-making, while not excluding the people who make it, is in a slot all by itself.

The James M. Vicary Company, a New York research organization, asked a variety of people to name the most unpleasant noise they could think of. No. 1 on the list: the racket made by children. And it wasn't only those without children of their own who put this up front. It was the parents' vote, too.

Screaming and yelling by adults came next, followed by animal and insect noises, banging, hammering, scratching, grating and screeching noise, and that old summertime pest, the blaring radio or TV set.

Q. Which people are most easily irritated?

A. Housewives, unskilled laborers and clerical workers, according to Professor Cason's study, are likely to come to a boil more rapidly. Appreciably less irritable were businessmen and skilled laborers. Students and farmers averaged still lower annoyance scores. And least irritable of all were the professional men and women. But thin men watch out! You get peeved more easily than fat men, while with women it's the other way around. Short men get exasperated more often than tall men, but how tall the lady is doesn't seem to affect her disposition at all.

Q. Do your pet peeves show anything special about your personality?

A. Psychologists say that the more gripes you have the more likely you are to be high-strung. If you have only a short list of gripes, you're probably a well-balanced personality.

The *kind* of things that upset is highly significant, too. Studies sponsored by the Rockefeller Foundation have shown that the person who tends to be neurotic is most annoyed by situations that threatened self-esteem: someone forgetting his name, being kidded, or discovering that he has made a silly mistake.

Q. What should you do when you feel you're getting angry?

A. When irritations scratch your nerves, what should you do to keep calm? Science says that the very worst remedy is to bottle things up — it's a chief cause of ulcers and hypertension

On the other hand you'll have few friends left if you give vent to every puff of ill-temper. Fortunately there are safe and sane means of dealing with anger-provoking situations. Here are some of them:

1. When someone bothers you, speak to him *gently* about it. In nine cases out of ten this approach will resolve the situation with no hard feelings on either side.

2. If this doesn't work grab a passing friend and tell him all about your gripe. This should be done as soon as possible. The longer anger is suppressed, the greater its power to harm you physically and emotionally.

3. Exercise is another tension-killer. Working out at the gym, a brisk walk, any active sport, helps relax you.

4. And if all else fails, allow yourself the luxury of telling the offending person off. But while this might prove a highly satisfactory method of letting off steam, it can also be dangerous especially if you choose to blast your boss — or your mother-in-law!

FRUSTRATE YOUR FRUSTRATION
You Can Get That Resentment Out Of Your System
By Letting Off Steam In An Acceptable Way

Few of us, if any, have never felt thwarted, baffled and
baulked in our effort to achieve some goal, great or small.
Therefore, most of us have been bedevilled by Old Man
Frustration for he is an inevitable consequence of such
feelings of disappointment.

If you are a well-adjusted person, on the whole — if you
have a well-balanced personality — you'll suffer less from him
physically and emotionally, than if you have neurotic tendencies.

In a neurotic person even a minor upset can induce a deep
sense of frustration — just a thing like being tied up in heavy
traffic while on the way to an important engagement. So it's
well worthwhile to make yourself over into a well-adjusted
person, if you aren't one already.

Psychiatrists have been studying this frustration business.
One thing they have determined is that the feeling can put
you into a state of such tension that your vital organs have
considerable trouble to function normally.

Your circulation can be slowed to a walk, your heart action
affected and the basis laid for what are called stress diseases —
they range from hypertension to colitis.

Life insurance tables show that the mortality rate for men
and women who have been seriously frustrated in love is two
to four times greater than for those who have not.

Dr. Richard L. Jenkins is convinced by his experiments that
one consequence of frustration can be schizophrenia. It is one
of the most serious mental diseases.

But remove the frustration and you cure the schizophrenia.
Psychiatrists J. M. Nielson and George Thompson have
demonstrated that.

One of their cases was a 36-year-old wife with all the
symptoms of schizophrenia. They found that she was frustrated;
her husband was so wrapped up in his business that he scarcely
ever showed her any attention.

He hadn't even taken the time for a wedding trip. So those

mental experts told him that if he wanted his wife to keep her sanity he'd better mend his ways.

Thoroughly shocked and scared, he did. He took his wife on a belated honeymoon of a month; he lavished sweets, flowers and theatre tickets on her. And when they came home she was completely cured.

She'd gained a badly-needed 20 pounds and felt wonderful. That was about three years ago. She has had no return of her trouble.

Don't jump to the conclusion that because you happen to be leading a life that seems to you filled with frustrations you're going to go psychotic.

Most people can endure even a tough dose of frustration and not have any such consequence. The point you need to remember is this: there is a definite relationship between frustration and the sufferer's mental health.

Usually, just getting rid of the condition or lessening it makes you better physically, mentally and emotionally. For one person who gets to be neurotic because he's frustrated there are plenty who don't.

A good home is valuable insurance against the effect of frustrating conditions often encountered outside it. In fact, studies have shown that where housing is poor, mental disorders are many times as prevalent as in better residential districts.

A good many of our frustrations cannot be eliminated, but their effects can certainly be neutralized.

What really does the damage is the feeling of resentment, anger or aggression that frustration instantly produces. If you give immediate expression to those feelings, in the same moment the frustration back of them is gone.

So all you've got to do to stop feeling frustrated is to find means of expressing these hostile feelings without winding up in jail or being ostracised socially.

If your host blocks your efforts to escape from a boring party, you can't very well just shove him out of the way and head for the door.

If you do what you feel like doing when the boss turns down

your request for a raise, you'll probably risk being fired and face a charge of assault and battery.

But you can find socially acceptable ways of venting your spleen and giving your resentment full expression.

You can get the feeling of aggression out of your system by engaging in competitive sports. You can do that vicariously by attending boxing or wrestling matches and imagining the loser as the guy you wanted to sock on the chin.

After a particularly frustrating day at the office, a certain leading executive always stops off at a nearby gymnasium where he works off his resentment by punching the bag or putting on the gloves for a round or two with a colleague. These methods have been thoroughly tested by psychologists. They work.

Why shouldn't they? They provide a release from the inner tensions caused by the resentment which frustration produces. They are a safety valve. And, as psychiatrist David Fink points out, anything that will relax your tension will banish that frustrated feeling. His studies show conclusively that you can't feel relaxed and frustrated at the same time.

Another way of relieving your frustrations is to give full expression in words to your feelings. Just pick out a confidant who's a sympathetic listener and pour out your grievances to him. Don't pull any punches.

Psychologists call this verbalising, and it works well. It's an emotional purgative that frees the frustration-produced tensions and keeps them from being bottled up inside you where they would fester and multiply.

You can't give all your frustrations the air just by airing them, but you can relieve a good many of them that way.

Incidentally, the next time you feel thwarted and have the urge to cut loose with a string of cuss words, science urges you to go ahead — provided the time, and place aren't too inappropriate. Professor M. Ashley Montagu has made a clinical study of this matter and he finds that swearing is a very effective antidote for that frustrated feeling.

In case you are sensitive to raised eyebrows, the professor's studies show a shout of laughter or a good cry have a similarly beneficial effect.

Tests show that on the whole children become frustrated much more easily than adults do. Moreover, the average child's desires are thwarted much oftener than a grown-up's are.

A child is always being told that he can't do this and mustn't have that. His natural reaction is one of aggressive resentment. He tries to give expressions to this resentment by unruly behavior. But his parents attempt to frustrate him on this score too. So the child's personality becomes a battleground.

So what to do? You can't bring a child up without discipline. And you can't discipline him without making him feel frustrated. But you can and should provide him with means of fully expressing the resentment and hostility that his frustration generates.

College psychologists tested out on nursery school children something that worked like a charm. The children were given clay doll models of each member of their family. They were told they could do anything they wanted to with them.

"Really?" said one little girl incredulously, "anything we want to?" And then she proceeded to give the doll replicas of her parents such an enthusiastic beating that they almost fell apart. The majority of other children followed suit. Clay heads were smashed, mothers and fathers and other relatives were spanked, scolded, made to stand in corners, and subjected to all sorts of indignities. By the end of the session there wasn't much left of the dolls. But the children felt wonderful.

There is a vague sense of frustration that very many housewives feel at least part of the time; a kind of "snowed under" feeling.

The endless succession of household tasks which must be done over and over again, day in and day out, seems to hem you in. Most of these chores provide no lasting satisfaction. They are conspicuous only when left undone — like planning meals, making the beds, scrubbing the floors.

So what should a housewife do? Well, she should include in her daily schedule tasks which result in some concrete and lasting effect. She can take up decorating; get busy with the paint brush or fashion a new couch cover; or plant things in the garden, or cultivate hobbies.

The field is practically unlimited. Another important thing she can do is to bear in mind that, though the performance of most routine household tasks may not provide much sense of achievement, it adds up to one of the most rewarding satisfactions life can offer: making a good home.

Suppose some insurmountable obstacle prevents you from achieving an important goal, or your life ambition. What to do then?

First, satisfy yourself that the obstacle really is insurmountable. If it is, then don't waste any time feeling sorry for yourself or batting your head against a stone wall. What you've got to do with your ambition is sublimate it; that is, choose an acceptable substitute. And there are plenty of substitutes, if you'll just look around for them with an open mind.

Frequently an alternate goal turns out to be even more satisfying than the first one picked. Anybody who can't learn to compromise is foredoomed to lead a pretty frustrating sort of existence. If you can't get pie, take cake. If you can't get cake, take bread pudding. Maybe the pudding offends you because it has raisins in it. Then pluck out the raisins.

If you can't make conditions adjust to you, then you've got to adjust to conditions. If you're trying to make a square peg fit a round hole — and most frustrated people are trying to do just that — you've either got to square up the hole, or else do some whittling on the peg.

ARE YOU NEUROTIC?
There Are Advantages And Disadvantages

Nearly everyone wonders, at one time or another, whether or not he is neurotic. Some regard being neurotic as a kind of badge of distinction, associated with special talent, creative ability, or genius. To others it suggests being odd or queer.

Few terms are more vaguely defined in the public mind.

Are people with neurotic tendencies less likely to succeed in life? Or can neurosis be an asset? And what are the most common symptoms of neurosis? How can a person determine if he is neurotic or well-adjusted? And if you are neurotic, what can you do about it?

Psychologists can provide authoritative answers to every one of these questions. Match your own opinions with the experts' conclusions. Just check each statement as true or false before reading the answer.

People with neurotic tendencies are less likely to succeed in life. (True_____. False_____.)

False. It's often the other way around. Though neurotics tend to scatter their energies because of emotional conflicts, they often have a strong drive to succeed. The British psychologist, Dr. R. Lynn, observes, "Neurotics are frequently very successful in what they undertake, for a person with neurosis-associated anxieties is likely to try to forget them in his work, and thus achieves a greater success than otherwise." Some of the world's greatest leaders have had neurotic tendencies.

It's neurotic to worry about things you can't do anything about. (True_____. False_____.)

False. Everyone is faced now and then with threats and dangers to his well-being, and it is a perfectly normal and natural thing to be concerned about them. As psychiatrists observe, to remain unworried when hazards or disasters threaten is often an indication of abnormality. Worry over *unreal* or *imagined dangers,* however, can be symptomatic of neurotic tendencies.

Chronic doodlers are likely to be neurotic. (True_____. False_____.)

False. A penchant for doodling, penciling forms or shapes on a pad while telephoning or waiting for someone, is likely to be a healthy sign. Doodlers have fewer emotional problems than nondoodlers. One psychiatric study has shown, for example, that "nondoodlers are mostly those who *repress* the emotions that they fear."

Grinding your teeth in your sleep is a sign you are neurotic. (True_____. False_____.)

False. At the University of Chicago investigators studied 40 chronic tooth grinders in all-night sessions in the research laboratory. Psychological tests subsequently showed that there were no significant personality differences between tooth grinders and nontooth grinders.

If you are chronically tired, even though you get enough sleep, it is an indication of neurosis. (True_____. False_____.)

True. Unless, of course, a medical checkup reveals a responsible organic condition. Chronic fatigue is often a telltale sign of neurosis. Inner conflicts and emotional frustration can produce tensions which deplete physical energies faster than the body can replenish them.

It is almost impossible for a person to determine the extent to which he is neurotic or well-adjusted. (True_____. False_____.)

False. It is not difficult if you have a reliable yardstick to use. One of the best yardsticks is furnished by the noted psychologist, Dr. Gardner Murphy, who defines a well-adjusted personality as "one which uses effectively and without conflict all that it possesses." The extent to which you are capable of doing this will provide you with an index of how well-adjusted or how neurotic you happen to be.

Neurotic persons are more subject to colds and other virus infections. (True_____. False_____.)

True. Cornell University researchers studied the health records of men and women from various walks of life. All subjects were given psychiatric interviews. It was found that those with neurotic tendencies were not only more subject to colds and other viruses, but had suffered far more ailments and afflictions of all types than subjects who were emotionally stable.

287

And studies at the State University of New York Medical Center strongly suggest that "an emotional condition may alter body chemistry in such a way as to make the body more susceptible to colds and other diseases."

If you are neurotic, there is little you can do about it except to accept the fact and make the best of it. (True_____. False_____.)

False. You can do much to overcome neurotic tendencies by cultivating the qualities and characteristics of the non-neurotic well-adjusted personality. The National Association of Mental Health provides a check list of the characteristics of well-adjusted people in three important areas of living.

How they feel about themselves.

They feel comfortable about themselves;

Are not bowled over by their own emotions: fears, anger, love, jealousy, guilt, or worries;

Can take life's disappointments in their stride;

Have a tolerant, easygoing attitude toward themselves as well as others; can laugh at themselves;

Neither underestimate nor overestimate their abilities;

Can accept their own shortcomings;

Get satisfaction from simple, everyday pleasures.

Relationships with others.

They are able to give love and to consider the interests of others;

Cultivate personal relationships that are satisfying and lasting;

Respect differences in people;

Do not push people around, nor do they allow themselves to be pushed around.

Attitude toward life.

They are able to meet the demands of life;

Accept their responsibilities;

Shape their environment whenever possible; adjust to it whenever necessary;

Plan ahead but do not fear the future;

Set realistic goals for themselves;

Think for themselves and make their own decisions;

Put their best effort into what they do, and get satisfaction in doing it.

DO YOU HATE YOUR JOB?
Do Most People Dislike Work?
Science's Report On You And Your Job

Practically every American man — and many American women — must "work for a living," that is, earn a salary. How successfully we do it depends on how shrewdly we channel our capacities into directions which will bring us maximum rewards.

Science has for some time taken an interest in the wage-earner. Here are some of its findings.

Q: Would you be happier if you didn't have to work for a living?

A: No. If you inherited enough money to quit your job and take it easy, the odds are that you would regret it. Psychologist George Ross Wells points out that to earn a living — to work and be paid for it — is positive proof of your value. And this reassurance is essential to that feeling of self-respect and self-confidence that is man's chief need. Studies have also shown that physical activity in the form of work plays a vital part in insuring a well-balanced personality. Work reduces conflict and frustration, gives us an opportunity for concrete self-expression. And it helps us keep our feet on the ground by compelling continuous adaptations to reality.

People are *not* happiest after they retire. Sociology Professor Judson T. Landis, who made a study of nearly 500 people from all walks of life, discovered, "The overwhelming majority of men and women were happiest during the time they were working the hardest and carrying the heaviest load of responsibilities."

Q: What type of work are you likely to be most successful at?

A: The kind of work you like to do best. Studies and surveys show that if you don't particularly like your work, the odds are exceedingly slim that you'll ever excel at it — no matter how hard you strive. A recent nationwide survey showed that the overwhelming majority of those who had risen to executive rank in their field were doing work they got a "kick" out of. But of those who had failed to rise, almost half considered their work "uninteresting" or "dull."

Q: Where can you do the best work?

A: Tests indicate that ideally every man should have one specific place which is used exclusively for his work – and for no other purpose. Studies conducted by Psychologist Harold E. Burtt, at Ohio State University, have demonstrated why this is true. "The idea is," says Professor Burtt, "that if one never does anything else at this place he forms a specific habit of working there. Such a strong connection is formed between the particular location and the work, that merely sitting down there is sufficient to start the man off." This advice may not help you on your regular job, but it may if you work at home.

Professor Burtt points out that it is not so important for all your work to be done at this particular place, as for this place to be reserved for nothing but work. If your desk is used for semirecreational activities, such as reading the papers, gabfests, eating, etc., that breaks the spell.

Q: Is there a best time of day for doing difficult work?

A: The consensus of scientific studies shows that the average person does his best work in the morning. For this reason, experts point out that we can increase our productivity by scheduling our most important work for the morning hours, and taking care of the more routine matters in the afternoon.

Q: At what temperature do you work best?

A: It depends on what kind of work you're doing. John Hopkins University scientists tried to determine at what temperature you can do the greatest amount of work with the least effort. Here are the results: Physically strenuous work, 60°; moderately hard work, 65°; and if you're a "desk man," your capacity for work varies with the seasons. Winter's best temperature was found to be between 68° and 73°; summer's, when the thermometer registers between 75° and 80°.

Q: How can you get the greatest benefit from rest periods?

A: Depends on the type of work you're doing. At the University of Cincinnati, Professor Arthur G. Bills found that if your work is largely physical, then complete relaxation is best. But if your work involves mental strain, complete relaxation is likely to take the edge off your faculties to such an extent that you'll find resuming work difficult. The mental worker, Professor Bills finds, should engage in some mildly stimulating activity — because such activity "serves to maintain alertness at an optimum and at the same time to relieve cramped muscles and jaded brain."

Q: Why is a person bored with his job?

A: If your job bores you, you've got lots of company. A wide-scale industrial survey reports that boredom is responsible for more absenteeism than all other causes put together. Most of these people are bored because their job fails to provide them with sufficient incentive or purpose. Any work — or play for that matter — will tend to bore you unless the rewards received are on a par with the effort you expend. The rewards may be money, satisfaction, pleasure, advancement, self-expression — or anything that seems worthwhile to you.

Q: Is it normal to hate work?

A: Some people have an active distaste for work — it's something to be avoided whenever possible. Psychologists say such an attitude is an indication of neurosis.

The noted psychiatrist, Dr. Bernard S. Robbins, has made a careful study of the type of individual who regards work as poison. "The work phobic," says Dr. Robbins, "may never openly rebel against work. He conforms with outward submissiveness. Yet mysteriously the work doesn't get done. It is easy for him to worry himself into a real illness in the face of a difficult job to be done."

At the other end of the scale is the work addict. He has an unquenchable passion for work, drives himself relentlessly and is incapable of enjoying leisure. According to Dr. Robbins, he drowns himself in unceasing toil to keep his anxieties and inner fears from coming to the surface and overwhelming him.

Normally work should be done with a good share of willingness and satisfaction. It's not normal to be a slave to work any more than it is to regard it with intense distaste. If your attitude falls in either one of these opposite categories, it indicates the likelihood of neurosis.

Q: Are most people satisfied with their jobs?

A: At Clark University, psychologists made a wide-scale survey of workers whose occupations ranged from the professional specialists to the lowliest ditch-digger. Their findings showed that only about 60% of the workers were satisfied with their jobs. The rest indicated that their work afforded them little satisfaction and scant opportunity for self-expression.

The vast majority of professional men and business executives were happy in their work, and found it both absorbing and rewarding. But the general attitude of the white-collar brigade of office workers was just the reverse. Less than 42% regarded their jobs with any appreciable satisfaction. The manual workers were much happier in their jobs than the clerical workers. This was particularly true of the skilled manual workers, such as carpenters, machinists, plumbers and so on. And even the semi-skilled workers enjoyed their work more than the average office worker.

Q: What are the main things that make a man dissatisfied with his work?

A: In the Clark University study, men in all occupations who were dissatisfied were asked why.

Almost 50% said they didn't like the nature of the work, and felt it didn't jibe with their abilities.

Thirty-six per cent were discontented because they weren't being paid enough, or that opportunities for advancement were lacking.

Only 8% admitted that dislike for the boss, or policies of management, was their primary reason for dissatisfaction. But many more added remarks to the effect that the boss failed to encourage personal expression or reward initiative, etc.

Q: Can overwork cause you to have a nervous breakdown?

A: No. Leading authorities agree that hard work never gave anybody a nervous breakdown. Things which *do* produce nervous exhaustion are fear, worry, anxiety, frustration — often about your job. Overwork can help *prevent* a nervous breakdown by giving you less time to worry.

WATCH OUT FOR BOREDOM
Or Pretty Soon You Won't Care What Happens To You

An air of utter boredom hung over a small town in the U.S.A.
From somewhere behind the buildings that lined the dusty main
street, the monotonous drone of a power saw sounded, blending
with the steady hum of insects in the still air of the summer
afternoon. A few residents idled aimlessly in front of the shops
or clustered in front of the post office. Their faces were dull,
blank.

Then suddenly, almost in a matter of seconds, the whole
atmosphere changed. A tiny cloud of smoke appeared in the
far hills. A boy was the first to see it. His excited cry swept
the town's lethargy before it like a giant broom.

Eyes gleamed with excitement as people milled about, pointing, gesticulating. Someone ran to the phone to make further
inquiries. Others climbed to the town's best vantage point, at
the top of an abandoned tower. The fire was spreading swiftly
now. Flames mingled with smoke as the blaze began eating its
way along a high pine ridge. The townspeople broke into
excited cheering as fire engines clanged through the town, and
roared up the road that led to the hills. Almost as a body, town
residents climbed into their cars and followed.

Next day worried State authorities conferred for the dozenth
time with the district ranger. Fires had been breaking out in
this area on an average of two or three times a week. And the
authorities suspected that the fires were being started by the
residents themselves. Investigators sent into the region ran into
a solid wall of conspiratorial silence. Nobody would talk.

A leading psychologist volunteered his services. "I've got a
pretty strong idea," he told officials, "and I'd like the chance
to follow it up." The baffled authorities were only too glad
to give the psychologist the green light. At first the hill people
regarded him the passive suspicion reserved for "foreigners."
He had to win their confidence slowly.

When he returned from his mission, the authorities were
astonished. "Those people start the fires, all right," he told
them. "In fact they take turns in starting them! They do it

because they are bored — bored to the point where they just don't care what happens. Those fires break the monotony of their tedious, humdrum existence. And they look forward to them as to a picnic or a circus. Their lives are painfully dull.

"There's only one way to stop those fires. Provide the people with other forms of diversion — give them something else to look forward to. If you'll send social and recreational workers there to introduce sports, hobbies, dances, social get-togethers and the like — if you'll show these people how to provide recreation for themselves — you won't have any more fires."

They followed the psychologist's advice. It took a little time, because you can't teach people how to amuse themselves overnight, but the formula worked. There's been only one fire since — and that was started by a careless tourist.

Psychologists estimate that a large percentage of the forest fires that break out in the United States are started purposely by irresponsible persons who are bored to the point where touching off a blaze seems the most effective way to break the monotony. Once, in the space of a single week, 400 fires broke out in the East Texas timberlands. And J. O. Burnside, aptly named fire chief of the Texas forest service, states there is evidence that nine-tenths were started deliberately.

Boredom is dangerous because men and women will do almost anything to escape from it. Actually, scientific studies show that simple boredom is responsible for most anti-social behavior. This include marital infidelities, excessive drinking, brawls, major and petty crimes and juvenile delinquency.

Little Johnny ran away from home simply because he was bored with himself, and the prospect of getting away offered adventure. Adults disappear for exactly the same reason.

Teen-age Tommy was bored and restless, so he took to stealing cars. The thrill it gave him provided escape from monotony. Tommy's mother was bored too. And when she couldn't stand it any longer, she took a slightly less anti-social form of escape. She started playing bridge for stakes that greatly exceeded the family income.

Ignorance of what boredom really is, and what causes it,

makes many people try to escape it by running away from themselves. Marion W. was the daughter of a socially prominent family. One day at dinner she said she had a headache and wanted to walk down the road and get a little air. She never came back. Six months later, detectives hired by her frantic family found her working as a waitress in a restaurant under an assumed name. When asked why she had done it, the girl said simply that she was "bored to death with everything and just had to get away from it all." The family regarded this as a trivial excuse, and tried fruitlessly to discover the "real" reason.

Many people feel that it would be easy to escape boredom if they had plenty of money to do the sort of things they've always wanted to do. Maybe so, but studies show that boredom is much more prevalent among those who have plenty of money than among those who haven't.

There was the case of Sylvia S. She was beautiful. On her twenty-fourth birthday she inherited a fortune. She built a fabulous castle on an island in the Caribbean; she travelled to Paris, Cairo, Rio, Buenos Aires, and everywhere she went her beauty and her fortune proved an open sesame. She met everybody; she did everything. After a few years of this she simply took an overdose of sleeping pills. Her doctor wrote, "She was bored to death, literally."

The files of doctors and psychiatrists yield many cases where extreme chronic boredom has directly or indirectly driven the person to suicide.

Studies show that in the advanced stages of chronic boredom, a person actually does not care what happens to him. While he hasn't consciously decided that he wants to end it all, he does find it diverting to flirt with the idea — to see how close he can come to it without actually killing himself. And the closer the better.

He'll drive his car around a hazardous curve at 60 miles an hour, knowing that it's a gamble whether he makes it or not. He flirts with oblivion for the same reason that a bored and fed-up husband may flirt with another woman. Consciously and sub-consciously he wants a change — and he's reached the point where he doesn't much care what it is. There's another angle too. Boredom can't exist in the presence of danger.

The shocking lengths to which this kind of thing can go is typified by a press dispatch from Sacramento: "A kind of roulette is frequently played by drivers along the road from Sacramento to San Francisco. When two drivers recognize each other as their cars approach they start weaving from side to side of the road. At the last moment each decides which side of the road he is going to be on when the cars actually meet. In the last incident, both drivers decided they would be on the left side. The terrific impact of the collision completely demolished one car. One driver was killed instantly."

While most of us are seldom bored to the point where we are driven to extreme measures, studies show that almost nobody is completely immune. As a matter of fact, psychologists estimate that the average individual is bored more than a third of the time.

Well, then, exactly what is boredom? Is there a cure — and if so, what is it?

Scientists have gone to great lengths to find out the answers to these questions. And it hasn't been easy, for boredom is one of the most curious phenomena known to man. They found, for example, people are bored most of the time without even knowing why.

Mr. X. lounges on the terrace of a luxurious holiday resort. He is a fugitive from the monotonous grind at the office. He's escaped from the office, but not from boredom.

"Yes," he confesses, "I'm bored stiff. There's certainly no reason why I should be, but I am."

We've all felt that way. Wanting to do something, without knowing what that "something" is, is one of the prime causes of boredom.

Take the case of Harry S. He loves the soil. He's really happy when he can plant things and see them grow. But he takes a job in the city. He can make more money there, and get ahead faster. He thinks that is what he wants. But Harry doesn't get ahead. He hasn't let himself do what he really wants to do — and he's never very happy. Harry's fenced-in feeling will persist until he recognizes his inner urge and provides it with some means of expression.

There are two kinds of boredom. One is the self-starting variety which bores from within and has its cause in one's own personality. The other type, just as painful and almost as prevalent, is caused by one of two things:

1. *Insufficient motivation:* You'll be bored by any endeavor which is not motivated by adequate incentive or purpose *according to your own standards.* And work or play will tend to bore you unless the reward received is on a par with the effort expended.

The reward may be money, satisfaction, pleasure, advancement, credit for any job well-done or anything which seems worthwhile to *you.*

Try to analyze any job which bores you — identify the reward, as intangible as it may be — and you'll be able to throw yourself into the work or play without fear of boredom. If you can't do that, spend some of the energy you waste in being bored (for tests show that acute boredom consumes more nervous energy than the most violent exercise) in figuring out how to leave the job altogether or how to *make* it interesting.

2. *Repetitive Action:* Everyone's job and daily living involves doing the same things over and over again. And the more repetitious your work happens to be, the more you are apt to be bored by it.

Science has discovered, however, a number of ways to make repetitious work less monotonous — even agreeable. If, for example, it's conveniently possible for you to do your humdrum work to music, that is precisely what your psychologist would order.

Clinical tests have also proved that if you make a sincere effort to *pretend* an interest in a dull job, the work can be made to seem actually pleasant. If certain tasks are below your intelligence, occupying your hands but not your mind — housework, for example — make little projects to keep your brain occupied. Think about the *larger* view of the job at hand — where the bolts you are packing will be used, how the wearer will enjoy the shirt you are ironing — and the "little" job will seem more important and interesting.

The only real cure, of course, is to pick a job that's consistent with your intelligence − or to think of monotonous work as a stepping stone to a more stimulating occupation. In any case, the best rule about outwitting boredom is never to fight it. Fight the cause, not the boredom itself.

How can this be done? All you have to do is relax, mentally and physically. It's as simple as that. And here's why. When a state of mental or emotional tension exists, the brain does not function as it should. Its awareness becomes sluggish. Its ability to recognize and interpret our subconscious wishes deteriorates completely.

To make your innermost wishes intelligible to your conscious mind, it is therefore necessary to relax. Then what you really want to do will become discernible to you, and you'll be able to find means of expressing the frustrated urge which is responsible for your boredom. Significantly, tests have shown that boredom is always accompanied by extreme mental and physical tension. You can't be bored without being tense − it's psychologically impossible. And conversely, studies of the noted psychiatrist, Dr. David H. Fink, have shown that boredom cannot exist if you are relaxed.

Give this proven principle a trial. Just relax, let go completely . . . stretch out in a warm bath for a few minutes . . . concentrate on nothing . . . and just feel the tension ease out of your mind and muscles. And even before you've got yourself completely relaxed, you'll find that your boredom is slipping away.

HOW BORED ARE YOU?

1. In the morning, when you get up, do you dread going to work?

2. Do you "need" much more sleep than the average person? Do you have trouble waking up in the morning?

3. If you had a windfall of $10,000 would you give up your job either to loaf about or to try for a better job?

4. Does time go slowly during the day? Are you usually glad when another week's work is over?

5. Do you rather dread the weekend?

6. In the evening, when you're ready to go home from work, do you hang about, perhaps stop at a bar for a drink or two?

*7. Do most people seem pretty dull and stupid to you?

*8. Do you dislike being alone, even for short periods of time?

9. Do you find it difficult to sit still without having something to occupy yourself?

10. Do you often find yourself wishing you could "get away from it all"?

HOW TO SCORE: *"Yes" answers to questions 1 to 4 indicate you're bored with your job; 5 to 6 that you're bored with your home-life; 7 to 9 that you're bored with yourself; and 10 that you're just plain bored. Do something about it!*

(Questions 7 and 8 may seem contradictory, but they're not. The bored person may or may not find people dull, but he has to mix with people.)

HOW'S YOUR SENSE OF HUMOR?
There's More To It Than Joking

Virtually everybody likes to laugh, to be amused, to have their funnybones tickled — but human beings vary tremendously in their capacity to appreciate humor and to respond to it. Some people go through life finding very little that strikes them as laughable. Others seek amusement and diversion as some people seek happiness — by running after it — and the result more often than not is disappointment. Still others have the ability to see the funny side of almost any situation.

It goes without saying that the better your sense of humor, the more enjoyment you're getting out of life. And scientists have also found that your sense of humor reveals a great deal about your character, personality, and general outlook on life. Let's take a look at some of the most interesting and significant findings.

Is it true that intelligence and a well-developed sense of humor tend to go hand in hand?

Yes. Studies at Purdue University and at Vassar have shown conclusively that a keen appreciation of wit and humor is indicative of a correspondingly keen intelligence. Persons who scored highest ratings on I.Q. tests likewise showed the greatest ability to see the humorous side of things; and students who achieved the highest scholastic marks had the greatest appreciation for various types of humor. All up and down the line, evidence indicated that people who were less well-endowed intellectually encountered the fewest things which they considered amusing.

Have psychologists ever discovered what kind of joke people find most diverting?

Yes. At the University of Illinois, psychologists picked the funniest jokes they could find from every category, tried them out on assorted subjects, carefully checking their responses. It was found that the "shock" or surprise element in a joke was most likely to determine its humorous impact. And that the funniest story for any given person is the one which provides the greatest shock which he can take with a playful attitude.

Can you tell a man's personality type by the brand of humor he prefers?

Yes. Studies at London's University College show that introverts prefer humor of the more subtle, sophisticated variety; while extroverts show the strongest reference for jokes and witticisms which are simple, uncomplex, and uninvolved. The latter prefer humor of the blunter, direct-to-the-point, guffaw producing type; while the introvert is most partial to jokes which are more artfully and ingeniously contrived. Extroverts, incidentally, showed the greatest fondness for off-color humor.

A further study showed a definite relationship between a man's body build and the type of humor he prefers. In this investigation researchers classified subjects according to the three Kretschmer body types: (1) the short, stocky, thick-necked, heavy-set type, (2) the well-proportioned, well-muscled, athletic type, (3) the tall, lanky, lean-faced type.

Each of these types tended to have separate and distinct

humor preferences in common. The short, heavy-set type enjoyed simple down-to-earth humor; while the tall and lanky individuals inclined toward subtleties, play on words, and delayed-action effects; and the athletic type preferred humor which was direct and lacking shading or nuance.

Is it true that laughter is an indication of social status?

Harvard sociologist Axel Inkeles finds that laughter is very definitely a barometer of social status, and that the more often you laugh, the higher you are likely to be on the social scale. "Contrary to popular belief," says Professor Inkeles, "the lower you are in social status, the less likely you are to report having laughed during the past day."

Is it true that a well-developed sense of humor tends to go hand in hand with a well-balanced personality?

Yes. Research at Yale University shows that it very definitely does. The investigators found that the better adjusted a person is, the more readily he responds to the humor in jokes, cartoons, and everyday situations. Maladjusted people showed a far greater tendency to miss the point in a joke or witticism, to take seriously things which are meant to be funny, or to regard humor with either apprehension or indifference.

A good sense of humor requires the ability to regard things in their proper perspective, and less well-adjusted individuals tend to be lacking in this department. And their inclination to take themselves too seriously extends not only to humor, but to other things as well.

Is it true that persons with a good sense of humor are the hardest to fool or deceive?

Yes. The better developed a man's sense of humor is, the harder it is to trick him by bluff, cunning, flattery, or subterfuge. Nor is he likely to be beguiled or misled by what he reads, since he has a marked ability to read between the lines, to separate the wheat from the chaff, the truth from the half-truth. This has been demonstrated by researchers at Purdue University, where students who made the highest scores on sense-of-humor tests also scored highest on tests designed to evaluate astuteness, perspicacity, and level-headedness.

If a person fails to get the point of certain simple, easy-to-

*understand jokes, does that indicate his sense of humor is
lacking?*

Not necessarily. Humor reaction studies at Yale University
show that failure to understand a joke may be the result of a
person attempting to protect himself from the anxiety which
the joke arouses. In cases of this kind it was found that "there
is really a hidden wish not to understand the humor."

The investigators cite many clinical examples, including the
case of a highly intelligent scientist, who was head of a university department. He was shown a cartoon in which the boss
of a company was shown approaching the office suggestion
box. On the top of the box was a bottle marked "Poison."
The scientist couldn't understand the cartoon.

When the bottle of poison was pointed out to him, he
reacted with surprise; he hadn't noted it as such — even though
the label was plainly marked. And though the meaning of the
cartoon then immediately became clear to him, he still didn't
think it was funny.

Analysis revealed that the cartoon touched on a point that
was causing the scientist extreme worry. He was deeply concerned over whether he was being too strict or too lenient
with his subordinates, whether they liked and respected him
or hated him. He didn't get the point of the cartoon because
of his subconscious wish to shield himself from its painful
personal impact. It hit too hard and too close to home.

*Is it true that people who have the greatest appreciation of
humor tend to have the most sympathetic insight into the
character of others?*

Yes. Studies at Michigan State University show that people
who are the quickest to perceive the comic elements in a
cartoon, story, or situation have the greatest ability to sense
the underlying motivations of others, and to put themselves
in the other fellow's shoes. They possess in marked degree
a quality known as empathy — the ability to tune in on the
other person's wave length and look at the picture through
his eyes and from his point of view.

*Is a sense of humor an important factor where physical
health and well-being are concerned?*

Yes. Findings of the Michigan State University studies as well as those of other leading investigations, make it clear that humor, and the ability to perceive it in everyday situations, provide a safety valve for the discharge of health-sapping tensions. Investigations have similarly shown that cultivating the habit of seeing the humorous side of things is an invaluable aid to promoting health, happiness, and longevity. Not only is laughter frequently the best medicine, but it's also the pleasantest to take.

OPTING FOR OPTIMISM
Even A "Born Pessimist" Can Find Ways To Change

You can make $1 million a year and find life dull. You can make $5,000 a year and find life exhilarating. You cannot change the world, but you can change your outlook. The choice ranges from the pessimist's murky gray to the optimist's rosy hues. Science has been looking into optimism and pessimism and has made surprising discoveries.

At Wesleyan University, psychologists James A. Vaughan, Jr., and Robert H. Knapp tested students to determine each one's outlook on life. Here are some of their findings.

Pessimists frequently complain of bad luck. They feel that they have more than their share of misfortunes. Is this true, or do they just imagine it?

It is quite likely to be true. The chronic pessimist tends to be failure prone, just as some persons are accident prone. The pessimist unconsciously sets himself life goals which will be extremely difficult for him to achieve. The pessimist also develops failure expectancy, and often seems genuinely disappointed when things turn out all right.

Is there more than one kind of pessimism?

There are three kinds. 1. Universal pessimism: the belief that the world, unsympathetic or indifferent to man, is an inhospitable place to live. 2. Moral pessimism: a distrust of the motives of others, a cynical attitude toward friendship and altruism. ("He has certainly gone out of his way to be nice to us. I wonder what *he* wants?") 3. Will pessimism: the belief that man is unable to control his emotions, but is driven by forces over which he has no control. This attitude is expressed in such expressions as "What's the use?" "The dice are loaded against you." "You're licked before you start!"

In the studies, the universal pessimists agreed with statements such as these. "The world is a great, cruel, impersonal machine, unresponsive to man's hopes, wishes, and fears"; and, "This world is a place of suffering. The mere absence of pain is man's greatest good."

Universal optimists, on the other hand, agreed with such statements as these: "There is a tendency toward order and goodness inherent in the world. Although evil or chaos might sometimes gain the upper hand, in the long run, goodness and order will prevail." "There are valid knowledge and wisdom which should guide our conduct, and man should devote his life to discovering them."

The moral pessimist agreed with these statements: "Man's advances in the world of science are likely to prove more harmful than beneficial, because man's ethics cannot keep pace with his intellect"; and, "Man is torn between two wills, a good and a bad; and the good is seldom able to overcome the bad."

The moral optimist rejects those statements completely. He checked off statements such as these: "The unique quality of man is his capacity of love. Human society is a monument to human sympathy and cooperation"; and, "Man is by nature a social animal; therefore it is only a matter of time until love and understanding conquer hate and suspicion, and wars will be no more."

The will pessimist shares the general outlook expressed by these statements: "In this great universe of ours man is a mere insect, an ant, and his mind is puny and ineffectual, as compared with the boundless universe around him"; and,

"Man's reason is, in the end, ineffectual in guiding his behavior. His life is determined basically by unconscious drives that he cannot know or control."

The will optimist does not look at it this way at all. Instead, he agrees that: "Man is unique among animals because he can reason, and therefore control and direct his own behavior"; and says, "Man alone, apart from all other creatures, is unique in the universe because he has a soul; he will live in some other form when all else has perished."

How does a pessimist get that way?

Environment has much to do with it. The person who experiences repeated failure during his formative years is likely to become a pessimist.

However, one of the most striking differences between pessimists and optimists revealed by the study was their attitudes toward themselves, and most particularly their relationship with their consciences. Pessimists tend to disregard the promptings of conscience, to regard it as something alien and malevolent, and to reject its demands. They conceived of conscience in terms of a strait jacket, a threatening father, a secret betrayer, a vicious bully.

Conversely, the psychologists discovered that the optimists looked upon conscience as a source of strength and of benign guidance, heeded its promptings, and were on good terms with it. They thought of conscience as a hidden lamp, a just judge, an accurate compass, a protective armor.

The investigators concluded that acceptance of the demands of conscience makes for optimism; their rejection leads to pessimism.

How does the optimist differ from the pessimist?

The studies showed that people who are interested in others, who have the capacity for warm relationships with people, are usually optimists. The pessimist's thoughts turn inward. He is interested in himself, often to the almost complete exclusion of others. One psychologist says, "Pessimism is essentially a feeling of inadequacy experienced by a person who is too self-centered." Another finding: optimists are much more religious; pessimists tend to be preoccupied with material things.

Tests also showed these differences. Optimists have, on the average, greater physical and mental energy than pessimists. They also tend to be more impatient, more excitable, and much more given to acting on impulse. Pessimists are more subject to depression, more troubled by phobias and compulsions.

If you are more of a pessimist than you would like to be, what can you do about it?

Be realistic about your life goals. It is fine to be ambitious, but do not set your hurdles too high. Setting goals which you can reach boosts optimism and self-confidence.

Since conscience seems to be an optimist's best friend and a pessimist's worst enemy, the most important step is to get on friendlier terms with it.

A LOOK AT LONELINESS
You Must Be Comfortable With Yourself
Before You Can Be Comfortable With Others

One of the strangest things about loneliness is its paradox. Nothing that human beings experience is more contradictory. You can be lonely without being alone. The loneliest type of loneliness is the kind you sometimes feel when you're with a crowd. And it follows that you can be alone without feeling the least bit lonely. In fact, if you're like most of us, there are times when getting completely away from people is one of the most blissful feelings on earth.

Is it true that some people are never lonely?

No. As one leading psychiatrist observes after evaluating a consensus of studies: Loneliness is a universal experience. Some people feel it only periodically. Others feel a sense of loneliness much of the time. Contrary to what many people believe, the loneliest people are *not* those with the fewest friends and acquaintances. You can be on a first-name basis with scores of people — as are countless celebrities, politicians, and others in the public eye — and yet actually be so lonely that you can't bear being by yourself for any length of time.

There is one aspect of loneliness that no one completely escapes. Psychologist James F. T. Bugental describes it as "the feeling of being a part of humankind, and yet apart from every other human being." For, as he points out, as a man comes to recognize himself as an individual, to identify himself as a unique being, he cannot help experiencing a sense of loneliness.

Is it true that many people are lonely because they have never discovered the art of being themselves?

Yes. There are many types of loneliness. One common variety has a simple cause and an equally simple cure. It invariably results when, instead of "being himself," a person plays a part which he fancies will make him more acceptable to others. This prevents people from getting to know the real person. In effect, they remain strangers to him. This precludes the possibility of any *real* relationship with others, and the result is loneliness.

Also his social masquerade causes him to lose touch with his own real feelings, thoughts, and experiences. Already estranged from others, he becomes a stranger to himself as well. This can be alleviated by the simple process of "being oneself."

Is it true that loneliness can sometimes be good for you?

Yes. Under some circumstances, loneliness can have a very positive value. Professor Paul Miller, University of California psychiatrist, has made a study of the effects of loneliness on people. His conclusion: Loneliness, within tolerable limits, provides a good opportunity for people to get in touch with themselves.

Many people feel cut off from both themselves and others because they have never taken the time to get acquainted with themselves, to look within and find out what they're really like.

Is it true that a lot of people are lonely because they don't like themselves?

Yes. As one specialist in human behavior has observed, "The man who rejects himself will be rejected by others. And the person who is hostile to himself will manifest it by hostility to his fellow men." Thus a vicious circle results, leaving little room for anything but loneliness, hostility, and self-pity. The cure for this kind of loneliness could be simple. Get on better terms with yourself, be more charitable to your weaknesses, and more generous regarding your faults. Remember no one is perfect and don't expect yourself to be. Remember also that you won't be estranged from others if you aren't estranged from yourself.

Are many people lonely because they feel they are too unattractive or inadequate to attract friends?

Yes. However, this psychological block which blights their lives is completely unnecessary. They have only to realize what sociologist Father Andrew M. Greeley points out in his treatise *The Friendship Game:* "The truth of the matter is that we are all attractive. There is no such thing, at least outside of the mental institutions, as a human personality that does not have the potential to attract other human personalities."

He notes that authentic human attractiveness, the kind that not only attracts friends but holds them, stems from the warmth of personality, the pleasantness of our attitude and outlook which communicates itself to others. These are things within our control, and they count for a great deal more in the long run than the shape of our nose or the color of our eyes.

Is it true that one of the best antidotes for loneliness is to take a trip, and meet new people, encounter new experiences?

No. As the noted psychiatrist, Dr. Klaus W. Berblinger, observes in summing up the findings of a study of loneliness, this is not the answer. "The airborne globetrotter may, in less than 36 hours, have been exposed to a variety of languages and landscapes, but has actually not made any meaningful contacts." The prerequisite for the avoidance of loneliness is the establishment of meaningful relationships, and this is dependent on our willingness to communicate on a two-way basis with fellow human beings. In simplest terms, this means sharing ourselves with congenial persons, exchanging our thoughts, concepts, and feelings. As this serves to renew our sense of well-being, we lose the feeling of being cut off, out of step with the world, out of context with our fellow man.

It has been truly said that many people are lonely because they build walls instead of bridges.

VI.

AS TIME GOES ON

Physical growth stops in the 20's for the average person, but mental growth can continue into old age. The patterns of that mental growth can be detected in the very young child as well as the pattern of his physical growth. Just as in the case of physical maturity, there is a mental maturity that man can reach, but the mental maturity is a sign of his continuing growth, not of its stoppage as in the physical body. How well you size up or understand another person depends to a great degree on how well you have learned what mental maturity he has reached. With that knowledge you can often forgive much, and just as often protect yourself from conditions you cannot otherwise control.

WHY CHILDREN ARE SO HAPPY
. . . And What You Can Do To Keep Them That Way

Poets and parents have suspected that children are happier than adults. For children seem to have an innate sense of wonder and goodness that adults have lost.

Pediatricians, psychoanalysts, and researchers have confirmed these suspicions. Their studies show that children's personalities are better integrated, their actions and attitudes more soundly motivated, than those of adults.

They also have concluded that you, as a thoughtful, observant parent, can learn more from your child than you'll teach him. Here are some of their most recent findings

What is the most important thing to give a child?

Love. No amount of toys, food, or hygiene can replace it. A very close emotional relationship between child and parent is vital to the child's sense of security and is the best insurance that he won't become neurotic in later years. So don't be afraid of spoiling your child by showering him with too much love and affection.

Is it dangerous to use fear to make a child obedient?

Yes. A child's fears should be allayed, not aroused. Fears and phobias can make a child withdraw inside himself, arresting his personality development, and undermining his all-important sense of security.

Medical studies show that a child reacts physically to abnormal fears. A youngster's insecurity can completely upset his metabolism. He may become thin and under-nourished as his fears interfere with digestive processes. Or, he may become obese because he is socially insecure. Fear of ridicule or criticism can make him avoid other children. To compensate for the loss of playmates, he begins to gorge himself with food. With time, the layers of fat seem to protect him from the outside world.

If your child seems sensitive to the jibes of schoolmates, listen sympathetically when he unburdens himself. Make him understand that it's natural for children to speak that way occasionally. Quiet his fears and bolster his ego.

Does time pass more swiftly for a child?

Yes. Your child actually lives more in one year than you do in a decade. Scientists have demonstrated that a child ages more between the years of 10 and 16 than he does in a 45-year period later in life. It may help you understand your child's moods if you remember that he experiences more joy, exaltation, sorrow, and disappointment in one single day than you do in a week.

Does a child live faster biologically?

Yes. A child's metabolism is much more rapid than an adult's. Tests show, for example, that a wound that takes 30 days to heal in a boy takes 76 days to heal in a man 40 years old.

Will the child who spends most of his time playing grow up to be irresponsible?

No. For the young child, play is a serious business. A University of California professor points out that the child at play is not only enjoying the activity for its own sake, but he also is wrestling with personal problems and anxieties of all kinds. He is often anxious about things which are unrelated

314

to his immediate activity, often frustrated by a world which, no matter how child-oriented, is still an adult's.

Can too much sleep make a child neurotic?

Yes. Consistent overdoses of sleep can cause your child to wet his bed, bang his head against objects, talk or walk in his sleep, and behave neurotically.

It's especially bad to force a child to remain in bed after he wakes in the morning. A healthy child of three awakes with the dynamic force of an animal and the vocal exuberance of a bird. When parents repress these animal spirits by making him stay in bed, the child feels cowed and completely inhibited.

Does an infant learn baby-talk from his parents?

Yes. Baby-talk, studies have shown, is not natural to babies. Actually, parents first teach their children baby-talk, then try to break them of it afterwards. Child specialists regret this situation. It's difficult enough for a child to learn to speak correctly and understandably, without having to unlearn bad habits.

Do some children misbehave because their parents want them to?

Yes. Psychiatrists explain that an ill-behaved child can act out a parent's hidden, forbidden, antisocial impulses. For example, a parent may resent that Jones down the block has a new color TV set or an expensive, plush rug. The parent can't express this resentment directly, but if his *child* spills something on the neighbor's rug or twists a dial off the TV set, there's not much anybody can do about it.

Should a child be encouraged to tell his dreams?

Yes. Children's dreams are almost always undisguised expressions of hopes, fears, and problems.

One of the best ways to know your child better is to encourage him to tell you his dreams. You may learn things about his mental and emotional processes that you would otherwise never learn.

How important are leisure-time activities for children?

Very. Researchers at California's Institute of Human Development demonstrate a definite relationship "between childhood leisure-time activity and satisfaction and psychological adjustment at age 30." By observing a child's development between the ages of 8 and 11, they can predict how well-adjusted he'll be at 30. The more a child is getting out of life then, the fewer personality conflicts and emotional problems he'll have later when he reaches his most productive years.

Do most children have qualities of genius?

They do indeed. The principal characteristic of a genius is his receptivity to subconscious and intuitive processes. Children share this uninhibited mental quality. Very often, they show genuine creativity when young, but lose their touch of genius when they grow up. Unfortunately, teaching a child to accept passively the ideas and conclusions of his parents or society seems to stifle original thinking.

So give your child a break. Encourage his creativity as you would nurture a delicate seedling.

WHAT CHILDREN FEAR
Mostly The Big Bad Wolf

One child psychologist says that you do not really know your child until you know what he is afraid of. Children's fears differ from those of most adults. Many of the things they find most frightening, adults find either laughable or inconsequential, and many of the things which cause adults deep concern seldom bother children at all.

What are the chief fears of most children?

University of California psychologist Adah Maurer systematically studied the fears of a random selection of children. "Many of the things they have been taught to be careful about, they do not fear at all, such as street traffic and germs," he concluded. "The strange truth is that they often fear what is an unrealistic source of danger in our urban civilization: wild animals. Almost all five and six-year-olds and more than half of seven to 12-year-olds says they are afraid of snakes, lions, and tigers. Not until age 12 do most children recognize real sources of personal danger."

Studies of children's fears conducted at Florida State University also showed animals to be a chief fear of most children. This included not only jungle creatures but also strange dogs, spiders, bugs, and other insects.

Other fears included "ghosts or spooky things"; being alone, particularly at night; as well as tornadoes, thunder, and lightning. Also ranking high were fears of getting lost, or of "something happening to mom or dad"; anxieties regarding personal appearance, of not being accepted by other children because of looks or dress; and being too fat or too thin.

Does birth-order affect a child's fears?

Yes. Psychological studies at Yale University show that first-born children tend to be much more frightened by the prospect of accident or physical injury than other children. They tended to avoid dangerous activity. Even in sports they were found much more likely than others to avoid those with high risks, preferring the activities involving the smallest physical hazard. But first-borns are no more fearful than others in situations where the threat is not physical. The answer to why this should be awaits further research. It has been suggested that first-borns may actually have a lower pain threshold than later children.

What about fear of the dark?

One study found about one child in five to be afraid in the dark, or reluctant to go to sleep without a light on. But this fear tended to disappear after the age of seven, researchers discovered.

Do girls have more fears than boys?

Yes. Girls are not only fearful of more objects and situations, but they are more deeply affected by them.

If your child is afraid of more things than the average boy or girl, does that mean he is likely to be neurotic?

No. At the University of Detroit the fears of normal and emotionally disturbed children, matched by age, sex, intelligence, and background, were carefully evaluated in interviews made by a team of psychologists. In all age groups, normal children

317

named more fears than did disturbed children. Even though the latter groups had fewer fears, they experienced them more often than did the normal children.

How do the fears of normal boys and girls differ from those with emotional problems?

The Detroit University study showed that emotionally disturbed boys were appreciably more fearful of being alone, more frightened of the dark and of fires than were normal children. Emotionally disturbed girls evidenced a much greater fear of ghosts, of growing up and getting older, of facing life and assuming responsibilities.

Do children's fears decrease with age?

Some do, some do not. The same study showed that "the fears of animals, the dark, being alone, ghosts, and scary games or movies decreased with age." Fears which increased with age were fear of making a mistake and having others laugh, reading or reciting in front of others, and fear of fires.

Is fear contagious? Do children "catch" many of their fears from their parents?

Yes, says Dr. B. M. Levinson of Yeshiva University. Whenever the parent shows fear, even covertly, the child will take on his mother's or father's anxieties in addition to his own. This is particularly likely if the child wishes to be like his parents and looks to them for security.

What can you do to help your child cope with his fears?

Make it clear to him that fear is normal. Encourage him to confide his fears to you. If he is reluctant, tell him some of the things you were afraid of as a child. When a child's fears are kept secret, they tend to multiply and magnify. When anxieties are shared with a sympathetic and understanding person, they are less frightening.

Assure your child that having fears does not make him different from others and does not mean there is anything wrong with him. You might point out to him that it would be abnormal for him *not* to have any anxieties.

HOW MUCH DO YOU KNOW ABOUT CHILDREN?
Maybe They Understand You Better Than You Do Them

Children often understand their parents better than parents understand their children. Psychologists and sociologists have been finding out things about children which can help parents toward a clearer view of their offspring's behavior. Here are some of the findings.

Should you worry if your child doesn't always make good grades in school?

Not necessarily. He has a lot of very distinguished company. Sociologist Henry Pang, who studied the matter, notes that "eminent persons who disliked school and whose performance was mediocre or poor include Isaac Newton, Leo Tolstoy, Winston Churchill, Frederic Chopin, Theodore Dreiser, Pablo Picasso, Ivan Turgenev, and others too numerous to mention. Many of these persons, Churchill and Picasso for example, refused to learn if they were not interested." Many eminent persons, he goes on, displayed no particular brilliance as youngsters even in the fields in which they later won fame. Teachers often disliked Einstein for his independent attitude and even thought him dull. After he became famous, he discovered that many of his former teachers could not even remember him as a student.

Conversely, the world is full of *A* students no one ever heard of, who have failed to distinguish themselves in any field whatever. So don't fret about your child if he is not at the top of his class. Studies show that people with a high degree of creative intelligence often are "late bloomers." It takes longer for their abilities to develop. Then, too, they often have difficulty adjusting their own "mental set" to the systems and methods of formal education.

At what point can you tell whether a child is likely to be early or late in developing?

At the Institute of Psychiatry, London, 4,000 boys and girls were given scholastic and ability tests, then subjected to standard-personality tests. The findings indicated that introverts tend to be late developers as compared with extroverts.

Parents should remember that individual personality factors determine a child's rate of development. To attempt to push him faster than his natural gait allows is to risk handicapping his progress. If he is made to feel that he is not progressing as fast as his parents feel he should, that can seriously undermine his self-esteem.

Oddly enough, parents can accept a child's learning to walk at a late age, but they worry when he does not advance in school with other children of the same age. But all studies show that some of the most intelligent children mature at a slow rate.

Who are best at exercising self-control and resisting temptations: boys or girls?

Psychologists at Southern Illinois University explored this interesting question by testing 114 children — 53 boys and 61 girls — aged six to eight. Each child was taken into a room by himself where 12 attractive toys and a jar of candy were displayed on a table. The investigator then excused himself for a few minutes, telling the child that he would play a game with him when he came back, and admonishing him not to touch the things on the table, explaining that "they are for a party in another grade." The attendant then stayed away for 15 minutes, while another investigator noted the child's actions from a concealed observation booth.

The children behaved in three characteristic ways: 1. One group showed complete self-control and did little more than glance at the toys and candy on the table. 2. Others showed strong interest in the array of sweets and playthings, and had difficulty keeping their eyes off them. 3. Some yielded to temptation, and played with the toys or sampled the candy. Some 39% of the children yielded to temptation, but the majority (61%) did not. There were "no significant differences between boys and girls in their ability to resist temptation." The report states, however, that girls resisted temptation longer, and when they did yield, they spent significantly less time at the forbidden behavior.

What makes some children accident prone?

The California Department of Public Health made a study

of 8,874 boys and girls aged four to 18, from which were selected 684 children representative of those who had a high, medium, or low accident record. Findings of the investigation: the higher the boys' accident rate, the more likely they were to be daring, active, exploring, and extroverted. The boys who had the most accidents also tended to be the most aggressive and hostile toward their peers, their teachers, and their parents. They were also characterized as "having a need always to win," and "to be impulsive, and to get angry when frustrated."

The personality profile for the accident-prone girls was much the same as for the boys, except that instead of hostility and over-rebelliousness, they exhibited a strong need to be the center of attention and to indulge in various forms of attention-getting behavior. The investigators also noted that "although physical disabilities such as poor eyesight and hearing are associated with higher accident liability for girls, this was not true of the boys."

Do children get stomach ulcers just as adults do?

Yes. A study of more than 300 ulcer cases among children has shown that a high-strung youngster gets ulcers for the same reason that a harried executive does: nervous tension. "Juvenile ulcer" was found to occur most typically in sensitive children subjected to stress or anxiety by problems at home or worry about school. Frequently, the study showed, such children failed to express their feelings and tended to keep them bottled up.

The findings suggest that if you have a sensitive child he may be affected by stresses and anxieties which you don't even suspect. Often he feels that he might be laughed at or misunderstood if he were to reveal his fears. Since pent-up anxieties can cause both ulcers and other stress ailments, it is important that you constantly reassure him and encourage him to get worries off his chest.

If a person has a happy childhood, is he likely to be less sensitive to pain?

Yes. Findings of a study conducted at the Mental Health Research Institute, in which pain-thresholds were compared with the kind of childhood experienced by subjects, showed that those with happy childhoods were appreciably less sensitive to pain than those who grew up under unhappy circumstances, or who in general did not enjoy life during their formative years. So the happier your child is while he is growing up, the less pain he will feel from a tooth or tummy ache, or even when he hits his thumb with a hammer.

Is it true that young children are often better judges of people than adults are?

Yes. A young child will often sense things about another's character which will cause him to form an instant like or dislike of the person. And the child's judgment is likely to prove more accurate than those of many adults who take longer to make up their minds, but who miss many of the clues which a child immediately perceives. A child's powers of observation are more direct, more acute, and less easily distracted by surface mannerisms and modes of speech. A child can often see through a magician's tricks and sleight-of-hand when a grown-up cannot.

More recent studies at the University of Florida demonstrate that young children are superior at judging character by the tone and quality of a person's voice, the way he speaks, rather than by what he says. They are, say the investigators, "more sensitive to nonlinguistic vocal cues than are older children or adults."

Will your child learn best by listening or by reading?

At New York University, investigators checked the performance of more than 200 boys and girls on standard reading and listening tests. Each was then given a personality test. The surprising results: children with introvert tendencies were better at listening, and got more out of verbal instruction than did the extroverts. The latter were much better readers than listeners.

Other studies have also shown that introverts are more "audio-oriented," more receptive to what they hear. This applied to music, speech, and other sounds around them. Tests showed them to be quicker to respond to a person's tone of voice or manner of speaking. Extroverts were found to be better in all tasks requiring a high degree of visual attention, which, of course, includes reading.

322

TAKE THE TEEN-TEST
Parents Can Get To Know Their Kids

Are boys more romantic than girls? Why do teen-agers dress that way? Are youngsters lazy? Here's a quiz for the whole family for and about teen-agers. It gives you a chance to see whether you understand teen-agers better than they do themselves. Could be. Your score will tell.

1. Most teen-agers are lazy. True ( ) False ( )

2. The smartest teen-agers have the least trouble coping with the problems of adolescence and adjusting to the realities of life. True ( ) False ( )

3. Teen-agers who go on to college are luckier in love than those who stop at high school. True ( ) False ( )

4. Teen-agers who dress the most conservatively tend to have the best-balanced personalities. True ( ) False ( )

5. In most cases, it's not the teen-ager who has the most brains and ability who is the most popular. True ( ) False ( )

6. Teen-age boys are more romantic than teen-age girls. True ( ) False ( )

7. Time goes by much faster for teen-agers than for older persons. True ( ) False ( )

8. Teen-agers with a high I.Q. are more affected by lack of sleep than others. True ( ) False ( )

9. Most teen-agers dislike being told what to do; they like to think things out for themselves and act on their own decisions. True ( ) False ( )

10. It's better for a teen-ager's parents to be too strict than too lenient. True ( ) False ( )

Answers:

1. *False.* Most teen-agers have energy to spare — and the desire to exert it. But they channel it in directions that hold interest for them. As the noted psychiatrist, Dr. David H. Fink, points out — provide a teen-ager with adequate incentive and purpose and he'll really apply himself. But if a project does not have these qualities for him, his reaction will be that of boredom and disinterest — but that is not laziness.

2. *False.* Studies of teen-age boys and girls conducted at

Ohio Wesleyan University showed that it's the other way around. Students with higher-than-average I.Q.'s tended to be less happily adjusted than those with more modest mental abilities.

3. *True.* Wide-scale studies sponsored by the National Office of Vital Statistics show that boys and girls who go to college have a much better chance of finding their ideal mate than those whose education ends with high school.

4. *False.* Psychological studies conducted at the Drexel Institute of Technology show that students who go in for gay and colorful attire tend to be much better-adjusted mentally and emotionally than those whose dress is more conservative.

5. *False.* Brooklyn College studies show that those who have brains, talent and creative ability have the inside track where popularity is concerned. Other studies show that teen-agers who are gifted in the I.Q. department are more interested in others, recover from the effects of quarreling more quickly, hold fewer grudges.

6. *True.* When boys reach the age when they become aware of the attraction of the opposite sex, they tend to be much more romantic than girls. In a sociological study of over 900 teen-agers conducted at the University of Redlands, it was the boys who were most inclined to be starry-eyed idealists where romance was concerned.

7. *False.* Studies conducted by Veterans Administration psychologists show that time tends to crawl at a snail's pace for adolescents. For the oldster, time appears to be fleeting. That's one reason why teen-agers tend to be restless and impatient. Time passes slower for them than for the rest of us — and they want to give it a shot in the arm.

8. *True.* Studies conducted at a leading research foundation show that not getting enough sleep increases feelings of frustration and aggression, and has a strong effect on social behavior — particularly among those in the adolescent and young adult age-group. It was found that those of higher intelligence are more adversely affected by lack of sleep than those with lower I.Q.'s.

9. *False.* The Purdue University Opinion Panel surveyed U.S.

teen-agers on this question. The majority indicated that they prefer to go along with the crowd. They didn't want to be "different" or "odd ball."

10. *False.* In studies conducted at Columbia University, youngsters were divided into two groups: 1. those who were brought up in good, loving but strictly disciplined homes, 2. those who were brought up in good, loving homes, but whose parents were extraordinarily permissive. The youngsters in the group where parental discipline had been the most permissive averaged significantly better personality scores. They tended to have more initiative and self-reliance, were more cooperative, had less inner hostility and more friendly feelings toward others; they also showed more spontaneity, originality and creativity. Note that "permissive" does not mean no discipline. It does not mean that parental rules and edicts are not enforced. But it does mean that they are more flexible. It means bringing insight and understanding to bear on a child's individual problems and needs. It means fitting the discipline to the child, rather than vice-versa.

FASCINATING FACTS ON
WHAT MAKES TEEN-AGERS TICK
What They Think About Parents,
About Going Steady, And About Taking Risks

Questions

1. Most teen-agers think they know more than their parents do, and feel that adults are "squares" who don't know what the score is. True (　) False (　)

2. Most teen-agers approve of boys and girls "going steady" while in high school. True (　) False (　)

3. When a girl really wants something, she'll take bolder risks to achieve it than a boy will. True (　) False (　)

4. Teen-agers who are most tolerant of others — where creed,

color and nationality are concerned — are the happiest and have the best-adjusted personalities. True ( ) False ( )

5. Most teen-agers feel it's okay for high-schoolers to smoke. True ( ) False ( )

6. Teen-agers who are least influenced by what the crowd thinks rate the highest with their fellows. True ( ) False ( )

7. Teen-agers from poor families are friendlier and more sociable than those from rich families. True ( ) False ( )

8. Teen-age boys are happier than teen-age girls. True ( ) False ( )

9. Teen-agers play an important part in influencing the kind of car the family purchases. True ( ) False ( )

10. Assigning a teen-ager individual chores and household duties to perform helps to build character and a sense of responsibility for his adult years. True ( ) False ( )

Answers

1. *False.* University of Chicago investigators surveying cross sections of both parents and adolescents, found that teen-agers actually tend to idealize adults, and rate them much higher than their parents do. The study showed that actually adolescents believe adults are superior to teen-agers in intelligence, general ability, fairness, and good judgment.

2. *False.* A teen-age opinion survey by Purdue University showed that a scant 50% of America's teen-agers believe it's a good idea for high-school students to go steady. The idea was least popular among teen-agers from "working class" families only 43% of them are in favor of it.

3. *True.* Recent studies by the National Institute of Mental Health show that when a girl really sets her heart on something she'll take bigger chances than a boy to achieve it.

For example, she may risk riding on the back of a motor-cycle if she feels that it will further a romance. For similar reasons, a girl who can't swim will go sailboat racing with a boy.

However, girls are much less prone to taking risks "just for the heck of it." The studies showed that unless she feels that the stake is vitally important, she plays her cards conservatively.

4. *False.* Studies of teen-agers conducted at a leading university show that those who were most tolerant of others

were not well-adjusted. Neither were those who were least tolerant. It was the boys and girls midway between the two extremes who were found to be the most happily adjusted.

5. *False.* A nationwide survey of representative young people by the Purdue University Opinion Panel showed that more than three-quarters of the nation's teen-agers disapprove of high-school students smoking. However, almost 40% of them admit they smoke. The survey also showed that though nearly all teen-agers disapprove of drinking, one-quarter of them admit they drink. Said one girl: "It's hard to say 'I don't care to' when all the rest of the gang are saying 'Ah, come on.' "

6. *True.* Recent studies sponsored by Vanderbilt University show that the more easily a teen-ager is influenced by his fellows, the less status he is accorded by them — and vice versa. In other words, the investigation showed that it's the fellow who thinks for himself who is the most looked up to.

7. *False.* Contrary to popular belief studies conducted at Vanderbilt University indicate that members of well-to-do families tend to be more gregarious, social-minded, and friendly toward others than members of poor families.

8. *True.* Evidence indicates that boys are happier. A survey of a cross-section of 1,100 teen-agers by the University of Oklahoma showed that girls average almost twice as many fears, worries, and anxieties as boys do. And other studies show girls to be the most subject to personality conflicts.

9. *False.* Marketing surveys evaluated at the University of Michigan's conference on consumer behavior show that Sis and Junior have little or no voice in the kind of car the family buys. Mom and Dad put their heads together, make the decision, and that's that.

10. *False.* Studies conducted by psychology professor Dale B. Harris, at Pennsylvania State University, show that — despite the cherished American tradition to the contrary — there is no necessary relation between the chores a teen-ager is assigned and the sense of responsibility he shows later.

No doubt chores are helpful, but only if properly assigned. The study showed that too many urgent and serious duties, assumed too early, can actually have an adverse effect on the teen-age boy or girl.

HOW EMOTIONALLY MATURE ARE YOU?
Find Out In Two Minutes

Your emotional maturity is directly related to how happy you are, how successful your marriage is, what kind of a friend you will make, and how you bear up under everyday existence.

How do you know whether you are mature or not? You can find out in two minutes, thanks to research completed under the direction of Iowa State University's sociologist Dwight G. Dean. Dr. Dean's early studies revealed that emotional maturity consisted of more than a dozen different qualities. He then devised a special test to measure those qualities.

Here is a simplified version of the test. It will tell you how emotionally mature you are, and help you to discover any problems you may have. It is difficult to see yourself as clearly as another person can, so it is best that you take this test with someone else. You rate him, and he rates you. If you are taking the test by yourself, pretend that you are someone else describing yourself. Be as objective as humanly possible while rating yourself on the characteristics listed. Place a check mark in the space after the statement which *most frequently* applies.

1. A. Accepts responsibility for unfortunate situations which he has brought upon himself, rather than blaming others. ( )
   B. When upset by being frustrated, resorts to fuming, feeling hurt, or acting peevish. ( )
   C. Sometimes is characterized by *A*, sometimes by *B*. ( )
2. A. Works off anger in sports or other physical activity. ( )
   B. When angry or disappointed, sulks, throws things, or takes it out on other people. ( )
   C. Sometimes is characterized by *A*, sometimes by *B*. ( )
3. A. Does not resent reasonable rules and regulations. ( )
   B. Resents regulations which restrict him, whether they are reasonable or not. ( )
   C. Sometimes is characterized by *A*, sometimes by *B*. ( )
4. A. Feels "all of a piece," and has a clearly defined sense of purpose. ( )

328

B. Has marked changes of mood; feels this way one day, that way the next. Has many enthusiasms, but they tend to be short-lived. (   )

C. Sometimes is characterized by *A*, sometimes by *B*. (   )

5. A. Does not make unreasonable demands for special privileges; doesn't mind waiting his turn; and if in a hurry, holds his impatience in check and doesn't make a fuss about it. (   )

B. Becomes a nuisance in order to get his own way. Likes to throw his weight around on occasion. (   )

C. Sometimes is characterized by *A*, sometimes by *B*. (   )

6. A. Seeks facts before making decisions. (   )

B. Acts impulsively without considering consequences.(   )

C. Sometimes is characterized by *A*, sometimes by *B*. (   )

7. A. Views the love relationship as beautiful and God-given. (   )

B. Seems unable to give love for fear of being hurt. (   )

C. Sometimes is characterized by *A*, sometimes by *B*. (   )

8. A. Is mentally alert and eager to learn. (   )

B. Seldom reads about anything outside his own particular field of special interests. (   )

C. Sometimes is characterized by *A*, sometimes by *B*. (   )

9. A. Carefully evaluates new ideas, rather than accepting or rejecting them blindly. (   )

B. Is unable to follow a line of thought to its logical conclusion; gets sidetracked or loses interest. (   )

C. Sometimes is characterized by *A*, sometimes by *B*. (   )

10. A. Is dependable, keeps his promises. Faces the consequences of his own acts without falling back on excuses. (   )

B. Makes commitments and then forgets to follow through on them. Often has to be reminded of his obligations. Frequently misses appointments without bothering to cancel. (   )

C. Sometimes is characterized by *A*, sometimes by *B*. (   )

11. A. Can enter imaginatively into the problems and joys of others. (   )

B. Is largely absorbed in self-interest, monopolizes conversations; tends to be unaware that others might like to speak. ( )

C. Sometimes is characterized by *A*, sometimes by *B*. ( )

12. A. Is able to communicate thoughts, ideas, and feelings of all kinds ranging from small talk to intimacy. ( )

B. Has difficulty in conveying thoughts to others; conversation is largely platitudes, cliches, and ineffectual expressions. ( )

C. Sometimes is characterized by *A*, sometimes by *B*. ( )

13. A. Can admit his own mistakes to others readily; and can accept criticism without becoming defensive or feeling it is a threat to his ego. ( )

B. Doesn't welcome ideas or suggestions which might force a revision in his thinking; feels he may lose face if he concedes he has been wrong. ( )

C. Sometimes is characterized by *A*, sometimes by *B*. ( )

14. A. Is self-confident in important situations, such as an interview for a job; does not feel nervous or flustered at the thought of meeting new people socially. ( )

B. Is self-conscious in groups. Feels uneasy and apprehensive in the presence of his superiors. ( )

C. Sometimes is characterized by *A*, sometimes by *B*. ( )

SCORING

Each of the 14 statements bears on one of the 14 factors which make up emotional maturity. Give yourself 7 points for each "A"; 3 points for each "C"; no points for each "B."

The emotionally mature person:

1. Is able to tolerate the normal stresses of everyday living without undue tension.
2. Is able to handle anger and irritation in a socially acceptable manner.
3. Is able to accept authority when necessary.
4. Has a belief or a philosophy of life which helps to stabilize his moods and gives him a measure of inner peace.
5. Exercises self-control and self-restraint.
6. Exercises good judgment.
7. Has a capacity for a deep and mutually satisfying love

relationship.

8. Is continually growing in knowledge and understanding, and has an open attitude toward new learning.
9. Has an ability to think, reason, and evaluate new ideas.
10. Is responsible, rather than irresponsible.
11. Is not self-centered, but is aware of and concerned with the feelings of others.
12. Is able to communicate effectively.
13. Feels secure emotionally.
14. Possesses social poise.

From 80 to 100 may be regarded as an excellent emotional-maturity rating; 60 to 80 is very good; 40 to 60 is fair or average. A score of under 40 indicates that you should take stock of yourself and concentrate on cultivating those qualities which are necessary for emotional maturity. You can find out exactly what those qualities are by going over the test and checking your "B" answers.

THE TIME OF YOUR LIFE
How To Make It Run Fast Or Slow

The time we really live by is not ticked off by our watches, but is measured by our "inner clocks." They can stretch time like a rubber band, making minutes seem like hours, or telescoping hours into minutes.

Psychologists have been examining the time we live by as measured by our mental clocks. Their studies can show you how to make time pass quickly, or how to slow it down, depending on your mood or the occasion. They can even test you to determine whether your mental clock runs fast or slow. They also show you what a stop watch reveals about your character.

At what times of the day can your mental clock tell time most accurately?

At Western Michigan University 75 adults were asked to

estimate the correct time of day without reference to clocks, at various times ranging from 8 A.M. to 8 P.M. It was found that their ability to sense the time varied consistently as the day progressed from morning to evening. There was a marked tendency for mental clocks to run faster in the early morning and evening (overestimating the time) and slowest from 12 noon to mid-afternoon. As the afternoon waned, the average speed of the mental clocks picked up, until by evening they were running faster than clock time again.

Times when most mental clocks were most closely synchronized with mechanical clocks: around 10 in the morning and 6 in the evening.

When a person is habitually late for appointments, does that mean his mental clock is slow?

It has nothing to do with the matter. No matter what kind of time a person's mental clock keeps, if he wants to be on time he usually is. People who are chronically late for engagements usually blame their mental clocks, but that makes a poor excuse since most people carry watches and there are three clocks in most homes.

Psychology professor Paul Fraisse of the University of Paris lists the following reasons for lack of punctuality. 1. A person may arrive late deliberately as a sign of his indifference to society. 2. He has an aggressive desire for independence. 3. He desires to annoy those who wait for him. 4. He likes to be the center of attention.

What effect does worry have on our mental clocks?

It makes them run so fast that by comparison the clock on the wall seems slow. Time appears to drag its feet. Danger, if sufficiently acute, can almost make time stop; a minute spent hanging from a cliff can seem like a year. Studies at Clark University show that nothing makes time pass more slowly than anxiety. And the greater the fear, the more nearly does time seem to come to a halt.

What can you tell about your character with a stop watch?

At Purdue University men and women students were given personality tests, then tested on their ability to estimate short intervals of time. Students who made the most accurate scores tended to have one particular characteristic in common: a strong achievement drive.

Women who were good at estimating time also tended to make high test scores on sociability: being outgoing, having many friends, willing to seek new ones, liking social activities.

Can you make time pass more swiftly for you by willing it?

No. This will have the opposite effect.

How can you make time pass more swiftly for you?

Studies show that one of the most effective ways is listening to music, which can make time pass faster or slower. When time is dragging for you, get some snappy rhythms from your radio or record player. The music doesn't need to be loud. Background music with a fast tempo is guaranteed to give time a shot in the arm.

If you want to slow time down, reverse the process. Play music with the slowest tempo you can find. For, as psychiatrist Dr. Joost A. M. Meerloo observes, our sense of rhythm is intimately linked with our sense of time.

Do most people's internal clocks run either fast or slow?

Yes. To persons whose mental clocks run slow, clock time seems fast. They are forever being surprised at "how time flies"; they look at the clock and shake their heads in amazement: "Where *did* the time go?" Then there are those whose internal clocks run fast, making clock time seem comparatively slow, "My," they say, "it took you a long time to get here!"

Various external factors can affect the tempo of our internal clocks. There are some people, however, with mental timepieces so closely synchronized with the clock on the wall that they can tell you almost the exact time at any hour of the day or night under all kinds of conditions.

How can you tell whether a person's mental clock is running fast or slow?

Give him this brief test, which is based on the Knapp Time Metaphor Scale. To take the test, simply check which metaphors most aptly describe your feeling.

I think of time as: a vast expanse of sky —; a road leading over a hill —; a speeding train —; a massive glacier —; a galloping horseman —; a fleeing thief —; a quiet, motionless ocean —; a fast moving shuttle —.

Western Reserve University studies show that persons whose
mental clocks run slower than mechanical clocks tend to pick
the swift images just listed as most fitting to describe the passage
of time. Those whose internal clocks run fast tend to choose
the static images.

WHICH ARE YOUR BEST YEARS?
Science Can Tell You When You May Expect Your Best, Mentally and Physically, When You'll Make The Most Money And When You'll Be Happiest

At what age are you the smartest? When are you most likely
to fall in love? At what age are you apt to make the most money?

To find out the answer to these and many similar questions,
scientists in leading universities and research foundations have
conducted exhaustive studies and surveys.

Q: At what age do you have the greatest physical strength?

A: You can expect your muscles to develop their greatest
horsepower between 20 and 25. It is then that your biceps are
likely to be the brawniest, your sinews capable of exerting the
greatest force. A consensus of leading university studies shows
that your physical strength increases steadily with each passing
year until you reach your early or middle 20's. But after the
age of 25, your muscular powers diminish — so gradually at
first that you are scarcely aware of being less strong than you
used to be. But as age increases, your strength declines at an
increasingly rapid rate.

Q: At what age is it easiest for you to learn?

A: Tests show that you can learn almost anything more
quickly and easily during your middle 20's than at any other
time in life. Studies conducted at Columbia University show
that a person's ability to learn increases from early childhood
up to the age of 25. After that time, it was found that a man's

ability to absorb knowledge begins to diminish at the rate of about 1% a year.

The late Professor Edward L. Thorndike, in reviewing the findings of the study, pointed out that contrary to popular notion, childhood is not the best age for learning. For example, any age between 20 and 45 was found better for learning than the early teens.

After 60, the ability to learn new things is appreciably lessened. Psychologist Thorndike found that a man of 65 can learn only about half as much per hour as he could when he was 25.

Q: At what age do you have the greatest mental ability?

A: Tests show that our ability to learn — to absorb new knowledge — begins to diminish gradually as we leave our 20's behind us. But our ability to *think and reason* keeps on increasing with age — provided these faculties are given sufficient exercise.

Studies conducted at several universities show that the average person's mental abilities decrease with age. But evidence indicates that this is largely due to the fact that most people let their brains "get rusty" after they get out of school.

At the University of Minnesota, investigators made a study of 5,500 extension-course students, whose ages ranged from 20 to 70, all of whom were engaged in occupations which made continuous demands on their intelligence. Tests revealed that in the vast majority of cases, mental ability definitely increased with age. The average man of 40 had appreciably more on the ball than the person of 30; the person in his 50's scored higher than the one of 45, and so on.

Q: At what age does your personality undergo the greatest change?

A: Between 25 and 35. Studies show that in this 10-year period our tastes, interests and attitudes change more rapidly than at any other period in our lives.

And the consensus of these surveys is that the older person possesses a definite set of tendencies which become more pronounced with each passing year:

1. He becomes more and more introverted, more given to self-examination, with a tendency to prefer his own company

to that of others. (These traits have been found to be more pronounced in women than in men.)

2. His interest in most former amusements (dancing, movies, sports, etc.) shows a marked decline. His interest in cultural activities (concerts, lectures, art galleries) increases.

3. He gets more and more enjoyment out of reading. But his interest in fiction decreases. He prefers magazine articles and newspapers.

4. His interest in politics and religion steadily increases with each passing year.

Q: At what age are you most emotional?

A: At Brown University, Professor William Royce Willoughby analyzed the personalities of nearly 1,400 persons of both sexes, ages 15 to 75 years. He found that women were the most emotional between 55 and 60; that their second highest emotional peak was reached at about their thirtieth birthday; that they were calmest and least emotional between 45 and 50.

The university study showed women to be more emotional than men at all age levels. The men showed little change in emotionality with age — except for a comparatively slight upsurge in the 40's and again in the 50's.

Q: At what age are you likely to do your most creative work?

A: The comprehensive survey on this question has been made by Harvey C. Lehman, professor of psychology at Ohio University. He made a detailed analysis of the years of greatest productivity in various professions, arts and sciences. Here are the findings of his monumental study, which took 20 years to complete:

The age of greatest proficiency in science, mathematics and practical invention is 33 to 44. The most productive years for physicians and medical researchers was found to be between 35 and 39. The peak years of productivity for psychologists was likewise found to be from 35 to 39.

Most painters and composers do their best work before the age of 35; and explorers make their most notable discoveries in their early 30's. Poets generally produce their best work between 26 and 30. The years of maximum productivity for most short-story writers are between 22 and 37. Novelists are most successful in hitting the literary jack-pot between 40 and 44.

Q: At what age are you likely to earn the most money?

A: Though your most creative years are likely to be the 30's, the odds are far better than even that you'll earn more money during your middle 50's than at any other period in your life. Wide-scale studies of the earning power of various age groups, conducted at Ohio University, have shown that under current conditions a man's earned income is likely to be the greatest at about 55 or 56. And a further survey made at the same university has shown that the age of most of the nation's top-flight executives ranges between 55 and 60. So if you haven't made your "pile" by the time you're 40, don't let it discourage you. The "golden fifties" are the jack-pot decade.

Q: At what age are you most apt to fall in love?

A: If you're a woman, studies show that you're likely to be most susceptible during your late teens, with 18 being the most vulnerable year. Men are most likely to be smitten between 20 and 25. After these peak periods are past, susceptibility of both sexes tends to wane until they reach their 40's. Then it takes a sudden upswing – particularly among women.

Q: At what age is a woman the most beautiful?

A: The National Institute of Public Opinion conducted a nation-wide survey, in which men and women of every age and walk of life were asked to vote on this question. Most people considered that a woman reaches the peak of her beauty in her early 20's. Less than one person in five considered the late teens the most beautiful age. Indeed, the bloom of youth and innocence as typified by the 18-year-old was esteemed even less by voters in the upper-age brackets. And only about one in eight subscribed to view that a lady is more fascinating when she reaches 30.

Q: At what age are you most sensitive to pain?

A: If you hit your thumb with a hammer when you're 40, it won't hurt nearly as much as it would have if you were only 20. The noted psychiatrist William P. Chapman tested the pain reactions of 200 persons, ranging in age from 10 to 85. He found that for the overwhelming majority of people, sensitivity to pain decreases progressively with age. His study showed that a young man of 20 is, on the average, 22% more sensitive to pain than a person of over 45. Moral: avoid getting hurt when you're young — it feels worse then.

Q: At what age are people most irritable and hardest to get along with?

A: To find out the answer to this question, Psychologist Hulsey Cason of the University of Wisconsin made a study of over a thousand subjects, aged 10 to 90. He found that middle-aged people (40 to 60) were more easily annoyed than any other age group. Young people were the least irritable, but each year that brought them closer to middle age found them more easily upset by trifles, and more inclined to be peevish and impatient.

But after middle age is passed, the psychologist found that people's dispositions tend to become more serene.

Q. At what age are your reactions the quickest?

A: University studies show that your physical reactions speed up with each passing year — until you reach your middle 20's, then slow up. By the time you are 60 you respond to things with just about half the speed that you did when you were 25. In other words, it takes twice as long for your brain to transmit an impulse and your body to act on it.

That's one reason why oldsters are more subject to accidents. They see danger coming, but their physical reaction to it is frequently several split seconds outside the margin of safety.

A young man hears an auto's horn and is out of the way almost at the same time the driver's hand touches the button. An older man hears the horn at the same time — but his reflexes are less instantaneous.

In view of science's findings, picking the best years of your life is not easy. The advantages and disadvantages of each age tend to almost offset each other.

Some of our faculties and abilities function better as we grow older; with others the opposite is true. Science can put the attributes of each age under the clinical microscope, but it takes a Solomon to add up the debits and credits and decide which of the years of your life are the best.

THE BEST STAGE OF YOUR LIFE
The Findings Of Science May Surprise You

Most people are discomfited by the little ticks of the clock which constantly transport them just a little farther from their youth. But youth is *not* the happiest or most fruitful time in life for a great many people, according to experts on human behavior. They have demonstrated that the best time in life is when you are old enough to appreciate it.

Does life get better as you get older?

Yes, for a great many people. To find out why some people live much longer than others and get much more out of life, one scientist studied scores of persons ranging in age from 87 to 103. Each was chosen for the study "because of their being in a good state of health, with a feeling of well-being, and because they were physically and mentally active and enjoying their lives."

These are the traits which they shared: they were singularly free from illness, particularly those which result from nervous or emotional causes. (Even the common cold was rare for them.) They showed no traces of accident proneness: their accident rate was far below that of the general population.

As for their personality characteristics, the investigator noted, "These people were not given to worry. They were deeply concerned about problems, but they took things in stride. For their vocations, consciously or unconsciously they seemed to have chosen those which gave them an opportunity to be their own boss and to maintain independence of choice. Thus they had avoided many frustrations."

A further characteristic of these people was found to be their ability to enjoy life. Boredom seemed to be unknown, and all were optimistic and had a good sense of humor.

This sounds like a recipe for a long and happy life, if you can just find the ingredients.

Does how well you like your job affect how long you will live?

Yes, as evidenced by the findings of a special study conducted for the Department of Health, Education, and Welfare. Indeed,

339

it indicated that the greatest single factor in longevity is not diet, how much exercise you get, whether you smoke or not, how long-lived your parents were, but the degree to which you are deriving satisfaction from your job. The other factors are important, but work satisfaction was the most significant.

Many other studies have shown a close link between morale and longevity, and good morale is not likely to be associated with job dissatisfaction.

Does your ability to think and reason increase as you grow older?

Yes, if you have a better-than-average I.Q. to start with, according to the findings of psychological studies. Smart people tend to get smarter as they grow older, but this is not true of people whose mental equipment is below average. A further finding is that the brain is somewhat like a muscle. The more you use it, the more it develops. And it is usually true that brainy people exercise their intellects to a far greater degree than others.

Does marital happiness affect longevity?

Yes. Studies show that compatible marriages, those which remain permanently intact, correlate with longevity. So picking the right companion to see you through life is one of the most effective ways of lengthening your life span.

Is the length of your life affected by how you react to stress?

Yes, as evidenced by the findings of a medical study of 3,000 American men. The subjects were first classified into two personality types A and B, based on their reactions to stress situations. Type A men were aggressive, hard-driving, competitive go-getters. Type B men took life easier. They tended to roll with the punches rather than meeting opposition head on, were more patient, thoughtful, deliberate, slow to anger, and much less inclined to take work home or struggle to keep up with the Joneses.

Each was then subjected to a complete physical examination. The great majority of those who were found to have a coronary heart condition were Type A men. And the A's were much more likely to develop heart disease even when the ordinary risk factors, such as high blood pressure, obesity, and so on, were not present. The B's, on the other hand, at least those who had normal cholesterol levels, appeared to be relatively immune to coronary heart disease, even in the presence of other high-risk factors, such as lack of exercise, bad diet, poor genetic history, and so on.

So people who live the longest are smarter, better educated, and better adjusted than others?

Yes. A 12-year study sponsored by the National Institute of Health has shown that people who average the longest lives tend to score higher on intelligence tests than shorter-lived people. They were also found to be more stable emotionally, and have better-adjusted personalities. Investigations have also shown that superior educational attainments tend to go with longevity.

WHAT'S THE BEST TIME OF THE YEAR
Psychologists Find There's A Best And Worst Season For Nearly Everything —
Thinking, Getting Robbed, Having A Baby

What's going to happen to you next year? Nobody, of course, can predict the actual events, but psychologists and other researchers can tell you the type of thing that's likely to happen — and when. They can help you plan for the year, because they've found that there are good and bad seasons for almost everything in the world.

Here's a question-and-answer breakdown of some of the most interesting recent discoveries about the calendar — and what it has in store for you:

Q: What time of the year are you likely to be the happiest?

A: Summer. Other factors being equal, that's when you're likely to have the greatest sense of well-being. The "level of good feeling" reaches its peaks at the beginning and end of the summer season. Columbia University studies show that most

341

people's morale is higher in warm, bright, sunny weather. Women's spirits, incidentally, were found to be affected even more than men's by these factors.

On the other hand, statistics show that more suicides occur during the spring than during the colder months.

So if you find yourself up against a serious case of the blues during the spring, remind yourself that summer's on the way.

Q: What time of the year is your health most likely to give you trouble?

A: The Metropolitan Life Insurance Company recently completed a two-year nation-wide survey to find the answer to this question. January was found to be the worst month for respiratory troubles, and February for ulcers and heart attacks.

March was the toughest month for people subject to rheumatism and arthritis, and circulatory ailments. More people had appendicitis attacks in October than any other time. August and October were the most aggravating months for people subject to rashes and skin ailments; and nervous disorders were most prevalent in mid-winter (January). Time of the year when people were most likely to "go off the deep end" emotionally was with the advent of spring. March was high in psychoneuroses.

Q: When are you the smartest?

A: Your brain functions most effectively during spring and fall. But winter is better for thinking than summer — you'll be able to think your way through problems in December that might stump you in July or August.

In a study by Ellsworth Huntington of Yale University, the findings of scores of studies have been evaluated. Thousands of persons of all ages were given mental tests during various months of the year. The daily marks of West Point cadets and the grades achieved in civil-service examinations were carefully evaluated.

It was found that people had the least capacity for mental effort during the summer months (lowest scores were made during August). Industrial surveys conducted in Chicago showed that stenographic errors alone increase 1,000% as the temperature rises. Virtually every other type of work surveyed showed similar decrease in efficiency. This slow-down is caused by a rise in fatigue during any extreme weather.

Thinking functioned at peak efficiency during spring and fall (highest scores of all were made in April and November).

Q: When is the best time to have a baby?

A: Summer. Infant mortality is lower then than at any season of the year. The most prevalent communicable diseases of childhood — pneumonia, other acute respiratory infections — are at their lowest ebb.

Also, as Dr. Louis I. Dublin, Consultant on Health and Welfare for the Institute of Life Insurance points out — a baby born during the summer months has time to gain strength and build up resistance before the onset of winter, when contagious infant diseases are most prevalent.

Q: What time of the year are you most likely to have an accident?

A: Studies show that June is the most hazardous time of the year for serious accidents of all types — with July and August running a close second. Worst month for auto accidents, however, is October. And December is the time when pedestrians are most likely to become mortality statistics.

Your chance of sustaining a serious accident due to a fall skyrockets as does the fire hazard during the winter. Incidentally, falls take the greatest toll of any type of accident except motor vehicle.

Q: When should you take the greatest precaution against burglary and theft?

A: During the winter. That's when you are most likely to have your house broken into, your pocket picked, or your purse snatched. Crimes against property — theft, forgery, embezzlement — climb in the cold season, drop sharply as soon as summer sets in.

Interestingly, crimes against persons — murder, mayhem, assault — do exactly the opposite. They hit the top during the warm season and drop off when winter sets in.

Q: At what time of the year are your children apt to get out of hand?

A: In the latter part of summer, during the last month of school vacation, according to studies conducted by psychologist Clinton E. Phillips, Associate Director of Counseling of the American Institute of Family Relations. Boredom reaches a dangerous peak as the thrill of vacation wears off.

Psychologist Phillips suggests either scheduling the family vacation for this time or planning a recreational program to keep the child interested or constructively occupied.

Q: When do the seasons begin?

A: This is a trick question. For astronomers and almanac makers, they begin on or about the 21st of March, June, September and December. But in the minds of American women they begin at altogether different dates.

These "psychological seasons" have reference not so much to the actual conditions of a particular season but to how women feel about them.

A survey of 5,400 women, conducted by James M. Vicary, reveals that spring begins in the feminine mind on January 13 — possibly with the first appearance of a spring-hat ad. Spring seems to be the favorite feminine season, because it keeps right on for nearly five months. For the ladies, summer starts two weeks early on June 7.

Fall, too, arrives just a fortnight ahead of schedule in the girls' minds, on September 7. Winter starts good and early, on November 17 — time to start Christmas shopping. Any way you look at the thing, it's an upside-down calendar!

WHAT MAKES TIME GO SO FAST?
If You're Complaining That It Whizzes By, You're Probably Lucky

Have you ever wondered what makes time pass so slowly at some times, and swiftly at others? It's a question that comes up especially often during the holiday season. "Good Lord," sigh harassed parents, "where has the year gone?" And on the other hand, the kids wonder if the hours will *ever* drag by till Christmas morning.

Mental time — the time you *really* live by — is not counted by cardboard calendars and mechanical clocks. It's measured by an extremely sensitive physiological clock that's mounted on the mental dashboard inside your head. Located in the time-measurement centers of your brain, this clock is powered by your individual metabolism, and regulated by the chemistry of your emotions. It keeps the time you live and feel by. *When it runs fast, it can make minutes seem like hours; and when it runs slow it can telescope minutes into seconds.*

Some people's mental clocks run consistently slow. They're always being surprised when they look at the clock on the wall to find that it's later than they think. They are habitually late for appointments, can never seem to get anywhere on time. "Here the day's almost gone," you'll hear them say, "and it seems like I just finished the breakfast dishes." Or, "Is it Saturday already? It just doesn't seem possible. Where *has* the week gone to?" For them mechanical time races so fast that they never quite catch up with it.

There are others whose internal clocks run fast, ticking off the minutes and seconds with such rapidity that Greenwich time seems to drag for them. For these people time seems to creep so slowly that 15 minutes may seem like an hour. Make an appointment with one of them, and the odds are he'll be there appreciably ahead of time. And every minute he has to wait for you will make him chafe with impatience.

On the other hand, there are some people whose mental timepieces are so well synchronized with the clock on the wall that time seems neither to race nor crawl. They can guess the time at any hour of the day or night — are are seldom more than five to 10 minutes off. Experiments at a leading university showed that about 50% of the subjects tested had such an accurate time sense that they could awaken from sleep at a previously designated hour a good precentage of the time!

It is true that some human clocks may tick off the minutes and hours at the same speed as Greenwich time, but they tend to do so only intermittently, running fast at one time and slow at another. For the clock inside your brain is so sensitive that it is affected by what you eat, whether you're working or at rest, worried or elated, how old you are, and whether you're successful or unsuccessful. One of the most amazing quirks is that time goes as much as five times as fast for adults as for children.

Your mental clock is also extremely sensitive to changes in bodily temperature. Experiments have shown that when we become overheated, time seems to pass much more slowly; and when we get a high fever, time passes at such a snail-like pace that it scarcely moves at all. Conversely, when we become chilled time passes at a much swifter pace. Indeed, when our bodily temperature drops to subnormal levels, time whizzes by with incredible swiftness.

Dr. Hudson Hoagland, then professor of physiology at Clark University, was one of the first scientists to discover how temperature can make time pass slowly or swiftly. Professor Hoagland had never given the matter any thought until one day his wife became ill with influenza and developed a fever of nearly 104°. She asked him to get something for her at the store, and though the errand took him a scant 20 minutes, his wife insisted that he had been gone for hours.

Dr. Hoagland decided to try an experiment on a volunteer group of subjects — controlling their bodily temperatures by artificial means. The results bore out his wife's reactions.

If time seems to pass for you with terrific speed day after day, you *may* have some type of disturbance. There are numerous physical ailments such as diabetes, glandular disorders and various nervous diseases which produce a subnormal bodily temperature.

One medical journal cites the case of a diabetic patient for whom time passed so fast that his first six days at the clinic he estimated at three days; an hour's conversation was judged to be only 15 minutes; and a period of 18 years which the patient had spent at his sister's home had flowed by so rapidly that he estimated it at only two years!

All states of mind have a bearing on your estimate of time. Nothing makes clock time pass more slowly than a state of anxiety or depression. The more "down in the dumps" you feel, the slower time drags by. In extreme depression, time seems to stop altogether.

How fast or how slow time passes depends also on how you're occupied. Tests conducted at the University of Washington show that, for a stenographer, time will pass a good 30% faster when taking dictation than when sitting at a desk doing nothing. And if you happen to be a bookkeeper or accountant, time will pass about 33% faster when you're actually working with figures than when you're idle.

The investigators also found, incidentally, that time passes much quicker for men than for women. Paradoxically, however, tests show that when the hours do drag, women are much less apt to be bored by the fact than men.

How fast your mental time ticks depends to a large extent on whether you are a success or a failure. Studies conducted at Arizona State College have shown that successful effort makes time zip by, while frustrated activity has the opposite effect. Indeed, mechanical time races so swiftly for the really successful man that the days seem all too short for him.

For the man of only mediocre success, time tends to slow to a dog-trot. The investigators also found that attitudes of confidence, hope and optimism make time move at an accelerated pace, while feelings of doubt and anxiety are apt to slow it down.

There are commonly prescribed drugs which play strange tricks on your time sense. Clinical tests show, for example, that quinine makes time appear to pass much slower than it actually does.

Next time you find time dragging for you, and you want to speed it up, just drink a cup of coffee. It will do the trick, for it

347

has a direct effect on the speed with which your mental chronometer measures the hours and minutes. Tea has a similar effect in making a time interval pass more quickly.

As for the effect of liquor, science now has an alibi for the man who gets home late for dinner because he stopped off "just a minute" for a quick one. Tests show that liquor has a bizarre and double-barreled effect on our time sense. It makes short intervals of time fly with incredible swiftness. It has been demonstrated, for example, that alcohol can make time pass *three times as fast,* causing an interval of 45 minutes to be estimated as only 15 minutes.

But for periods longer than this, on the other hand, liquor slows time down and makes it appear to pass *much* slower than normally.

At the Psychological Laboratory at the University of Graz, the noted German scientist Professor Othmar Sterzinger conducted a series of tests on all types of persons. His studies show that for a great many people alcohol waits only about 20 minutes to do its abrupt about-face. So, all things considered, liquor can scarcely be recommended as a means of giving time a "shot in the arm."

How fast time passes for you is also determined to a very large extent by your age. When you are young – during childhood and adolescence – mechanical time crawls at a snail's pace. It marches with steadily increasing swiftness with each passing year until, as old age approaches, time really rushes past. Indeed, scientific tests show that time moves five times as fast for us at the age of 60 as it does at the age of 10. And time passes even more swiftly for elderly people when they are fully and actively occupied.

This sounds amazing, but exhaustive studies of the famed scientist, Pierre Lecomte de Noüy, have furnished mathematical biological proof of the fact. Indeed, Dr. de Noüy's findings show that in the course of 60 minutes a child has lived physically and psychologically as much as the man of 60 would have in five hours.

Therefore, as the scientist has pointed out, it is not surprising that it is difficult to sustain the attention of a child for more than a few minutes; to him 10 minutes takes as long to pass as 50 minutes for the older man.

The scientist's studies also show that the speed with which our mental clocks measure time is directly tied in with vital biological processes, such as the healing of wounds, and the body's power to recuperate. He has demonstrated that a wound which will take a month to heal in a man of 20, will heal in less than three weeks in a boy of 10, and will require over three months in a man of 60.

Scientific evidence all up and down the line makes this fact crystal clear: the time we really live by is not mechanical time, but time as it is measured by the mental clock inside our brain. And so, if you're one of the many who are watching the year run out with groans of "where did it go?" you can at least have the satisfaction of knowing you had a pretty good time after all.

SECRETS OF LONGEVITY
How To Stay Young For A Long Time

Science has been exploring some of the factors which contribute to a long and happy lifetime of successful living, and looking into the habits, attitudes and personality traits which cause some people to age faster and others to stay young longer.

Why do some of us "age" faster than others? Do those with a higher I.Q. die at an earlier age? Is a pressure-packed position likely to prevent you from ever living long enough to enjoy the fruits of retirement? How important is your marriage partner to a long life? Science has come up with some surprising answers.

People who are mentally relaxed — who are careful not to over-exert their mental processes — live the longest. (True____, False____)

False. A 12-year longevity study conducted by the National Institute of Health has shown that people who are the most mentally active, whose brains are the busiest, coping with problems, exploring and evaluating new ideas, tend to live appreciably longer than others — and are the least likely to become senile as their age advances.

A high I.Q. however, is a handicap where longevity is con- ?rn-cerned. (True_____, False_____)

False. In the same study, in which a specimen group of healthy elderly men (mean age 71) were followed over a 12-year period, intelligence tests were made when the investigation was launched. The men who were still alive when the study was completed a dozen years later — many of them well into their 80's by that time — made appreciably higher scores on the I.Q. tests. On a standard adult intelligence scale, for example, the longer-lived group averaged almost 15 points higher than the others. The investigation showed, moreover, that the surviving group showed no significant lessening of mental powers — which were carefully checked by test performances over the years. Conclusion of the investigators: *survival is definitely associated with retention of intellectual vigor and capacities.* It has long been observed that the human body will *rust* from insufficient use much quicker than it will wear out from activity. And scientists' findings indicate that this is equally true of our mental powers.

The more successful you are, the longer you're likely to live. (True_____, False_____)

True. Consensus of studies shows that people who are the most successful, who distinguish themselves in their profession or occupation, average significantly longer lives than others. It's pointed out that the man who excels at his calling, who takes pride in what he does, enjoys a healthy self-esteem and a high morale. And authorities agree that these are extremely important factors in longevity.

Your choice of a marriage partner plays an important part in determining the length of your lifetime. (True_____, False_____)

True. Researches at the Center for the Study of Aging and Human Development, Duke University Medical Center, show

350

that the happier your marriage is, the more birthdays you're likely to celebrate; that marriages that are stable and remain intact are definitely related to longevity.

A further study of men and women over 60, conducted at the same university, also showed that satisfaction with one's occupation and general happiness are the two most active determinants of longevity.

People who live the longest are the most active socially. (True_____, False_____)

True. The National Institute of Health study showed that the longer-lived group whose lives were followed over a 12-year period were much more socially active than the others and showed no tapering off of their various outside interests or their contacts with others.

You can grow older without getting "old." (True_____, False_____)

True. Chronological age as measured by the calendar often has little in common with a person's capacity for living dynamically, and enjoying life to the fullest. Many people are younger — in a very real sense of the word — at 70 or 80 than others are at 30 or 40. For every youthful oldster in the public eye, such as Jack Benny, Pablo Picasso, Maurice Chevalier, Arthur Rubinstein, Jimmy Durante, etc., there are thousands of ordinary private citizens also in their 70's and 80's whose personalities are as vibrant, whose zest for living is as keen as ever.

How much you enjoy living has a direct bearing on how long you are likely to live. (True_____, False_____)

True. Investigations have shown that people who stay young the longest, and celebrate the most birthdays, have this in common: a positive rather than a negative outlook, a capacity to enjoy life, and the ability to count their blessings rather than brood over disappointments and frustrations.

A survey of the attitudes of older people sponsored by the National Institute of Mental Health cites marked differences in outlook (quoted from random interviews): "I don't like being old. I haven't got a thing to do and I can't stand it . . .. I got a lot of aggravations for no reason . . .. I'm not happy." "I've never found time on my hands. There are just so many things that I

351

want to do that I haven't found time to do. And I've got stacks of good books around that I want to read and study." "I feel I don't exist anymore. I'm just living out my life. What else is there to do when you're getting old?" "My cup is overflowing. There are so many opportunities to do things for people. These are the happiest days of my life. I do what I want to, when I want to. I don't think there is anything I long for. I enjoy things."

How long you're likely to live depends to a large extent on what you do for a living. (True_____, False_____)

True. It goes without saying that people in high-risk occupations are more subject to becoming mortality statistics than others, but there are many other factors in addition to physical hazards which cause a man's work to have a bearing on the length of his life-span. Some of the elements are intangible and difficult to pin-point, such as the peace of mind and satisfaction derived from the work. A wide-scale study conducted by statistical analysts of a leading life insurance company has shown that educators and scientists, church officials and clergymen rank among the most prominent contenders for the longevity sweepstakes.

Feeling young is even better than being young. (True_____, False_____)

True — in many respects. As Dr. Bernice L. Neugarten, Professor of Human Development at the University of Chicago, observes in summing the findings of a study of a cross-section of one hundred men and women, middle-aged and older, who had distinguished themselves in their callings: One of the most prevailing themes expressed by these people is that this is the "period of maximum capacity and ability to handle a highly complex environment and a highly differentiated self. Very few express a wish to be young again. As one of them said, 'There is a difference between wanting to *feel* young and wanting to *be* young. Of course it would be pleasant to maintain the vigor and appearance of youth; but I would not trade those things for the authority or the autonomy I feel — no, nor the ease of inter-personal relationships nor the self-confidence that comes from experience.'"

"GROW OLD ALONG WITH ME"
Scientific Studies Back Up Robert Browning's
Attitude On The Geriatrics Problem

Most people would like to stay young forever if they could.
They think that youth is the best part of life. The disadvantages
of growing older are so obvious that the many advantages are
overlooked. But recent evidence indicates that in many respects
life gets better as we grow older! Here are the findings of
science.

Is it true that pain doesn't hurt as much when you get older?

Yes. A stomach ache that would tie a teen-ager in knots, an
older man takes in his stride. It hurts you far less when you hit
your thumb with a hammer than it would if you were younger.
For the man who has graduated from his 50's, a toothache that
once sent him screaming for an ice pack can now be borne with
equanimity.

In a study sponsored by the National Research Council at the
University of Manitoba, subjects were selected from all walks of
life, ranging in age from 12 to 83 years. Their sensitivity to
various types of pain was measured. It was found that a person's
sensitivity to pain diminishes appreciably during his middle years.
The study also showed that this change begins at different ages
for different parts of the body. In the forehead and forearms,
for instance, sensitivity is significantly less after a man passes
45. When he reaches 60, over-all sensitivity to pain or physical
dissensitivity to pain or physical discomfort begins a sharp
decline, which continues with each passing year.

Is it true that time tends to drag for us as we grow older?

No. It's the other way around. Scientific studies show that
all units of time — minutes, hours, months, years — pass more
swiftly for us with each birthday. For the youngster, even a
few hours may seem to take forever. But the older we get the
more likely we are to say, "Susie's married and has two
children? Why, it seems only yesterday she was a little girl in
pigtails!"

Studies conducted at the Massachusetts Institute of
Technology indicate that the reason time goes by faster for

the more mature adult is that he places a higher value on it.

Does physical exercise significantly help to assure us a long, happy life?

Says Dr. George Gallup in reporting the findings of a special survey designed to explore the why of longevity: "One of the important secrets of living to a ripe old age was found to be physical exercise. In a sampling of persons 95 years of age and older (including 164 who were 100 or older) nearly all had engaged in occupations which require much physical exercise."

Exercise does much more than improve one's physical condition. It provides a valuable outlet for the release of emotional tension, improves morale, and contributes to a greater sense of well-being. These factors have been found to affect not only how much we enjoy life, but how long we enjoy it.

But aren't older persons more subject to boredom? And don't our tempers shorten as we get older?

No. Cornell University sociologist Lois R. Dean cites the findings of a continuing study which shows that irritations steadily decrease as we get older.

As for boredom, the findings surprised even the investigators. "We had anticipated," says Dean, "that an increase in boredom would be reported with advancing age. However, not only was this *not* the case, but those in the older age groups report the opposite!" The fact that time passes so quickly for the aging is probably the chief reason.

How old is old?

It varies with each person. No one is old until he feels old. Some people feel old, act old, and seem old before they're 30. On the other hand, a recent study of centenarians showed that many of them are so young in mind and spirit that they have no sense of being old at all. To a great many people being "old" is a shadow that keeps comfortably ahead of them as they progress through life.

Harvard sociologists studied 200 men and women, all over 65. The subjects constituted a roughly typical cross-section of the older segment of the total population. Only 21% of the men and just 20% of the women thought of themselves as elderly.

Other studies show that people who don't think of themselves as old tend to be far better-adjusted mentally and emotionally than those who do.

Is there any point in living to be 100?

Dr. S. George Santayana, professor of sociology at Stirling College, made a 15-year study of 300 centenarians, selected at random from various parts of the country, and ranging in age from 100 to 121.

With a very few exceptions, he reports, these people were anything but feeble. The group as a whole was remarkable for its enthusiasm, physical strength, and willingness to strive for new experience. Most showed a keen interest in world affairs, spare-time pursuits, and plans for the future.

A 105-year-old Minnesotan was an ardent student of ancient and modern languages. In addition, she had an almost encyclopedic knowledge of English and American literature. She had begun these studies in her 90's through university extension courses and adult-study groups.

Many had full-time jobs; about 30 were part-time workers. Five operated their own farms. Others conducted their own businesses. All described themselves as being happy in their work.

One, a Pennsylvania centenarian of 109, was planning to marry a man of 102. She had been married and widowed four times.

With a few exceptions, the centenarians manifested a keen sense of humor, an attitude of tranquility, and social poise. They also had an unshakable confidence that their lives would always be useful and productive no matter how long they lived.

VII.

THE BATTLE OF THE SEXES

THE BATTLE OF THE SEXES

*The staple of cartoon-comic art has always been
the rolling pin brandished or the flower pot thrown
by the enraged "Mrs." of the comic strip personnel.
In the comics the battle is usually all in good fun —
at least up to now a husband beating a wife has
never seemed funny to the cartoonist or his followers.
The battle in real life is fought with subtler weapons.
The weapons are the distinctive and exclusive
differences implanted by nature in man and woman
to enable one to cope with the other. The quarrels
of lovers and most newlyweds can be traced to these
differences. It is only with maturity that the man
or the woman understands the opposite number
well enough to settle down to happiness instead
of periodically outraged bliss.*

THE MENTAL DIFFERENCES BETWEEN
MEN AND WOMEN
Science Confirms What Everybody Always Knew

Women do find it easier to understand men, and most men
are quick to admit that they simply don't understand women.
Still, there are many things about men that women find
confusing. Though the sexes will probably always be something of a puzzle to each other, science has recently made some
discoveries which may some day make it easier for men and
women to understand one another.

Do men and women see themselves as completely different?

Yes. University of Nebraska researchers studied the self-
concepts of men and women in a cross-sectional survey.
Women, the investigators reported, tended to see themselves
as having more warmth, tenderness, and sense of satisfaction
than men. But they also saw themselves as more tense,
excitable, and insecure. Men tended to describe themselves
as more assertive, practical, and adventurous than women.

Are women more romantic than men?

To explore this subject scientifically, researchers at Florida State University made an in-depth study of the attitudes of hundreds of men and women, using questionnaires specifically designed for the purpose. The findings: "Although both men and women tended to be somewhat more realistic than romantic in their attitude toward love, women tended to be more realistic than men."

Is it true that women who read a great deal tend to be "loners," preferring the pages of an absorbing book to the society of people?

No. University of California studies have shown that women who get the greatest enjoyment out of reading tend to be the easiest to get along with, and to be happier than women who don't care for reading. Psychological tests showed that they make the best companions, and are much more likely to be quiet-spoken, thoughtful, feminine, and agreeable.

No husband, of course, likes to be henpecked?

Not true. Studies show that some men are attracted to dominating women. They would feel emotionally insecure if their wives didn't boss them around, take the lead in making decisions, tell them what to do. The husband who is always saying "I'll-have-to-ask-my-wife" may complain that he is browbeaten but he would not really feel comfortable with a wife who didn't dominate.

Do women have more emotional conflicts than men?

Yes. All studies show that women are much more subject to conflicting emotional drives than men are. And perhaps precisely because they have a greater degree of self-awareness and are more conscious of their innermost feelings than men are, they are more likely to be bewildered when their heads and their hearts fail to agree.

Recent psychological studies at New York University have shown that this difference exists even among children. Boys and girls of various ages were given the Emotions Profile Index, a test which yields conflict scores in four different emotional dimensions. The results showed that little girls had significantly more emotional conflicts than did little boys.

360

Is a woman's handwriting harder to read than a man's?

No. Studies of representative samples of men's and women's handwriting have shown that women's penmanship is not only more legible, but more likely to be beautifully flowing script. Men's handwriting was characterized by undecipherable scrawls, obliquely formed letters, and so on.

Which sex is the best at coming up with new ideas?

To explore this interesting question, behavior scientists at California State Polytechnic College made a study of men and women of all ages and various walks of life. Each was given an "Ideaphoria" test, one designed to measure the flow of ideas. When the scores of both sexes were examined, the women were found to have the most active imaginations, the most abundant flow of new ideas. What's more, they were able to communicate them with greater ease. If fewer women than men distinguish themselves in creative fields, perhaps it is because women are less strongly motivated, finding greater satisfaction in being wife, mother, homemaker.

MEN AND WOMEN ARE DISTINCT IN PERSONALITY
But Some Popular Ideas
About Their Dissimilarities Are Incorrect

Psychologists and sociologists are constantly looking into the personality differences between men and women. Here are some more of the things they have found out.

Is it true that men are easier to understand than women?

No. All psychological studies show that women are more gregarious, more outgoing, and more communicative. They are more willing to exchange confidences, and to reveal themselves to others. And similar tests show that men are more inclined to conceal their emotions.

Are women easier to fool than men are?

Yes. University studies have shown that women are significantly more persuadable than men, more susceptible to smooth talk, and more likely to be influenced by a glib sales pitch.

Do men try to lose weight for different reasons than women do?

Yes. A survey by London University has indicated that most men who try to lose weight do so for health reasons. Women were concerned with their appearance. A survey of 1,500 doctors, which went into the case histories of their overweight patients, showed that women were less successful in losing weight despite their dieting. Conclusion: their reason for trying to lose weight is not strong enough incentive to make them stick to their diets. The men who were reducing to save or prolong their lives did much better.

Are women more given to feeling blue than men are?

Yes, at least that is true of college women. In a survey by the University of Michigan, students were asked, "Do you ever get very depressed?" Twice as many females as males answered Yes.

Is a man usually happier with what he sees in the mirror than a woman is?

Women look in the mirror more often than men, but don't like what they see as well. Studies at both Duke University and the University of Wisconsin show that men are much more satisfied with the way they look. Not so with a woman. When she looks in a mirror her eyes rove critically over every feature, wincing at each real or imagined imperfection. The expression on her face often seems to say, "If I only had the receipt, I'd like to exchange it for something else."

Are most women better readers than most men?

Yes, according to a nationwide survey which looked into the reading habits of men and women of various ages and stages of life. The survey did not try to consider literary taste, but did show that women read more books than men.

Other studies show that women not only read appreciably faster than men, but that they enjoy reading more, finding it easier to become completely absorbed in a book.

Is it true that women are more sensitive to weather changes?

In tests at Kansas State University Institute for Environmental

Research, students were exposed to temperatures ranging from 60° to 98° and humidities ranging from 15% to 85%. Men were found to be more sensitive to weather changes than women were. They felt uncomfortably warm at temperatures that women still found agreeable. And it was found that "humidity plays a significantly more important role in how men feel than in how women feel."

Do women have a better sense of direction?

No. Studies show that it is much easier for a woman to get lost, or to confuse directions. Psychologists at one university gave sense-of-direction tests to 300 men and women students. The men averaged significantly better scores than the women.

Do men remember their dreams better than women do?

Investigators at the University of South Carolina tested the ability of a group of 145 men and women to remember their dreams. The findings: women had significantly more dream recall than men. Other studies have shown that women also are much more likely to dream in color.

There are other differences in the dreams of men and women. Men's dreams are usually pleasanter than women's. The reason is that women have a greater tendency to transfer their fears and worries into dreams. Women, it was found, were twice as subject to nightmares. The study also showed that women's dreams are much more vivid and emotional.

But in one respect women have an advantage over men: it's much easier for them to resume a pleasant dream after awakening. With most men, this proves impossible.

In placing blame, do men give women a better break than women do?

In studies at St. Louis University, students acted as judges, evaluating the offenses of other students (cheating on an examination, various infractions of rules). Findings: "Both sexes prescribed similar punishment for males, but males were more lenient than females in prescribing punishment for females." Apparently men like women much better than women do.

Is it true that a woman's glance takes in more than a man's does?

Yes. At the University of California at Los Angeles, the vision of 17,000 men and women drivers was tested. Women demonstrated a significantly larger field of vision without turning their heads or moving their eyes.

Is it true that women drivers don't get an even break?

They do not, according to driver-reaction studies at Purdue University. In the tests, 123 drivers selected at random pulled up behind cars that were used by investigators to purposely cause a traffic delay. Findings: the sex of the frustrating driver was the big factor in determining the other driver's reaction. Only 52% of the drivers honked at the delaying cars when they were driven by a man: 71% honked at a car having a woman at the wheel.

Which sex is more finicky about eating?

Women have far more food dislikes than men have. At the University of Cincinnati 500 men and women were tested on 145 different kinds of food. The women disliked a far greater number of things than did the men. They also were much more demanding about how the foods were prepared.

Among the many foods that men liked, but most women didn't, were lobster, spaghetti, caviar, clams, quail, pigeon, and hominy. Tests also showed that watermelon, cantaloupe, and tomatoes were disliked by twice as many women as men.

The few things that women showed a greater preference for included artichokes, cottage cheese, olives, cucumbers, and turnips.

DO MEN REMEMBER BETTER THAN WOMEN?
Researchers Have Recently Uncovered Some Surprising Things About What You Remember And What You Forget. They've Even Found A Foolproof Way For You To Remember Things!

While millions of dollars are being poured into research on the already fabulous memories of electronic computers, science hasn't forgotten our fallible human memories. Recent research has made fascinating discoveries about what sticks in and what leaks out of your mind. Here are some of the questions explored by psychiatrists and psychologists. Their conclusions may surprise you.

How far back can a person remember?

Psychiatric studies conducted at the University of Pennsylvania Medical School by Dr. Leon J. Saul, Thoburn R. Snyder, Jr., and Edith Sheppard show that it's not unusual for a first memory to go back to the age of two years — or even earlier. It was found that some first memories are amazingly accurate, some completely distorted. Others simply never happened. They are based on hearsay, dreams, and wishful thinking.

Do women remember things better than men do?

They have better social memories — that is, they remember people better. Tests conducted by psychologists Walter A. Kaess and Sam L. Witryol at the University of Connecticut show, for example, that women have a marked superiority over men when it comes to remembering faces. It was also found that women are ahead of men when it comes to remembering people's names.

Are men better than women at remembering the names and faces of pretty girls?

Strange as it seems, the answer is No. The University of Connecticut makes it clear that a woman looks at a pretty girl harder and more appraisingly than a man does — and remembers everything about her.

Introduce a man to a good-looking lass and later ask him what he remembers about her. Ordinarily it's that "she was sort of blonde, had a turned-up nose and wore a sweater."

Make the same test with a woman and she'll give you complete run-down: face, figure, dress, voice, make-up — you name it.

Curiously, the study showed that men remember *men's* faces much better than they do women's.

Is it true that your memory gets worse as you grow older?

As middle age approaches, many people worry needlessly that their memories may deteriorate. Usually their concern is baseless. Even if you're well past middle age it's very unlikely that there's anything wrong with your memory.

In a McGill University study directed by Dr. V. A. Kral, 169 men and women — all past middle age — were given a battery of memory tests. In the 60-to-70 group 69% were found to have excellent memories. However, in the very oldest group (over 90) most, though not all, of the men and women did have memory defects.

Another point: other studies show that people who remain active in some kind of occupation as they grow older retain their memory function better than those who retire.

When does your memory work best?

Studies conducted by psychiatrist David Harold Fink and other authorities show that your memory functions at top efficiency when you relax as completely as possible.

Next time you're trying to remember something and can't, stretch out on a couch and really let yourself go. Relax your mind and muscles. The odds are that what you were trying to recall will flash back in jig time.

Conversely, tests show that the more tense and anxious a person is, the poorer his memory functions. People suffering from extreme anxiety may lose so much of their recall ability they are temporarily unable to remember their street addresses or telephone numbers.

Does a poor memory reflect on your intelligence?

Not in the least. Studies show that people of below-average intelligence often have better memories than persons in the high I.Q. brackets. Many of the world's brainiest people have been absent-minded and forgetful.

Is there a sure way to remember?

There certainly is. The simple principle of automatic association can be your "memory insurance policy." Here's how it works: Let's say you're dropping off to sleep and suddenly remember something important that you must do first thing in the morning. Reach over to the bedside table and turn your alarm clock around so that it faces away from you. That's all. Or, tie a knot in one of your socks. Or tip the shade on your reading light askew — anything you're sure to notice in the morning. The minute you wake up and see that the clock's turned around you will automatically recall the thing you wanted to remember.

Dr. Martin Grotjahn, professor at the University of Southern California and author of *Psychoanalysis and the Family Neurosis,* says, "This system is soundly grounded in psychological principle. It is highly effective." With a little ingenuity you can use this principle almost any time it is important not to forget something. For example: as you leave your car in the office parking lot you notice the gas gauge says your tank's almost empty. How do you insure against forgetting to get gas when you come back?

Simple. Just put your car keys in a different pocket — right instead of left, or back instead of front. Later, when you find your keys in an unaccustomed place your memory instantly snaps awake and says, "Look, Jack, let's get some gas!"

If you're eating in a restaurant and are afraid you'll forget your overcoat, hat or umbrella, take one of the bills in your wallet and fold it sideways over the others. Later, when you pay your check, you'll get your automatic reminder exactly when you need it.

The number of ways in which "memory insurance" can be used is limited only by your own resourcefulness. Husbands might even use it to remember wedding anniversaries!

WHO DIETS BEST – HUSBANDS OR WIVES?
Everybody Knows There Are Differences Between Men And Women, But You Probably Don't Realize How Many! Which Sex Is Embarrassed Easier? Which Enjoys More Sleep? The Questions Are Easy. But Watch Out For The Answers!

	TRUE	FALSE
1. When it comes to losing weight, men outclass women.	[ ]	[ ]
2. Men make better jurors than women.	[ ]	[ ]
3. Though "girl watching" is thought of as a male avocation, women actually do more of it than men.	[ ]	[ ]
4. Men enjoy meeting new people more than women.	[ ]	[ ]
5. Women are better judges of human nature than men are.	[ ]	[ ]
6. When it comes to buying a new car, it's the wife who usually has the final say.	[ ]	[ ]
7. Men like men a whole lot more than women like women.	[ ]	[ ]
8. Women are more shy and modest than men.	[ ]	[ ]
9. Men have better heads for figures than women do.	[ ]	[ ]
10. Men enjoy sleeping more than women do.	[ ]	[ ]

1. *True. Men are better at reducing.* Weight-reduction studies conducted by the University of Pennsylvania School of Medicine and the Department of Nutrition at New York Hospital show that males tend to be far more successful than females in losing excess poundage. And the more excess avoirdupois involved, the more the men outdistance the women in shedding it.

2. *True. Men make better jurors* than women. Recent studies conducted by the Law School of the University of Chicago show that male jurors participate more actively and effectively in jury deliberations than female jurors. Women jurors were found to spend more time exchanging personal experiences and making disruptive remarks. Men tended to show greater competence in

368

objectively reviewing and evaluating trial evidence.

3. *True. Women are tops at "girl watching."* Researchers have found that men don't spend nearly as much of their time eyeing pretty girls as women do. In studies conducted at Harvard, for example, when movies were shown to groups of men and women subjects (in situations where their eye movements could be observed) it was found that women spent more time than men watching the heroine. Other studies have noted that when a woman joins a party, she almost invariably takes stock of all the women present before she even looks at the men.

4. *False. Men do not enjoy meeting new people* as much as women do. Sociological studies conducted at Tufts University show that women like the society of other people much more.

Men were found more inclined to take an antisocial attitude toward their environment, and to be more wary of relationships with others. Women were more inclined to regard the world as being pleasant, friendly and sociable.

5. *True. Women are better judges of human nature.* Dr. Van Cleve Morris, of Rutgers University, has made a study of this matter. Females, Professor Morris finds, are far more keen and sensitive to interpersonal relations than males; they can see more, feel more of what is going on, what motivations are at work, what lies behind a person's thoughts or deeds. Women, he says, have a superior ability to "tune in on the wave length of other human beings."

6. *False. The man is the boss when it comes to cars.* Results of nationwide marketing surveys, evaluated at the University of Michigan's conference on consumer behavior, show that wives don't place the value on having a new car that husbands do, and often suggest cheaper models or secondhand cars. But the husband usually goes out and buys the car he prefers.

7. *True. Men like men better than women like women.* Studies conducted at the University of California show that men in evaluating their own sex tend to emphasize men's most *desirable* qualities. But when women were asked about their own sex, they tended to emphasize *undesirable* characteristics, such as narrow-mindedness and being rattle-brained.

8. *False. Women are not more shy and modest.* Studies of the

noted psychoanalyst, Dr. Martin Grotjahn, show that women are far less likely to become flustered or embarrassed in an awkward or delicate situation.

In his textbook, *Beyond Laughter*, Dr. Grotjahn cites this amusing incident. A group of college students (half men and half women) undertook a series of long hikes sponsored by their college.

"I went along," the psychoanalyst relates, "as an interested observer. We passed a nudist camp on one of our hikes and when we were near the gates, I could not resist asking, 'Why don't we visit the camp?' "

"It was clearly understood that while we were in Rome we would have to do as the Romans did. A vote was taken, and all of the girls — unanimously! — voted in favor of a visit. All of the boys — just as unanimously! — voted against it."

9. *True. Men are better at figures* — faster and more accurate. Wives, stay away from that checkbook!

10. *True. Men do seem to enjoy sleeping more than women do.* Studies conducted at the Alabama Polytechnic Institute show that men's dreams tend to be far more pleasant than women's. Women's dreams are apt to be dreams of disappointment and frustration, whereas men's dreams are on the happy side.

It was also found that a man is more likely to dream about doing something his spouse wouldn't permit him to do if she knew about it.

WHO GETS FOOLED MOST — HUSBANDS OR WIVES?
You May Be Surprised! Try This Quiz To See
How Much You Know About
Men, Women, Love And Marriage

Practically everybody is an amateur expert on love and marriage — but how does your "expertness" stack up against the facts uncovered by scientific investigators?

Husbands and wives, prepare to defend yourselves — some of these may start arguments:

	TRUE	FALSE
1. A husband is asking for trouble when he discusses other women with his wife.	[ ]	[ ]
2. The axiom, "Absence makes the heart grow fonder," applies more to women than to men.	[ ]	[ ]
3. It's more difficult for a man to deceive his wife about something than vice versa.	[ ]	[ ]
4. There is one thing all husbands have in common: they hate being henpecked or dictated to by their wives.	[ ]	[ ]
5. Women lie about their ages more than men do.	[ ]	[ ]
6. Women workers give their employers more trouble than men workers do.	[ ]	[ ]
7. When marital upsets occur, wives are less willing to accept their share of the blame than husbands are.	[ ]	[ ]
8. Beauty has little to do with a woman catching and holding a husband.	[ ]	[ ]
9. Husbands have less voice in family decisions when the wife works.	[ ]	[ ]
10. Men expect more from their wives than women do from their husbands.	[ ]	[ ]

Answers.

1. *True. Discussing other women puts a husband on dangerous ground.* No matter what the husband says about the other

woman he runs the risk of causing misunderstandings and ruffled feelings.

2. If the husband speaks *favorably* of another woman, his wife may suspect him of being "too interested." If he speaks *unfavorably,* that's not good either. For, as sociologist Paul H. Landis points out: "A man must always be careful in making any criticism of women in the presence of his wife or sweetheart, for she immediately feels that his abstract criticism is really meant for her."

2. *False. Absence makes her heart grow fonder — of somebody else?* Psychological studies conducted on a cross section of men and women students at the University of Redlands show that when the object of a *woman's* affections is absent over a protracted period of time, her romantic feelings for him tend to wane. However, the *opposite* tendency was found true for *men.*

3. *True. Wives don't fool easy.* When a husband comes up with a phony alibi, chances are his wife will spot it from his voice. Psychological tests conducted at DePauw University show that women are much better than men in judging whether a person is lying from the way his voice sounds. The study also shows that when a woman tells an untruth, her voice doesn't give her away.

4. *False. Some men want to be henpecked.* Studies conducted by the American Institute of Family Relations show that many men have a need to be dominated by their wives in order to feel secure. Such a man wouldn't be happy with a wife who didn't tell him what to do.

5. *False. Men fib more about their age.* An eight-year study by Dr. Nathan Mansor indicates that men are more given to lying about age than women.

The method used in making the study was simple: when each patient left the doctor's office a file card was filled out with his name, stated age, and marital status. On subsequent visits, at least 12 months later, the same information was elicited and recorded on the file card. A lying patient was considered to be anyone who deviated from the truth one or more times.

6. *True. Women workers cause employers more trouble than men.* To find out the answer to this question, the National Office Management Association recently polled heads of 1,900 business and industrial organizations in the U.S. and Canada. Seventy-five per cent of the firms said they had more "problem" workers among women.

7. *True. Husbands admit they're wrong.* A study by the Survey Research Center at the University of Michigan showed that when marital problems are involved, husbands admit being at fault far more readily than wives do. Wives were more disposed to rationalize the situation in a way that put the blame exclusively on the husband.

8. *True. Beauty's not the big thing.* Psychologist Richard H. Klemer, member of the American Institute of Family Relations, finds that good looks actually play a minor role. He studied two representative groups of women, of similar ages and backgrounds. All the women in one group were married and those in the other group were still single. And 25% of the single women were easily better looking than any of the married women.

What really counts? According to Dr. Klemer's investigations, it's a woman's disposition.

9. *False. Girl breadwinners don't take charge.* Surprisingly enough, recent surveys of married couples from various walks of life, conducted by Florida State University Research Council investigators, have shown that husbands have considerably *more* voice in family decisions when the wife is a breadwinner than when she isn't. This finding has investigators puzzled. Possibly it is because by the time the wife works all day, comes home and gets the house tidied up and dinner on the table, she is too tired to argue about family matters.

10. *False. Wives expect the most.* The Michigan Survey Research Center found that women demand more from their husbands, and criticize more if they don't get what they want.

ARE MEN MORE CONCEITED THAN WOMEN?
Are They Smarter? More Sincere?
Here's A Quiz Loaded With Fighting Words —
But Science Has Some Surprising Answers

Everybody knows that men are the less-emotional sex, and that women are more prone to laughter and tears. But are these suppositions true? Here's a quiz that's likely to upset a few popular notions. Check true or false.

	TRUE	FALSE
1. Men are more egotistical than women are.	[ ]	[ ]
2. Men have more appreciation for the beauty of nature, the call of the wide-open spaces, than women.	[ ]	[ ]
3. Women have more poise than men.	[ ]	[ ]
4. Men are most often to blame for marriages that go "on the rocks."	[ ]	[ ]
5. Women have better imaginations than men.	[ ]	[ ]
6. The average woman can't tell a funny story as well as a man.	[ ]	[ ]
7. Women are more emotional than men.	[ ]	[ ]
8. Women are more sincere than men.	[ ]	[ ]
9. Women's mental reflexes are slower than men's.	[ ]	[ ]
10. Most husbands are henpecked.	[ ]	[ ]

Here are the answers

1. *False.* Women are more egotistical. Psychological studies conducted at the University of California evaluated self-opinions of men and women on such items as self-reliance, sense of personal worth, feeling of belonging, social skills, and family and community relations. These tests showed that women are far more prone to have an inflated idea of their own importance.

2. *False.* Women have far greater appreciation of the beauties of nature than men. Thus, despite the fact that both convention and a housewife role may cause a woman to spend most of her life indoors, according to studies conducted at Stanford University by psychologist Dr. Catherine Cox Miles and the late

Dr. Lewis M. Terman. Men have a greater affinity for pursuits which take them outdoors — such as hunting and fishing. But when it comes to the grandeur of nature, forests, streams, sunsets and awe-inspiring vistas, the women were found to respond with much keener appreciation than the men.

3. *True.* Women have more aplomb and composure than the average male, particularly in social situations, say University of Southern California psychologists. Despite men's reputation for being the most self-possessed sex, tests showed that they are much more easily flustered and disconcerted than the ladies are. In fact, women averaged much better scores when it came to taking embarrassing situations in their stride. Studies have also shown that men blush more easily.

4. *False.* In most cases *both* parties are equally at fault when a marriage cracks up. A study of over 10,000 divorce cases conducted by Judge Thomas R. Blaine bears out this fact.

5. *True.* Tests show that the women definitely have it over the men when it comes to imagination. Psychologists at Harvard and two other leading universities have evaluated the results of leading studies on this question. Consensus: women definitely excel. Women were also found to surpass men in vividness of mental imagery and on story-completion tests. The evidence would seem to indicate that far more women would excel in such fields as poetry, literature and art if they applied themselves in this direction.

6. *True.* Men are better story-tellers. University of Southern California's professor of psychiatry, Dr. Martin Grotjahn, sums up the findings of his studies on this interesting matter in his textbook *Beyond Laughter.* First, he points out that the woman of today is supposed to be warm, understanding, charming and attractive — but not witty. Women are traditionally supposed to be incapable of even retelling a joke properly, and his studies show that with the majority of women this assumption is perfectly valid.

There are, he observes, a few women who are as skillful as any man in inventing and retelling jokes. But they are in the distinct minority — and most men are afraid of them and run for cover. Most women are aware of this — at least unconsciously — and are inhibited by it.

7. *False.* Men are every bit as emotional as women, according to recent studies conducted at the University of California Institute of Personality Assessment and Research. They feel things just as deeply and poignantly and are as much upset by them as the opposite sex. The only difference is that men don't *express* their emotional feelings as freely and openly as women do. This is largely due to the fact that social custom provides for two different behavior patterns for men and women. For example, a woman may burst into tears to express hurt or grief, but such behavior in a man is not socially acceptable.

The findings of the study made it evident that the differences in the display of emotions between men and women are not due to innate differences in feeling.

8. *False.* Consensus of psychological findings shows that men tend to be far more sincere in their relations with others than women. Women are much more prone to disguise their true feelings with an insincere remark than men are. And a woman's penchant for treating another woman whom she dislikes with simulated cordiality is axiomatic. In fact, evidence all up and down the line indicates that women are much more inclined to be two-faced — particularly with members of their own sex. A leading psychiatrist recently displayed a Franklin Folger cartoon in which three women are shown departing from the house of a friend. "I wonder," muses one, "how much she paid for those awful slip covers I admired so much."

9. *True.* Women's mental reflexes are slower than men's. Recent studies reported by the American Psychological Association show that men can size up a situation and act on it quicker than women can. It even has been observed in restaurants, for example, that the female of the species takes longer to decide what she wants than the average male. And a British survey showed that it takes a man five to ten minutes to buy a hat when he shops alone, twice as long if he's with a girl friend, 30 to 40 minutes if he goes with his wife.

10. *False.* Only one husband out of every three can be classified as henpecked, says the American Institute of Family Relations. Of the remaining two thirds, an appreciable percent-

age were subjected to some mild nagging on occasion, but that's about as far as it went.

The survey showed, however, that the majority of the henpecked one-third were brow-beaten and dictated to to such an extent that the term "head of the house" could be applied only as a form of courtesy, without any basis in fact.

THE SUPERIOR SEX IS . . . ?
The Contest Shows No Signs Of Ceasing, But New Facts Are Providing New Weapons

Some of the liveliest arguments in the history of men and women have been over which sex is superior, and in what ways. Some discussions end with the throwing of dishes as well as adjectives. Here are the findings on the subject in scientific studies conducted by universities and research centers.

Do women worry more than men?

Yes. Men may get more ulcers, but women do more worrying. A nationwide interview survey found that women worry far more than men do about everything that touches their lives. They worry more about their personal shortcomings, marriages, children, and their children's children. One of their chief worries was that all their worrying might bring on a nervous breakdown.

Can women stand noise better than men can?

Yes. Public-health studies of men and women exposed to the clamor of industrial machinery have shown that women can take far more noise than men without suffering physical ill effects, such as hearing loss. Husbands who come home to find the wife shouting to make herself heard over the household bedlam, children yelling at each other, the baby testing its lung power, the blare of the TV set, the roar of the vacuum cleaner may wonder how she can take this daily pandemonium without becoming deaf. Fortunately, she has what science terms "a greater resistance to noise trauma."

When a husband is intemperate, is it usually a nagging wife who has driven him to drink?

No. "The type of woman who will drive her husband to drink" has no being in fact. At the University of Washington School of Medicine, investigators made an extensive study of wives of alcoholics and nonalcoholics. They found that the personality types of wives of temperate husbands were no different from those of alcoholics.

Are women more thoughtful of others than men are?

No. All evidence indicates that most women's thoughts seldom stray far from themselves. This is particularly evident in their conversation.

Investigators at the University of Cincinnati studied the speech habits of men and women of various ages, in various I.Q. ranges. Conversational samples of each subject were recorded and studied. Most women's speech was found to a far greater extent than men's to contain words referring to herself. "Me," "Mine," "I don't like this," "I don't like that," "My such-and-such," and other phrases abounded in the conversation. Although this situation held true for the vast majority of women, those of higher I.Q. were often exceptions.

Do women feel pain more than men?

Yes. When a woman has a pain, it hurts more than when a man has the same pain. Toothache, stomachache, stubbed toe, whatever — if a woman has it, the pain is more acute and lasts longer. Veterans' Administration psychologist Donald V. Petrovich subjected men and women of various ages to the recently developed Pain Apperception test. In all cases women rated higher both as to intensity and duration of pain than men did.

Can women taste things better than men?

Yes. A human being has only four distinct tastes: bitter, salt, sour, and sweet, and each is perceived by a different part of the tongue. In a recent study, investigators measured the taste sensitivity of nearly 400 men and women. Women had a very definite superiority.

The only things that men could taste better than women

were vinegar, lemon, and sour grapes!

Can men on the average hear as well as women?

No. Studies conducted at the University of Michigan show that men can hear lower-pitched sounds as well as women, but they can't hear higher-pitched sounds nearly as well. So when a husband says, "But I didn't *hear* you call me to dinner, dear," there's a good chance that he didn't.

Are women more secretive than men?

No. Studies directed by University of Florida psychologist Sidney M. Journard show that women reveal far more of themselves to their friends than men do. It was found that a man is far more inclined to keep much of his real self hidden from others.

Would most people rather confide in a man than in a woman?

No. The University of Florida studies show that women are confided in by members of both sexes to a far greater extent than men are. Indeed, the investigators found that the average woman is the repository of more secrets than the average male. Despite her reputation for being unable to keep a secret, there is something about a woman that invites confidences. Men will tell things to a woman that they wouldn't dream of confiding to another man. And a woman, when letting her hair down to another, is likely to become silent when a man is within earshot, even and perhaps especially if he is her husband. This same principle of the man being the "last to know" was found to hold true with fathers and their children's confidence.

THE TRUTH ABOUT QUARRELS
Do Some Couples Like To Fight?
What's The Best Way To Win An Argument With Your Spouse?
Should You Raise Your Voice?

Clear the family arena for action. This quiz may start as many arguments as it settles, but it's guaranteed to banish boredom from the fireside and provide fuel for some lively family discussions. In addition to testing your knowledge about what gives with the battle of the sexes, it provides answers to questions you've always wondered about — and some you've probably never thought of.

1. Many marriages are held together simply because the couples enjoy fighting with each other. (True____, False____)

2. Your husband is less likely to blow his top about those bills you've run up, or that fur coat you have on your mind, if you break the news to him while he's lying down. (True____, False____)

3. Wives are prone to exaggerate when they try to needle hubby about how many other men they could have married. (True____, False____)

4. The older a man gets, the younger he wants his wife to look. (True____, False____)

5. It's difficult for a man to tell whether a woman honestly means what she says or whether she's just pretending and "putting on an act." (True____, False____)

6. When your spouse raises her voice during a discussion, the best way to win the argument is for you to raise yours, too — and shout her down. (True____, False____)

7. With young married couples, altercations involving in-laws are likely to exceed all other husband-and-wife skirmishes. (True____, False____)

8. When it comes to decisions on how the family income is spent, husbands have better judgment than wives. (True____, False____)

9. Most husband and wife quarrels are senseless — their differences could easily be settled by discussion. (True____, False____)

Answers

1. *True.* Recently psychiatrists at the Menninger Foundation made an intensive study of long-standing discordant marriages. They picked the stormiest, most strife-ridden they could find, the kind that always seem as though they are heading for immediate crack-up — yet unaccountably endure. Why? The psychiatrists concluded from their findings that the almost constant friction and fighting in these family arenas served a psychological purpose for both husband and wife; that seemingly incompatible couples may stay married indefinitely to have someone to fight with.

In such turbulent marriages, the investigators found what seemed to be a tacit agreement that threats of divorce or separation were not to be taken literally. In many cases, perennially sparring couples claimed they were staying together for the sake of their children — but further probing revealed this to be subterfuge; the claim was made only because it was more socially acceptable than saying they needed "sparring partners."

2. *True.* Your chances of getting your way in any kind of situation are better if you can maneuver your husband into a reclining position before you throw the works at him. For science has found that husbands (wives, too, for that matter) are much less likely to stand up for their rights when they're lying down. Studies conducted by psychology professor Hugo G. Beigel at Long Island University show that people react far more passively and resignedly to unpleasant or disturbing verbal utterances when they're in a reclining position. The study showed that a sitting position is conducive to a more vigorous and active reaction. But the worst time to tackle your husband with a controversial subject is when he's standing up. Then, the tests showed, he's most likely to over-react and "blow a gasket."

3. *True.* In a survey conducted by the American Institute of Family Relations, women from various walks of life were polled on the number of "possible husbands" they had known. Findings of the study indicated that the average woman is lucky if she chalks up more than three *bona fide* proposals during her entire husband-hunting career. Certainly there are exceptions, but for every lass who makes a high score in the marriage proposal

381

department, there are many who married the only man who ever popped the question to them.

4. *True.* He may not say anything about it to his wife, but evidence indicates most husbands do feel this way. Dr. Paul H. Jacobson, director of population and family research for a leading life insurance company, has analyzed the findings of leading sociological studies and surveys. He finds that, generally speaking, the older a man gets the more he tends to prefer a woman appreciably younger than himself. This preference of the aging male for a more youthful-appearing partner than himself is similarly evidenced by other investigations, which show that when older men marry they tend to pick women younger than they are.

5. *True.* Sociological studies conducted at Harvard show that men are far more apt to reveal their true feelings than women are. The investigators found that a woman is much more apt to conceal what she really feels, to register the emotion she feels will best fit the occasion and say what she feels her listener expects. It is pointed out that this tendency not only bewilders the male, but often confuses the lady herself. As sociologists Carle C. Zimmerman and Lucius F. Cervantes point out: "A woman's life is much more of a masque or play than a man's is. She is so helpless and yet strangely she is the one who is most frequently in control. In courtship, for example, custom has made her as helpless as a mousetrap — it dare not pursue the mouse; yet strangely enough it is the mouse and not the mousetrap which is ensnared."

6. *False.* The smartest thing you can do is just the opposite — *lower your voice.* This is a strategy that takes advantage of two psychological principles: (1) the mere act of raising your voice in a discussion tends to make the other person angry and intractable — even if he may agree with what you say; (2) when you raise your voice, tests show that the other person just can't help raising his, too — unless he makes a special effort. Shout at another person and he will shout back. Speak in a low tone and he will automatically answer softly. And when you subdue your spouse's voice to a low tone, you also subdue his resent-

382

ment and animosity. He can't help but become more receptive to your point of view. And also the fact that he raised his voice and you didn't is likely to throw him a bit off stride. These advantages markedly increase your chances of winning the argument.

7. *True.* Evidence all up and down the line indicates this to be the case. For example, sociologist Judson T. Landis reports a study of 544 married couples from various walks of life. They were asked to list their most difficult marital problems. In-law frictions were rated the No. 1 villain — topping the list of all other causes of discord. Typical comments: "They try to run our home"; "They treat us as children"; "They try to influence our lives", "According to them, nothing I do is right." The couples were asked to indicate which in-law was chiefly involved in the friction. Mothers-in-law figured in the majority of cases, with sisters-in-law running second in the trouble-makers' sweepstakes. Fathers-in-law ran a close third and brothers-in-law figured as an also-ran — their contribution to tense in-law relationships being rated as negligible.

The attitude of many douples to in-laws is definitely on the bitter side and is mirrored to an appreciable extent by the following joke: An example of mixed feelings — a man watching his mother-in-law go over a cliff in his brand new Cadillac convertible.

8. *False.* At the University of Michigan's conference on consumer behavior, findings of coast-to-coast marketing surveys were carefully evaluated. It was found that in most cases wives are more astute and show sounder judgment in administering the family income than husbands. They were discovered to be more realistic where expenditures were concerned, placed more emphasis on such practicalities as putting money aside for emergencies, furnishing the home, providing for the children, etc. Husbands were more prone to advocate extravagances, to lobby for luxury purchases that would stretch the family budget out of shape. Typical examples: The husband believes the family can afford a new car, a power boat, or whatever, while the wife says, "I don't see where the money is coming from. We'll have to wait a while."

9. *False.* Human nature being what it is, this would be completely impossible in most cases. Says sociologist E. E. LeMasters, in summing up his findings on the subject in his recent textbooks on marriage: "It may be that some couples, although not very many, settle their differences through *discussion* and in this sense, avoid *argument,* but this implies more self-control than most of us are capable of. If we are to grow in marriage, then we must learn from each other, and this requires differences between the spouses." As other authorities have pointed out, the trick for married couples to learn is not to avoid arguments, but rather to learn how to argue constructively.

WHO STARTS THE FIGHTS?
Is It Usually The Man Or The Woman?
Who's Most Ready To Forgive And Forget?
A Round-Up On A Fascinating Topic

Clear the family arena, grab a pencil and see who knows most about what gives with the opposite sex. Each question is guaranteed to produce a reaction — although we don't guarantee what kind. The answers are based on leading surveys and studies.

	TRUE	FALSE
1. Women are more inclined than men to provoke arguments deliberately.	[ ]	[ ]
2. A woman is more likely to start smashing dishes and throwing things when she gets mad than her husband is.	[ ]	[ ]
3. Wives are more critical of their husband's faults and shortcomings.	[ ]	[ ]
4. A husband is more apt to blow his top before meals than at any other time.	[ ]	[ ]
5. Women are more narrow-minded than men		

and lack a man's capacity to see the other side
of an argument.   [ ]   [ ]
6. Women can't see as well as men.   [ ]   [ ]
7. Wives are notorious for infuriating their
husbands by being late for appointments. This
is because it makes them feel important.   [ ]   [ ]
8. Women are more dissatisfied with their
lives than men are.   [ ]   [ ]
9. Women tend to be more neurotic than men.   [ ]   [ ]
10. Wives get along better with their in-laws
than husbands do.   [ ]   [ ]
11. After a family argument, wives are quicker
to forgive and forget than husbands.   [ ]   [ ]
12. Wives who get along best with their husbands
are those who are well-endowed with "woman's
intuition."   [ ]   [ ]

Here are the answers

1. *True.* As the noted psychiatrist Dr. David H. Fink points
out, women thrive on attention, feel emotionally insecure when
they think they aren't getting their share of it. Thus a wife
may start a row simply as a means of gaining her share of
attention. And while this drastic method doesn't exactly
contribute to domestic harmony, it does achieve the desired
effect.

2. *False.* Despite the fact that it's the wife who is usually
depicted in cartoons as hurling a vase at her husband, or
smashing up the crockery, in real life it's more apt to be the
husband who is given to destructive impulses. This fact has
been demonstrated by psychological studies at the Hartford
Seminary Foundation in Hartford, Conn.

3. *True.* In a nationwide poll of married couples, wives were
found to be far more critical than husbands. Seventy-one out
of every 100 women singled out some trait in their husbands
to criticize, as compared with 54 out of every 100 men who
found fault with their wives.

4. *True.* And this applies to the wife as well. Columbia

University studies show that people are more irritable at this time than during any other period in the day. Tip to wives: don't keep him waiting for dinner. And should there be domestic differences to iron out, don't try to do it just before meal-time.

5. *True.* Psychologists have found women to be by far the more subjective-minded sex, tending to direct their thoughts inward toward themselves. This self-preoccupation causes a woman's whole outlook to be much narrower than a man's. And since men are by nature more objective-minded it's easier for them to understand someone else's viewpoint.

6. *True.* Studies conducted by University of California researchers showed that almost twice as many women as men became significantly near-sighted by the time they reached their early 30's. In the opposite direction, it was found that women also had a greater tendency to become far-sighted.

7. *False.* The fact is that women have a different sense of time than men do. Studies conducted at Arizona State Teachers College show that time goes by much faster for a woman than for a man. If husbands and wives could just figure out some way to synchronize their mental clocks, it would eliminate a lot of domestic friction.

8. *True.* Surveys conducted by the American Institute of Public Opinion show that women tend to be far more discontented with their lot than men are, and feel that men lead the more interesting lives, and have an easier time of it. And in one survey men and women from all walks of life were asked: "If you had a choice, which would you rather be — a man or a woman?" While only 6% of the men said they would prefer to be women, 29% of the women said they would much prefer to be men.

9. *True.* Wide-scale studies conducted by the National Association for Mental Health show that women are much more likely to become emotionally maladjusted, develop deep-seated personality conflicts and assorted phobias than men are. The studies also showed that, regardless of their age bracket, women are more apt to lose touch with the real world around them than men are. The fair sex also led the field in the

hypochondria department (the gentle art of magnifying little aches and pains out of proportion and imagining you're physically ill when you're actually fit as a fiddle).

10. *False.* Exhaustive studies conducted by sociologists both at Stanford and at the University of Chicago, show that men get along with their in-laws much better than their spouses do. It was found that men tend to regard their mothers-in-law in a much more sympathetic light than women do. As a matter of fact, many husbands felt that their in-law relationship actually strengthened their marriage; but most wives didn't go along with this view.

11. *False.* Studies show that women tend to be far more introspective and given to brooding over real or fancied grievances.

12. *False.* Despite the fact that intuition is popularly supposed to facilitate human understanding, studies conducted at Stanford University show that it is actually a handicap to getting married, and staying that way. Indeed, it's easy to imagine situations where a woman's ability to sense her husband's innermost thoughts and desires could lead to domestic strife. And most of us harbor impulses — at least fleetingly — which would not set at all well with the wife, were she intuitive enough to divine them. At any rate the investigators found — quite significantly — that intuitive perception is far more prevalent among the single and the divorced than among the happily married.

So don't envy the woman who can "read her husband like an open book"! As often as not this ability pays off in negative dividends.

CAN WOMEN GET ALONG WITHOUT MEN?
And Are They More Mercenary?
More Intelligent? Better Drivers?

Nothing's better than a little lively home discussion — as long as nobody starts throwing things — so here's another battle-of-the-sexes quiz. It's designed to answer that age-old argument as to who knows more about men and women: men, or women?

The topics covered have been fought over for centuries and will probably provide inspiration for many fine tussles in centuries to come. Of course, *we* think *we've* got the right answers — they've been based on the latest findings of responsibl surveys and researchers. Anyway, match yourselves off, get you selves a couple of pencils, and see which sex can score the highes And remember to count ten!

	TRUE	FALSE
1. Men are easier to live with than women.	[ ]	[ ]
2. The best way to find out what a man's really like is to ask his wife.	[ ]	[ ]
3. Men have a better sense of humor than women.	[ ]	[ ]
4. Women are more mercenary than men.	[ ]	[ ]
5. Generally speaking, women are more level-headed than men.	[ ]	[ ]
6. Women are more bashful than men.	[ ]	[ ]
7. Men are better drivers than women.	[ ]	[ ]
8. Women have better memories than men.	[ ]	[ ]
9. Most women think they are more intelligent than men.	[ ]	[ ]
10. Men can get along without women better than women can get along without men.	[ ]	[ ]

Here are the answers:

1. *False.* Wide-scale studies conducted by sociologists Ernest W. Burgess of the University of Chicago and Paul Wallin of Stanford show that in most marriages it is the husband who is the more rigid and set in his ways, and that it is the wife who is called upon to make most of the adjustments. The study also

388

makes it clear that if women were not willing to go more than half way in making these adjustments, a great many more marriages would go on the rocks.

Women like to get their way just as much as men do, but they go about it more subtly and more diplomatically ("I'll talk to him about it when he's in the right mood," etc.) They're also more willing to compromise when the situation seems to indicate it.

2. *False.* "If you want to know what a man is like, the *last* person to ask is his wife," says psychologist Verne Kallejian, who has made a study of the matter at the University of California at Los Angeles. A woman may be expert in judging others, but when it comes to her husband it's an entirely different story. Dr. Kallejian's studies show that a wife tends to believe that she understands best the person that she likes the most; but that actually she has the greatest difficulty in understanding anyone she strongly likes. She tends, evidently, to see her husband not as he actually is, but the way she wants or expects him to be. And the same principle was found to apply to men.

3. *False.* Psychologists at Wesleyan University subjected hundreds of men and women to a sense of humor test, evaluating each subject's reaction to 100 representative jokes — ranging from the extremely funny to the completely pointless. The men tended to laugh at *all* of the jokes, and rate them all higher than the women did. The women were more discriminating. They laughed at the funniest jokes, and gave them even higher ratings than the men did. But they were less inclined to laugh at the feeble jokes than the men were.

The study indicated that while men may be more *easily* amused than women by assorted varieties of humor, the ladies tend to be sharper and more discerning in the sense-of-humor department.

4. *True.* Surveys show that women are far more inclined to regard "plenty of money" as the prime requisite for happiness than men are. Sociological studies conducted at Purdue University showed that the most marked difference between the sexes, when it comes to picking a marriage partner, is the

woman's concern with her prospective mate's financial status. Nationwide polls conducted by the American Institute of Public Opinion bear out this finding, and also show that the thing wives quarrel most often with their husbands about is — yes, you guessed it — money!

5. *False.* A question as controversial as this is most acceptably resolved by permitting the nation's male and female citizens to settle it themselves. A coast-to-coast Gallup survey has done just that. Representative sample groups of men and women were asked to indicate which sex their experience has shown to be the most level-headed. The men got almost twice as many votes as the women.

6. *False.* Psychological studies conducted at the University of Southern California have shown that men are shyer, more bashful, and more timid than women: and that women very definitely have it over the males when it comes to social poise, self-confidence, and the ability to handle embarrassing situations.

7. *True* — at least in the opinion of most Americans. In a nationwide poll, the American Institute of Public Opinion asked men and women from every walk of life if they'd rather ride in a car driven by a man or woman. Forty-nine per cent said that they'd definitely feel more comfortable riding with a man; 43% weren't particular; but only 5% actually preferred to ride with a woman. (Three per cent had no opinion.) The controversy over which sex is the most competent to sit behind a steering wheel has been going on for a long time. But when the vote is put to the American people, the male of the species wins hands down. (Oops, watch that fender, Jack!)

8. *True.* University of Oregon psychologist Leona E. Tyler has evaluated the results of leading scientific studies on this question. Consensus of the findings: female superiority in the memory department. Men forget things faster — not because they don't *try* to remember — but because they're just built that way.

9. *False.* In spite of all the feminine talk about how much better the world would be if women ran it, University of Pennsylvania studies show that women very definitely tend to regard men as their intellectual superiors (the study also showed that the majority of men agree enthusiastically). Other

390

investigations show that the average woman prefers to look up to her husband intellectually — whether he rates it or not.

In short, a woman likes her man to be smarter than she is; and if he isn't, she'll try to convince herself that he is anyway.

10. *False.* Wide-scale studies conducted by the Metropolitan Life Insurance Company show that spinsters are much more capable of adjusting to the single life than bachelors; and that the latter are far more subject to physical and mental breakdowns. Also, the mortality table for those studied showed a much higher rate for men who lose their wives than for women who lose their husbands.

In other words, women think men are bright, level-headed and good at driving cars — but not indispensable!

VIII.

WHAT IS THIS THING CALLED LOVE?

WHAT IS THIS THING CALLED LOVE?

*Without romantic love permeating human life as
it does, we would have very little poetry, literature,
art – even less war, to judge by the age-old story of
Troy. The ancient Greeks, followed notably by
Fulton Sheen and Martin Luther King, Jr. distin-
guished three kinds of love:* <u>agape,</u> <u>philia,</u> *and* <u>eros.</u>

*Agape meant religious love; philia, marital or
friendly attachment where the partner was
irreplaceable; eros, physical-sexual attraction where
the partner did not much matter. But under whatever form, love interferes with the calm course of
nearly every normal person's life. How to diagnose
it and what to do about it, should obviously be part
of every thinking man or woman's background of
knowledge.*

ROMANTIC LOVE
Researchers Are Taking A Scientific Look At
"The Supreme Theme Of Art And Song"

Sociologists and psychologists have been making surveys to
find out as much as possible about love, and why it affects us
the way it does. Their findings answer questions you've
undoubtedly asked, and some you've probably never thought of.

Is it true that many people don't believe in romantic love?

Yes. Many who pride themselves on being "practical" scoff
at the idea of romantic love, or even associate it with emotional
instability. But romantic persons can find comfort in recent
scientific findings. At Capital University, a sociological study
has shown that, contrary to whatever you might think, a
romantic attitude goes with good emotional adjustment. Other
investigations show that people who look down their noses at
"starry-eyed love" are frequently repressed individuals who
grapple with inner conflicts.

How can you tell if someone you meet is romantic?

The same study showed that the more romantic a person is the more he is likely to agree with such statements as these: "One can't help falling in love if he meets the right person" and "One can truly love only once." The "practical" respond to statements like these: "One doesn't fall in love, it has to be achieved" and "Love can develop after marriage."

When a girl considers a man her best friend, does that mean she's likely to fall in love with him?

No. Studies at the University of Wisconsin show that men tend to select the same kind of woman for a friend as for a wife. But not so with women! Most girls have one set of specifications for a male friend, and an entirely different one for the kind of man they can fall in love with and marry. When a girl tells you she considers you "a real friend," you haven't a hope of winning her hand.

Is it true that absence makes the heart grow fonder?

Yes and No. At the University of Redlands, Prof. Charles W. Hobart studied the effects of separation on the courtships of a random selection of men and women students. It was found that when couples were separated for any length of time men and women reacted in opposite ways. In most cases, a man's romantic feelings for his girl friend increased; but with most women, absence did indeed make their hearts grow fonder — of somebody else.

Does the strong, silent man find the path of true love smooth?

No. American Institute of Family Relations studies show that one of the biggest problems in courtship and marriage is the taboo in our culture that views tenderness as effeminate. It prevents many men from freely expressing their true feelings. The strong, silent man refuses to tell his wife that he loves her because, he says, "I told her that when I asked her to marry me, and it holds good until revoked." His attitude is a menace to himself, his wife, and his marriage. Few things are more important, say the investigators, than for a couple to show their love for each other.

Are lovers' quarrels a danger signal?

People are fond of saying that lovers' quarrels shouldn't be taken seriously. The experts disagree. Says the University of

California sociologist, Dr. Judson T. Landis, "When a romance isn't going smoothly that's one of the most serious danger signals." When associates in business often disagree, he points out, the parties concerned usually see a sign that the partnership isn't workable.

But young people tend to ignore their lovers' quarrels and dwell on the happiness of making up afterward. But their quarreling should tell them that there is something wrong somewhere.

If a couple are certain they are really in love, does that necessarily mean they should marry?

No. Dr. Landis finds that many people rush into marriage because they are in love, and thus are "made for each other." The trouble is that you can be in love with people you couldn't live with happily. "The more research I do," he says, "and the more I work with young people, the more convinced I am that they should approach marriage slowly. Some of the most serious danger signals do not show up in early relationships at all."

When do couples face their biggest crisis?

The American Institute of Family Relations made a study of the various kinds of crises which couples face during courtship and marriage. "The No. 1 crisis is most likely to occur," says director Paul Popenoe, "at the time of the wedding. During the courtship period, each has put his best foot forward, and each has looked for the best in the other. What was said was usually said in praise and love. But as soon as the ceremony is over, there is too often a sudden change in the atmosphere of expressed admiration to one of continual criticism, part of which may have been stored up for many weeks."

What is most necessary to be happy in love?

Each partner must be his real self. As psychologist Sidney M. Jourard points out, most of us have two selves: a public self and a real self. In any love worth the name, each person must be capable of revealing his real self to the other. To be his real self means to express honestly what he feels, needs, wants, expects, and believes.

"Such mutual authenticity is vital," says Dr. Journard, "if

the relationship is to be called love."

Is it true that no two people experience love in the same way?

After a lifetime of study, psychiatrist Dr. Clemens E. Benda insists that there is not just one kind of love, but as many kinds as there are people, all differing in intensity, vitality, strength, and scope of emotional experience. Love is different in each season of life. Its expression is never twice the same.

LOVE AND INFATUATION
Which Is The More Romantic Sex?

Science has been looking at love. Since most people fall in love between the ages of 18 and 24, a University of Pennsylvania professor of sociology, Dr. William M. Kephart, studied men and women in this age group. He wanted to find out how romantic love affects people. There were 576 women and 503 men.

Only 3% of them said that they didn't know what love is. Romantic love is thought to mean different things to different people, but Dr. Kephart found that to those people love means much the same.

Many people are afraid of falling in love because they may be hurt. Nevertheless, the study found that romantic experience was regarded as much more gratifying than painful. Fewer than five persons in 100 felt that it had brought them more heartache than happiness.

How do you tell the difference between love and infatuation?

Most people had trouble distinguishing one from the other for a time. Psychological investigations have shown that there is only one sure way to tell: love lasts, infatuations do not. Most reported infatuations lasted only four to six weeks.

Which sex falls in love more often?

Both the women and men in the study started dating at about the same time (median age 13). The girls were likely to become infatuated almost immediately, frequently with one of the first

397

ey dated. The boys seldom developed any infatuations
ney had been dating for at least a year. Most girls
perienced falling in love for the first time shortly after their
17th birthday. Boys tended to remain uncommitted until
about 18.

Dr. Kephart found that the women averaged more romantic
experiences than the men up until the age of 22, but by age
23-24 this difference had disappeared. "Romantic experiences
for females decreased with closeness to marriage, while the
opposite was true for males," he says. "As a woman passes
from the teens to the 20's and nears the matrimonial state,
emotional experiences tend to be rejected because they impinge
on the monogamic ideal."

*Which sex is more likely to fall in love with someone just
because of physical appearance?*

Men. Girls were found less likely to be influenced by physical
appearance, and thus less subject to disappointment.

*Does this mean that women are more attractive to men than
men are to women?*

Yes, according to the Kephart study, which reports, "The
percentage of those who said that they were 'very easily
attracted' to the opposite sex was nearly twice as high for men
as for women." Other studies have shown similar findings. So,
romantically speaking, men find women more interesting than
women find men. Perhaps they are. Women are more outgoing
than men, more fluent in expressing themselves, and more at
ease in social situations, all qualities which make a person more
interesting to others.

*Is it true that most girls find men older than themselves more
attractive?*

Yes, but it is also true that many prefer men younger than
themselves. In the survey, 31% of the women reported
romantic attachments to younger men. Some 61% of the men
had been either infatuated or in love with girls older than themselves.

The women who had been romantically involved with men
younger than themselves showed some evidence of maladjustment
(relatively poor college grades and poor personality-test scores).

But men who were attracted to older girls did not show signs of maladjustment.

Which sex is more likely to marry without love?

Women are the greater advocates of romantic love, but they are more likely to marry without it. Each person in the survey was asked, "If a man (or woman) had all other qualities you desired, would you marry this person if you were not in love with him?"

Nearly two thirds of the men answered No, but fewer than one fourth of the women did. A co-ed quoted by Professor Kephart said, "I'm undecided. It is rather hard to give a Yes or No answer to this question. If a boy had all the other qualities I desired, and I was not in love with him, I think I could probably talk myself into falling in love!"

So men are apparently more romantic-minded than women are. Women are more likely to let their heads rule their hearts.

Dr. Kephart concludes, "Contrary to a rather strong popular impression, the female is not pushed into marriage by her romantic compulsions. On the contrary, she seems to have a greater measure of control over her romantic inclinations than the male."

HOW CAN YOU TELL IF YOU'RE REALLY IN LOVE?
Wait A While

Love, illusive and mysterious, is the most powerful force on earth, and the most puzzling. In universities and research foundations, psychologists and sociologists have been making studies to find answers to questions that everyone asks about love.

What is love?

No word in the English language is harder to define. Psychoanalyst Erich Fromm, who has made an intensive study of love, says it is a feeling of infinite closeness to the heart of another. "If I love the other person," says Fromm, "I feel one with him or with her." He finds that if two persons are able to let the wall between them break down and "feel close, feel one, this moment of oneness is the most exhilarating, most exciting experience in life." He concludes that the desire for closeness with another person is the most powerful striving in man.

How can you tell if you are really in love?

All over the world, millions of people, from duchess to ditch-digger, are asking themselves this question: how can I tell the difference between true love and infatuation? It is the simplest thing in the world. You don't have to do anything, or consult anybody. All you need to do is wait a while, because an infatuation lasts on the average less than two months, and a great many are over in three or four weeks.

Is there such a thing as love at first sight?

There is sharp disagreement on this question, on the part of both experts and laymen. Those who have never loved at first sight, say it is a romantic myth. But those who have had it happen to them, and who found lasting, true love, cannot be shaken in their conviction. Pick out couples of any age who are happily in love, ask them how they felt about each other when they first met, and you will get three kinds of answers.

1. "We really didn't feel much of anything at first. Jim was just another date. It was some time before we discovered that we really liked each other. And then gradually that liking grew,

until finally we both realized that we were really in love."

2. "Love at first sight? With us it was the very opposite!
I thought he was an insensitive clod, and he felt I was impossibly
conceited. I am sure that for a while we really loathed each
other. But we still met now and then, and little by little we
began discovering things about each other we really liked.
Then we realized that we were meant for each other, and that's
the way it turned out to be."

3. "The minute I saw him across the room I knew he was
the man for me. And I could tell from the way he looked that
he felt the same way. He told me later it was as if lights flashed
and bells rang. We've been married 15 years, and I can remember
it as if it were yesterday. Joe can, too. When you fall in love
at first sight, it's like being hit so hard by something that everything around you stops except your heart, and that beats like
a sledge hammer. There's so much feeling inside you that
you're almost numb, and it feels too wonderful to be true."

How do most people think of love?

At Wesleyan University, psychologist Robert H. Knapp and
his colleagues made a study of the reactions of hundreds of
men and women. Each was asked to select from a group of
metaphors or phrases the one which best described their idea
of love.

These metaphors were selected by the psychologists for the
differences they revealed in attitudes toward love. The subjects
were then instructed to "read them over and then rate them
according to how they evoke for you an effective image of the
nature of love."

Here are the images which scored the most votes:

A pink planet inhabited by two.

A stairway to paradise.

A tiger in a cage.

Violins and golden trumpets.

Bubbles in champagne.

A dainty box of sweets.

A churning sea.

A bittersweet drink.

Brave and joyful eyes.

A person's choice of images tells much about his attitude. The person who thinks of love as a stairway to paradise or violins and golden trumpets lives in a completely different world from the man or woman who regards it as a dainty box of sweets or brave and shining eyes.

Who understands love best, men or women?

It has been said that however dull a woman may be, she will understand all there is in love; but however intelligent a man may be, he will never know the half of it.

Psychological studies bear out this saying. A woman lives in a world of emotion to a far greater extent than a man does. She is more intuitive and more subjective. More sensitive to interpersonal relations, she is quicker than a man to recognize the presence of love. Women realize this, and make allowances for it. Often a girl will say, "Yes, he is in love with me. But he doesn't know it yet."

What are your chances of finding and falling in love with your Dream Girl or Dream Man?

Very slim. Sociological studies show the person you fall in love with is likely to be totally different from your preconceived ideal mate. Sociologist J. Richard Udry says that what often happens is that we attribute those characteristics to the mate we ultimately select; or our ideal image may be changed by our relationship with the person we fall in love with, so that the ideal comes to resemble him.

Psychiatrist Joost A. M. Meerloo says that we may easily fall in love with the fictional attributes we project into the other, and not with the person he or she really is. Many a hasty marriage fails because of this.

How can you make yourself more attractive to someone you are interested in?

It all depends. Suppose you are the girl-or-boy-next-door kind of person. If so, you will make yourself the most attractive to that certain someone by putting your best foot forward, emphasizing your positive qualities, and trusting that they will overshadow your negative ones to such a degree that the other person will not notice them until he or she has grown so fond of you as to disregard them. However, if you are a brain or a hero, psychological studies conducted at the University of Minnesota show that you will make yourself much more attractive by falling into some clumsy or embarrassing social blunder now and then, or doing something which makes you appear awkward or ridiculous, like spilling a cup of coffee all over your new suit.

This gambit is described by the investigators as the "prat-fall technique," and the study showed that such occasional blunders on the part of a superior person have the effect of heightening his attractiveness. "It increases his approachability, makes him seem less austere, more human, and much more likeable," say the researchers. The same blunder tends to decrease the attractiveness of a person of average ability, and makes him seem that much more ordinary.

Does falling in love change your sense of values?

Yes. A man in love scarcely feels the same about anything.

His world outlook becomes, at least for the time being, altogether different. Things he gave little thought to before now assume overwhelming importance. As Balzac said, "There are no little things with the heart."

WHAT DO YOU REALLY KNOW ABOUT LOVE?
It's Man's Favorite Subject And Now Psychologists Have Taken More Of An Interest In It Than Casanova

Since affairs of the heart have always interested more people than affairs of state, it's gratifying to learn that science has redoubled its efforts to discover as much as possible about love. And while leading psychologists and sociologists haven't been able to analyze completely the stuff Cupid dips his arrows in, they've come up with some interesting findings. Let's take a look at the most revealing:

Q: Is there such a thing as "love at first sight"?

A: No. As psychologist Vernon W. Grant observes after evaluating findings of leading investigations: "Only *attraction* can occur at first sight"; genuine attachment, expressing a fully matured emotion, must have time to develop. University of California's sociologist Judson T. Landis finds that what happens "at first sight" is infatuation. Sometimes these sudden infatuations may develop and ripen into love. But more often than not, he finds, the elements necessary for the ultimate growth of love are not present — and the attachment is short-lived.

Q: Is it true that the most important step in achieving love and happiness is choosing the right mate?

A: No. Dr. Harold T. Christensen, Chairman of the Sociology Department of Family Life at Purdue University, finds that too many people are under this illusion. His studies show that picking the right mate is only part of the story, and that of even more importance is being a good mate. This means being willing to go at least half-way in making the multitude of necessary marital adjustments and making allowances for your partner's faults and imperfections.

Q: Is a high I.Q. a handicap where love and romance are concerned?

A: On the contrary. Studies conducted by sociologist Paul C. Glick, of the U.S. Bureau of the Census, show that persons of higher education and intelligence tend to be far "luckier" in love than the rest of the population. A recent survey of married couples showed that among those who had not completed their high-school education, better than one marriage out of four had gone on the rocks; while with those who had gone to college, only one marriage out of every ten had failed to work out.

Q: Should you try to persuade the "Girl of Your Dreams" that she's in love with you?

A: No. Professor F. Alexander Magoun warns men in his latest textbook, *Love and Marriage,* not to make the mistake of persuading a young woman that she is in love. "Courting," he points out, "ought not to be a conquest, but a mutual search by two people to discover together what they have in common." And it doesn't serve either party's interest to sweep a girl off her feet at a time when it's most important that she have her feet solidly planted on the ground.

Q: Is it true that the more a couple have in common, personality-wise, the better their chances for love?

A: Professor Christensen's studies show that it can be dangerous for a couple to be too similar in character and temperament. The course of love runs smoothest when they have opposite faults, similar virtues. (For example: if both are idealistic, that's fine; but if both are stubborn or hot-headed, that's bad.)

Q: Is it true that southern gals have the inside track over their northern sisters?

A: Studies conducted by psychiatrist J. A. Morris Kimber show that southern women have a decided edge on northern women in matrimonial chances; and that northern men frequently marry southern women, but few southern men marry northern women. In another study, made by Florida State University psychologists, personality tests were given to more than 1,500 co-eds from both north and south. The results showed the southern belles to be far more romantically feminine in their attitudes.

Q: Does love mean a different thing to a woman than it does to a man?

A: Studies of psychologists and sociologists have probed this question from every angle. Consensus of their findings backs up what Byron said over 100 years ago: "Man's love is of man's life a thing apart; 'tis woman's whole existence." The more a couple can understand this fundamental difference between the sexes, the happier their whole relationship is likely to be.

Q: Is it true that the better adjusted a girl is the sooner she's likely to fall in love and marry?

A: No. It's likely to be the other way around. Sociology Professor Floyd M. Martinson studied a cross-section of young women in their early-to-middle 20's, and found that those who had not yet married averaged the best personality scores. The single girls showed better emotional adjustment, greater self-confidence, and a better-developed sense of security. They also averaged better physical health scores. Professor Martinson concludes that it is the immature or not-so-well adjusted person who is the most anxious to get married.

Q: What if your "one and only love" turns you down?

A: Your chances for love and happiness are just as good as they ever were, if you will only realize the fact. As Dr. Claude C. Bowman, Temple University sociologist, points out: the "one and only love" is a myth, and studies have completely exploded the illusion that there is a single "soul mate" to whom one is attracted by cosmic affinity. If you are jilted, get back in circulation.

Q: What is this thing called love?

A: Perhaps the best answer to this question has been provided by a Harvard University sociologist, Carle C. Zimmerman, and the Rev. Lucius F. Cervantes, director of the Sociology Department of Regis College, Denver, in their textbook, *Marriage and the Family,* which sums up the findings of a monumental study. They define "Love" as "the most complete response of which a human being is capable, reaching its fulfillment in a total community of life between one man and one woman. Married love is, then, the highest union possible between human beings."

WHAT'S NEW ABOUT LOVE
Are You Ever Too Old To Fall In Love?
Can The "Other Woman" Steal Your Husband?

It is doubtful that any subject under the sun has more interest for people of all ages than this thing called love.

Teen-agers are troubled by its turbulence. Young married couples are both bewildered and enthralled as they become initiated into its mysteries and try to adjust to its complexities. The middle-aged face the problem of keeping it alive, and the elderly face the realization it is in many ways more essential to their happiness now than it ever was.

For this reason psychologists and sociologists continue to explore love's uncharted labyrinths, discovering new facts and exploding old fallacies. Here are some of their findings:

Question: Are you ever too old to fall in love?

Answer: No. The noted authority, Dr. Flanders Dunbar, surveyed a representative cross section of the oldest men and women in the U.S. By questionnaire and personal interviews, Dr. Dunbar and her associates compiled personal data on the lives of 20% of all persons in the country 100 years old or older. Consensus of her findings showed that centenarians not only maintain a lively interest in matters pertaining to love and romance, but they also tend to keep their potency. There were a number of cases where men and women fell in love and re-married, even though past the 100 mark.

Q: What type of person are you most likely to fall in love with?

A: Studies of Professors Ernest W. Burgess and Paul Wallin — as well as those of other leading sociologists — show that handsome men tend to be drawn to good-looking women; and that the plain-looking tend to fall in love with each other. Like has been found to attract like so far as body build is concerned too.

Q: Does this like-tends-to-attract-like principle in love extend to personality characteristics?

A: In some respects, yes. But studies conducted by Stanford University show that introverts tend to be most attracted to extroverts; and that men and women who are opposites in this respect are apt to have the greatest mutual allure. It was also found that the heart-rules-the-head type tends to be most strongly drawn to the "thinker" type.

Q: Can the "other woman" steal your husband's love?

A: If, like many women, you have vague fears on this score, let a leading authority reassure you. Dr. Alfred Blazwer, New York psychiatrist and author of the book, *What's Your Problem,* says no woman married to a normal man where there is friendship, love and a healthy sex life has anything to worry about. He feels it is important for a woman to bear in mind the following points which apply to all husbands:

Being a man, he is by nature polygamous. Being in love with his wife does not blind him to all women. However, for the sake of his peace of mind he is willing to forego them. (Unless he is, say, away from home with his physical needs incited by too many cocktails and too many miles between him and his true love.)

The fact remains that no man ever uprooted himself from a good relationship. The other woman can wear black lace scanties and use any perfume she wants; it won't make any difference, providing his relationship with his wife is satisfactory

Q: Does the moon actually have a stimulating effect on love and romance?

A: Poets have long sung of the magic spell the moon is supposed to exert on lovers. Recent scientific investigations, instead of exploding this notion as a myth, indicate that it may be completely valid. Findings show there apparently is a definite connection between the moon's changes and human emotions.

At Duke and Yale Universities, for example, the noted psychiatrist, Dr. Leonard J. Ravitz, made a careful study of university students and found that peaks of emotional stimulation coincided with full and new moons.

And the noted British scientist, Dr. J. L. Harrison, after a four-year study of the nocturnal behavior of jungle animals, reports "a burst of conception in animals with the approach of the full moon."

In view of these findings, it would appear the moon has all the powers the poets attributed to it — and then some.

Q: What per cent of love affairs end in heartbreak for one of

the persons involved?

A: No survey of all age groups has ever been made on this score, but investigators at the University of Minnesota made a careful study of 896 love affairs of men and women college students. Of these, 644 (or close to 70%) had been broken off.

In almost half of the broken love affairs there were no heartaches involved for either party. When asked "How did you feel about the way it ended?" nearly 50% indicated that they were "indifferent," "relieved," "satisfied" or "happy." And only slightly over 8% described themselves as being "bitter" or "angry."

Q: Is lasting love assured when a man marries "the girl of his dreams"?

A: No. Just the opposite, says Dr. H. V. Dicks in reporting the findings of his studies to the Fifth International Congress on Mental Health.

The trouble with marrying a dream mate, says Dr. Dicks, is that too often the person does not love and marry a real person, but a distorted image of inner fantasies projected onto the partner. When the other person fails to measure up to this dream picture, disappointment, frustration and conflict are bound to follow.

Q: Is love an important factor in longevity?

A: Probably the most monumental study ever undertaken relative to love and its effect on human beings was done at the Harvard Research Center by the noted sociologist, Dr. Pitirim A. Sorokin. His investigations show that, other conditions being equal, the man who loves and is loved throughout his lifetime will live appreciably longer than the man whose love relationship is frustrated.

Life-insurance studies have likewise shown that couples who are happily in love — and stay that way — are consistently healthier and longer-lived than those who are single, divorced or estranged.

Q: Do love and peace of mind go hand in hand?

A: Not always. It depends on the *quality* of love. In his book, *The Ways and Powers of Love,* which reports the Harvard Research Center's findings, Dr. Sorokin says:

"When love is slight and impure, peace of mind is slight and fragile . . .. But when love is unbounded and pure . . . the love experience is equivalent to the highest peace of mind and happiness."